Exploring Inclusive Educational Practices Through Professional Inquiry

Exploring Inclusive Educational Practices Through Professional Inquiry

Edited by

Gordon L. Porter
Inclusive Education Canada
The Education Training Group

Déirdre Smith
Ontario College of Teachers, Canada

With Contributors

Vianne Timmons
University of Regina

Brian Kelly
New Brunswick Department of Education

Diane Richler
Inclusion International

SENSE PUBLISHERS
ROTTERDAM/BOSTON/TAIPEI

A C.I.P. record for this book is available from the Library of Congress.

ISBN: 978-94-6091-556-7 (paperback)
ISBN: 978-94-6091-557-4 (hardback)
ISBN: 978-94-6091-558-1 (e-book)

Published by: Sense Publishers,
P.O. Box 21858,
3001 AW Rotterdam,
The Netherlands
www.sensepublishers.com

Printed on acid-free paper

DEDICATION

*To the children, families and communities
that benefit from a truly inclusive education*

TABLE OF CONTENTS

Foreword xiii

Acknowledgements xv

Introduction 1

Case Matrix 5

1. Diversity, Equity and Inclusion: A Challenge and an Opportunity 15

2. Commitment to Inclusion 31
    Case One: Craft a Quilt 32
    Professional Inquiry 34
    Case Commentary Reflections 35
    Case Commentary 1 35
    Case Commentary 2 36
    Case Commentary 3 36
    Case Commentary 4 37
    Connecting to Professional Practice 38

    Case Two: Building Bridges 39
    Professional Inquiry 41
    Case Commentary Reflections 41
    Case Commentary 1 42
    Case Commentary 2 42
    Case Commentary 3 43
    Case Commentary 4 44
    Connecting to Professional Practice 45

    Case Three: I Just Want to go to School Like a Normal Kid 46
    Professional Inquiry 49
    Case Commentary Reflections 50
    Case Commentary 1 50
    Case Commentary 2 51
    Case Commentary 3 52
    Case Commentary 4 53
    Connecting to Professional Practice 53

    Case Four: One of my Greatest Challenges 55
    Professional Inquiry 57
    Case Commentary Reflections 58
    Case Commentary 1 59
    Case Commentary 2 60
    Case Commentary 3 60

Case Commentary 4 61
Connecting to Professional Practice..62

Case Five: Sam...63
Professional Inquiry 64
Case Commentary Reflections 65
Case Commentary 1 65
Case Commentary 2 66
Case Commentary 3 67
Case Commentary 4 68
Connecting to Professional Practice..69

3. Professional Knowledge and Practice 71

Case Six: Getting Frustrated 72
Professional Inquiry 75
Case Commentary Reflections 75
Case Commentary 1 76
Case Commentary 2 76
Case Commentary 3 77
Connecting to Professional Practice..78

Case Seven: Hopeful Eyes 79
Professional Inquiry 81
Case Commentary Reflections 82
Case Commentary 1 82
Case Commentary 2 84
Case Commentary 3 84
Case Commentary 4 85
Case Commentary 5 86
Connecting to Professional Practice..87

Case Eight: I Did My Best 88
Professional Inquiry 90
Case Commentary Reflections 91
Case Commentary 1 91
Case Commentary 2 92
Case Commentary 3 93
Case Commentary 4 94
Connecting to Professional Practice..95

Case Nine: Six Girls and a Bully 96
Professional Inquiry 98
Case Commentary Reflections 99
Case Commentary 1 99
Case Commentary 2 100
Case Commentary 3 101
Case Commentary 4 102
Connecting to Professional Practice..103

4. School Level Planning and Practices 105
    Case Ten: Language or Behaviour? 107
    Professional Inquiry 109
    Case Commentary Reflections 109
    Case Commentary 1 110
    Case Commentary 2 110
    Case Commentary 3 111
    Case Commentary 4 112
    Connecting to Professional Practice..113

    Case Eleven: Planning Ahead 114
    Professional Inquiry 116
    Case Commentary Reflections 116
    Case Commentary 1 117
    Case Commentary 2 118
    Case Commentary 3 120
    Case Commentary 4 120
    Case Commentary 5 121
    Connecting to Professional Practice..123

    Case Twelve: Planning for Inclusion 124
    Professional Inquiry 125
    Case Commentary Reflections 126
    Case Commentary 1 126
    Case Commentary 2 128
    Case Commentary 3 129
    Case Commentary 4 131
    Connecting to Professional Practice..132

    Case Thirteen: Striking a Balance...133
    Professional Inquiry 134
    Case Commentary Reflections 134
    Case Commentary 1 135
    Case Commentary 2 135
    Case Commentary 3 137
    Case Commentary 4 138
    Connecting to Professional Practice..139

5. Challenges and Barriers to Inclusion...141
    Case Fourteen: Bridging the Gap..142
    Professional Inquiry 144
    Case Commentary Reflections 145
    Case Commentary 1 145
    Case Commentary 2 146
    Case Commentary 3 147
    Connecting to Professional Practice..148

Case Fifteen: Dirt Bikes and Computers...149
Professional Inquiry 151
Case Commentary Reflections..152
Case Commentary 1 153
Case Commentary 2 154
Connecting to Professional Practice...155

Case Sixteen: Who is Blind?..156
Professional Inquiry 159
Case Commentary Reflections..160
Case Commentary 1 160
Case Commentary 2 162
Case Commentary 3 163
Connecting to Professional Practice...164

Case Seventeen: Hit Hard 165
Professional Inquiry 166
Case Commentary Reflections..167
Case Commentary 1 167
Case Commentary 2 168
Case Commentary 3 169
Case Commentary 4 171
Connecting to Professional Practice...172

6. The Voice of Parents 173
Case Eighteen: Parental Demands 175
Professional Inquiry 176
Case Commentary Reflections..177
Case Commentary 1 177
Case Commentary 2 178
Case Commentary 3 180
Case Commentary 4 180
Case Commentary 5 181
Connecting to Professional Practice...182

Case Nineteen: Parent Faith in Schools 183
Professional Inquiry 187
Case Commentary Reflections..188
Case Commentary 1 188
Case Commentary 2 189
Case Commentary 3 189
Case Commentary 4 190
Connecting to Professional Practice...191

Case Twenty: It was a Memorable Day in Our Family 192
Professional Inquiry 194
Case Commentary Reflections..194
Case Commentary 1 195

Case Commentary 2 195
Case Commentary 3 196
Case Commentary 4 197
Case Commentary 5 198
Connecting to Professional Practice..198

Case Twenty One: Educating Emily 199
Professional Inquiry 201
Case Commentary Reflections...202
Case Commentary 1 202
Case Commentary 2 203
Case Commentary 3 204
Case Commentary 4 204
Connecting to Professional Practice..206

Case Twenty Two: Of Chess and Life 207
Professional Inquiry 210
Case Commentary Reflections...211
Case Commentary 1 211
Case Commentary 2 212
Case Commentary 3 213
Case Commentary 4 213
Connecting to Professional Practice..214

Case Twenty Three: Rosa's World 215
Professional Inquiry 222
Case Commentary Reflections...222
Case Commentary 1 223
Case Commentary 2 224
Case Commentary 3 224
Case Commentary 4 225
Connecting to Professional Practice..226

Case Twenty Four: The Personal Program Plan 227
Professional Inquiry 232
Case Commentary Reflections...232
Case Commentary 1 233
Case Commentary 2 234
Case Commentary 3 235
Case Commentary 4 236
Case Commentary 5 237
Case Commentary 6 238
Connecting to Professional Practice..239

Case Twenty Five: Scattered Notes from a Scattered Mom 240
Professional Inquiry 242
Case Commentary Reflections...243
Case Commentary 1 243
Case Commentary 2 244

    Case Commentary 3 245
    Case Commentary 4 246
    Case Commentary 5 247
    Connecting to Professional Practice...247

Significance of Lived Experiences for Inclusive Education...................249

Final Reflections 253

About the Editors 255

About the Contributing Partners 256

About the Commentators 257

Bibliography..275

FOREWORD

Gordon Porter and Déirdre Smith have written a complete book on inclusion. It is rich in concepts, rich in case examples, rich in inquiry and rich in application.

Exploring Inclusive Education through Professional Inquiry is first and foremost grounded in cases—not only 25 cases that capture the frustrations and joys of inclusive education that give the book a graphic and personal picture, but also in the series of commentaries on each case that furnish so many insights and perspectives. This is a book that is deep in inquiry.

While the cases give individual reality to inclusion, the framework is both comprehensive and coherent. The book is organized into five big chapters that capture: the values and ethics (chapter 1, Commitment to inclusion); the knowledge base (chapter 2, Professional Knowledge and Practice); what it looks like at the school level (chapter 3, School level plans and practice); frustrations and obstacles (Chapter 4, Challenges and barriers); and the role of parents (Chapter 5). These five chapters provide a reflective guide for schools, school districts and communities that are committed to making inclusion a reality for all students and families.

Exploring Inclusive Education through Professional Inquiry is unique because it combines individual cases with cross-case insights about assumptions and beliefs, professional inquiry, culture, and leadership practices. It also leaves the reader with insights, reflections, and questions to ponder. This text would serve as a valuable professional learning resource for teacher education, ongoing teacher development and leadership preparation.

This is a book on inclusive education that leaves you with hope and ideas for action. It takes a very difficult and highly charged topic and demonstrates that it is possible to see both the trees and the forest.

Michael Fullan
Professor Emeritus, OISE/University of Toronto

ACKNOWLEDGEMENTS

Exploring Inclusive Educational Practices Through Professional Inquiry is intended to serve as a catalyst for opening the types of conversations that will enable inclusive education to become a lived reality for all students.

It is hoped that the inclusion of multiple voices and perspectives in this text will help foster deep reflection, inquiry and critique into the educational practices that result in the inclusion or exclusion of students and families. This book clearly illuminates the experiences of students, parents and educators, as they journey alongside one another, in the mutual quest for truly authentic inclusive educational opportunities.

The Canadian educators and parents who wrote the narratives offered in this book are committed to supporting inclusive education. They reflected upon their own experiences and made these accessible for others through the format of a written narrative case. The highly diverse educational contexts that exist across Canada are brought to light in this text. The stark similarities in the lived experiences related to inclusive education are also crystallized in the cases written by educators and parents from across Canada.

The reflections and critiques of case commentary writers provide additional lenses to understand the deep complexity and collaboration necessary for successful inclusion. The wealth of insights, perspectives and questions provided by the case commentary writers serve to extend, challenge and enhance educational practices. Their involvement in this shared project contributes to the illumination of the implicit and explicit influences upon inclusion within educational settings.

The assistance provided by Carmen Dragnea helped this book become a reality through her thoughtful and careful formatting and editing. Her generous support has enabled the written experiences of the case and commentary writers to be shared in a format that invites inquiry.

The vision and commitment of Sense Publishing in recognizing the importance of a book that privileges the voices and lived experiences of educators and parents alongside those of scholars and policy makers is acknowledged as a significant educative model for publishers. This innovative model results in an authentic and rich exploration of inclusive educational practices. The honoring and inclusion of a diversity of perspectives and experiences within this text is a living example of inclusion and collaboration.

The leadership of the Canadian Association of Community Living, in creating the conditions for these stories of struggle, triumph and justice to be told, becomes a gift to the education community. It is hoped that this gift is unwrapped and read with open hearts and minds. These dispositions will help nurture deeper commitment towards inclusive education.

INTRODUCTION

Exploring Inclusive Educational Practices Through Professional Inquiry is a collection of experiences, practices, commentaries and educative pedagogies designed to support the development and enhancement of inclusive processes and practices within education. This text was created by integrating the experiences and insights of educators, parents and academic scholars. Educators and parents wrote about their experiences related to supporting learners with diverse needs within various Canadian educational contexts. These stories are re-told to help facilitate deep conversations and extend learning related to inclusive education.

Exploring Inclusive Educational Practices Through Professional Inquiry is organized into five interrelated sections. Each section focuses on a different theme or influence associated with inclusive education. The five thematic sections include,

Section 1: *Commitment to Inclusion*
Section 2: *Professional Knowledge and Practice*
Section 3: *School Level Planning and Practices*
Section 4: *Challenges and Barriers to Inclusion*
Section 5: *Voice of Parents*

These five thematic sections provide a conceptual lens for investigating the efficacy of educational practices towards the advancement of an inclusion agenda. Each section invites readers to explore the significance of a specific thematic influence upon inclusive education.

CASES OF EXPERIENCE

Portraying and representing the *lived* experiences of educators and parents through the narrative genre of a written case enables the beliefs, thinking and actions of individuals to be made visible. This written illumination of experience can be then be used as "records of practice" (Smith & Goldblatt, 2009). The value of having available, illustrative educational cases enables the teaching profession to use these "records of practice" for the enhancement of professional practice. The efficacy of case inquiry for advancing professional knowledge and skill in education continues to be acknowledged by practitioners and scholars (Smith, 2010; Smith & Goldblatt, 2009; Ontario College of Teachers, 2009; Cherubini, Smith, Goldblatt, Engemann, & Kitchen, 2008; Shapiro & Gross, 2008; Strike, 2007; Goldblatt & Smith, 2005; Strike, Haller & Soltis, 2005; Merseth, 2003; Darling-Hammond & Hammerness 2002; Stake, 1995; Shulman, L. 1992; Shulman, J. 1992).

The collection of narratives and commentaries in this book has been developed as a curriculum and pedagogical resource for teacher education, leadership formation and professional learning. The case narratives honor the voices, perspectives and experiences of educators, school support personnel, parents and students. This text respects the insights and role of practitioners, academic scholars, community advocates and parents as they collectively make visible the *lived* knowledge and experience of educators and families.

Processes for the integration of theory and practice using inquiry methods that foster meaningful and useful educative applications for inclusive practice are also included in this text. Most importantly, this text illustrates that the *lived* experiences of educators, parents and students can be effectively used to advance educational knowledge regarding inclusive practices. The professional practice and lived experiences of educators provides effective sources of pedagogy and professional learning for exploring the many dimensions of inclusive educational practices.

The use of case narratives is especially important in the study of inclusive education. Cases are effective means for capturing the layered and rich thickness of meaning that is integrated within educational experiences and practices. Educational cases offer a rare window into the often private and extremely complicated journeys of educators and parents trying to foster an inclusive education for students. Through opening or uncovering complex educational practices, educators can be provided with an opportunity to gain deeper insight into professional practice. Cases provide a unique entrance into the experiences of the individual practitioner or parent. Collaboratively reading, reflecting and discussing an individual narrative can initiate a process of dialogue: a shared experience of focused professional inquiry.

A collection of twenty five cases are presented in this text for the purpose of illuminating the dilemmas intrinsic within inclusive education practices. These cases written by practicing educators and parents reveal the diversity and complexity of conundrums, tensions and issues lived out daily in a variety of educational contexts. Many of the tensions encountered by this group of educators and parents are ethical in nature. As the reader recognizes, understands and reflects on the issues within each narrative, s/he is invited to respond to the case through a variety of perspectives: ethics, justice, democracy, pedagogy and leadership. These are all key dimensions of inclusive education.

The cases in this text provide multifocal lenses into the thinking, values, commitments and actions of educators from a wide range of different educational settings. The *lived* experiences of the educators depicted in these cases serve as a professional learning text for principals, teachers and policy makers. The cases provide explicit representations of practice. These representations can be read, reflected upon, discussed and critiqued in an attempt to extend professional knowledge and understanding of inclusive educational practices.

PROFESSIONAL INQUIRY

A variety of *Professional Inquiry* methods are integrated within this text to facilitate investigation into the authentic tensions, issues and dilemmas experienced by educators and parents. Examining professional practice by using illustrative scenarios provides a genuine context for educators to explore the meaning of both individual and collective commitments to inclusion. Educators can gain additional insight and awareness regarding inclusive practices by inquiring into 'real' dilemmas and issues that have actually occurred within practice.

Engaging in diverse inquiry processes helps educators to deepen professional knowledge, consolidate professional identity, strengthen sensitivity towards moral responsibilities and activate actions based on social justice principles. The professional inquiry methods that are incorporated in this text include reflection, dialogue, collaboration, case analysis, commentary critique and making connections to professional practice. These methods invite further investigation into principles, concepts, pedagogies, processes, decisions and practices associated with inclusion.

Each case narrative in this text is followed by a *Professional Inquiry* section that provides a series of reflective questions. These questions and frameworks are designed to guide readers through processes of reflection and analysis. Engaging in dialogue with colleagues regarding the dilemmas and forms of exclusion can support ongoing professional learning. It also fosters the co-construction of deeper insights regarding inclusive education.

CASE COMMENTARIES

A set of *Case Commentaries* also accompany each case scenario. The commentaries were written by educational scholars, teacher educators and practitioners. They provide a multiplicity of perspectives to the re-counted *lived* experience written by an educator or parent. The commentaries offer alternative reflections, interpretations and critiques of educational practices that are re-constructed through the parameters of a written case. Readers are invited, through the commentaries, to re-examine the case scenario from a different viewpoint and to contemplate additional issues and implications that may not have been previously considered upon the initial reading and discussion of the case. The alternative lens and voice of each commentator helps readers to explicate the complexities and issues inherent within inclusive education.

These commentaries may stretch and challenge a reader's initial responses and assumptions to the case. Or, they may affirm deeply rooted values and principles. They may evoke feelings of discomfort associated with a specific action or decision made within the context of the case. The commentaries are catalysts for additional insight, reflection and understandings. They may function as educative and dialogic methods in revealing the deep complexity inherent within inclusive education practices.

The commentaries provide alternative views to the written case. They invite the reader to review the issues in the case from additional perspectives. Perspective taking is an important professional skill to continually refine and exercise. Effective educators invite and include the perspective and voices of all those involved in the education of students.

The commentaries serve as additional reflective process to further explore the myriad of dimensions associated with inclusive educational practices. The written commentaries invite analysis and dialogue (Smith & Goldblatt, 2009). They support the development of professional knowledge and judgment associated with inclusive education. This form of understanding can enhance empathy, extend thinking and inform decision making. Ultimately, the attainment of new understanding and insight can also help change assumptions and beliefs.

CASE COMMENTARY REFLECTIONS

Case Commentary Reflections is one of the many inquiry processes used in this book to assist readers in acquiring additional knowledge and skill related to inclusive educational practices. Each commentary section is preceded by reflective questions designed to invite readers to identify new insights gained from reading the comment-aries. These questions are also intended to help facilitate discussions regarding the impact of the commentaries on the personal and professional understandings the reader regarding inclusive education.

CONNECTING TO PROFESSIONAL PRATICE

Connecting to Professional Practice follows each set of case commentaries. This section of the text summarizes key concepts or issues identified by the case commentary writers. Educators are invited to reflect on their experiences in relation to these issues and concepts. This section of the book is intended to foster deeper reflection and further inquiry into professional practice. Educators are encouraged to revisit their own professional experiences and consider how their values, commit-ments, actions and decisions support inclusive education. Educators can enhance their understandings, practices and beliefs of inclusion through critically examining their own assumptions and the assumptions of others in light of research, evidence from practice and their own experiences. Educators that thoughtfully contemplate issues of social justice, human rights, diversity, full participation, and access are more able to provide learning environments free of discrimination.

CASE MATRIX

A *Case Matrix* (See Figure 1) has been developed as a pedagogical resource to support the use of the cases, commentaries, and professional inquiry components of this text within teacher education, leadership development and professional learning courses. The matrix provides an at-a-glance overview of all sections of this text. Brief information on the cases, commentaries, professional inquiry sections and the key concepts identified by the commentary writers are included in the matrix. Course facilitators or instructors may choose to use the matrix as a planning and instructional tool.

CASE MATRIX

Theme 1. Commitment to inclusion

Case	Case Overview	Professional inquiry focus	Commentary writers	Concepts from commentaries
Craft a Quilt	A principal describes the processes and actions involved in the inclusion of an elementary student with significant needs.	Leadership and Professional Knowledge School Culture Inclusive Practices Assumptions and Beliefs	Heather Hogan Amanda Watkins & Cor Meijer Zana Lutfiyya John Loughran	School Culture Leadership Practices Core Beliefs Shared Responsibility Collaborative Team Work
Building Bridges	A new principal attempts to develop a trusting and supportive relationship with a grade eight student. The student experiences significant academic challenges and behaviour issues.	Professional Knowledge Challenges to Inclusion Commitment to Inclusion Inclusive Practices Educational Programming	Bendina Miller Marie Schoeman Tanya Whitney Seamus Hagerty	Authentic Inclusion Teacher Capacity Differentiated Instruction Open Learning Communities
I Just Want To Go To School like a Normal Kid	A young adolescent student dealing with significant family issues and drug abuse returns to secondary school after dropping out of school. The student is provided with an individualized school experience, support of community agencies and is surrounded by individuals who care and are committed to her success. The provision of this extensive support results in considerable success for this student. The possible return to her family by the court is a concern for the educators involved.	Professional Knowledge and Commitment Instructional Practice Professional Responsibility School and Community Supports	Kendra MacLaren Audrey Lampert Tracy Beck Anke Grafé	Emotional Abuse and Neglect School Level Planning Legal and Moral Responsibility Counselling Support to Foster Families School Level Interventions Community Supports Role of Student Success Initiatives

CASE MATRIX

Theme 1. (Continued)

One of My Greatest Challenges	A resource teacher committed to inclusion describes the school's collaborative approach to supporting a ten year old student. The well intentioned strategies of the school are not being implemented at home. The commentary writers for this case challenge the school's pedagogical strategies to promote inclusion based on equity, socialization and theories associated with emancipation.	Inclusive Pedagogies Working with Parents Educational Programming	Margaret Kress White Alice Bender Darlene Perner Scott A. Thompson	Inclusive Education Pedagogies Emancipation Equity Social Engineering Relationship with Parents Person Centered Planning
Sam	A resource teacher describes the educational program for a student with cognitive, physical and social needs. This teacher is concerned with the lack of shared commitment, responsibility and involvement of staff in the education of this student.	Creating an Inclusive Learning Environment School Culture	Sharon Rich Catherine Montreuil Edith Clarke Jacqueline Karsemeyer & Jaya Karsemeyer	Community Love of teaching Professional learning Collegial support Caring teachers Elimination of labels Flexible groupings Differentiated materials Collaboration and shared responsibility Educational programming

Theme 2. Professional knowledge and practice

Case	Case overview	Professional inquiry focus	Commentary writers	Concepts from commentaries
Getting Frustrated	A principal attempts to support a learner with significant behavioural challenges. The actions and decisions employed invite considerable reflection by the principal.	Beliefs and Assumptions Ethics Inclusive Education	Chris Treadwell Sarah Elizabeth Barrett Julie A. Stone	School Planning Professional Knowledge Case Manager Individual Education Plan Student Interests Student Involvement
Hopeful Eyes	A resource teacher describes the school history of a grade four student who is recently identified with autism spectrum disorder. The case raises issues related to developing trusting relationships with parents, formal identification of student needs and professional responsibilities.	Identification and Support Educational Programming Relationship	Pamela C. McGugan Jude MacArthur Melanie Panitch Krista Carr Sheila Bennett	Relationship Building with Parents Leadership Collaborative School Culture Trust Welcoming School Communities Parent Meetings Parental Grief Parental Efficacy Meaningful and Effective Instruction
I Did My Best	A grade three classroom teacher attempts to support a student displaying significant anxiety. This case reveals that more than a teacher's best efforts are required in supporting and including students with multi-dimensional needs.	Commitment to student learning Professional Knowledge Challenges to Inclusive Education School Processes and Practices Professional Responsibility	Odet Moliner Garcia Barbara Wenders Stephanie Zucko Tiffany Gallagher	School Protocols Collaboration with and Involvement of Families Transitional Planning School Problem Solving Teams Medication Individual Education Plans Professional Responsibility

CASE MATRIX

Theme 2. (Continued)

	Case overview	Professional inquiry focus	Commentary writers	Concepts from commentaries
Six Girls and a Bully	A principal outlines an issue involving exclusion through bullying in an elementary school. The principal is concerned that s/he did not address all aspects of this issue in terms of student needs.	Professional Knowledge and Practice Leadership	Pamela C. McGugan Sheila McWatters & Shirley Kendrick Cindy Finn Ulla Alexandersson	Inclusion and equitable school environment Character Education Collective responsibility for the safety of students Restorative Practices Forgiveness Self-reflection Unequal relationships Professional Knowledge

Theme 3. School level planning and practices

Case	Case overview	Professional inquiry focus	Commentary writers	Concepts from commentaries
Language or Behaviour?	A student level team meeting involving parents reveals that the parents, classroom teacher, speech and language pathologist and resource teacher are not aligned in their understanding of the issues related to a young student.	School Problem Solving Teams Communication Instructional Practice Parent Involvement	Kathryn Noel Tammy Dunbar John Lundy Isabel Killoran	Communication with Parents Shared Understanding Team Member Communication Meeting with Parents
Planning Ahead	A principal describes the school's approach to supporting a learner with autism. The principal is concerned that the school's planning and programming are not promoting inclusion.	Beliefs and Assumptions Leadership Practices Inclusive Practices	Anthony H. Normore Lois Kember Joanne MacNevin Dan Goodyear Emily Dwornikiewicz	Assumptions Knowledge of Student School Leadership School Planning Meetings Transition Planning

Theme 3. (Continued)

	Case overview	Professional inquiry focus	Commentary writers	Concepts from commentaries
Planning for Inclusion	A principal begins to question the school's approach to supporting a learner with autism. The involvement of teachers in the planning process, the role of the resource teacher, parent perspectives and the holistic needs of the student are areas for reflection by the principal.	A Commitment to Inclusion Leadership Inclusive Pedagogies	Pamela C. McGugan Darren McKee Lois Kember Carson Allard & James Moloney	Relationships Appreciative Model Professional Knowledge Definitions and goals of inclusion Visioning exercises with schools Professional Learning School level planning Accountability Transition Planning Individual Education Plan
Striking a Balance	A parent shares her expectations for her child at a school team meeting. The new principal is perplexed at the parent's apparent change in mind regarding her child's school placement and program.	School Level Planning School Culture Leadership	Carla DiGiorgio Ann Marie MacDonald Brent Langan Jerry Wheeler & Darquise Leroux	One to one support Programming Collaborative planning School Leadership

Theme 4. Challenges and barriers to inclusion

Case	Case overview	Professional inquiry focus	Commentary writers	Concepts from commentaries
Bridging the Gap	A grade eight teacher outlines the issues and challenges associated with supporting a student with autism from the elementary to the secondary level.	Transition Planning Inclusive Practices Challenges to Inclusion Self-Advocacy	Jean J. Ryoo & Peter McLaren Jacqueline Specht Zuhy Sayeed	Ethical Practice Transition Planning Advocacy Professional Responsibility Parent Involvement and Leadership Student and Family Empowerment

CASE MATRIX

Theme 4. (Continued)

Dirt Bikes and Computers	A grade eight student with learning challenges is disengaged from school. The practices, school culture, attitudes of teachers and educational programming appear to contribute to the student's disengagement.	Leadership Practices Teaching Practices Instructional Strategies School Culture Professional Judgement Assumptions and Beliefs Ethical Practice	Lauren Hoffman JoAnne Putnam	Moral Responsibility Curriculum Relevancy Relationship Building Teacher Commitment Community Involvement Commitment to Inclusive Education Self-Efficacy Ethic of Care and Compassion Peer Engagement Motivation and Self-Esteem Differentiated Instruction School Problem Solving Team
Who is Blind?	A secondary school educator outlines the school's perspectives regarding a learner with visual impairments.	Language Assumptions and Beliefs Programming Professional Knowledge and Practice Working with Parents	Sheila Bennett Jackie Fewer-Bennett Alicia de la Peña Rode	Disability language Blind mystique Programming Changing attitudes and beliefs Positioning of students and families Professional Knowledge Individual Education Plan
Hit Hard	A mother and a family advocate are hit hard by the actions and words of school personnel who do not appear to be open and supportive of inclusion.	Ethical Practice Challenges to Inclusion Advocacy Leadership	Jean J. Ryoo Gordon Kyle Shelley Arsenault Krista Carr	Equitable access to education Human Rights Treatment of parents Individual Education Plan Exclusionary practices Parent advocate Voice of parents School leadership

Theme 5. The voice of parents

Case	Case overview	Professional inquiry focus	Commentary writers	Concepts from commentaries
Parental Demands	A classroom teacher with a highly functioning class is challenged by a parent for not meeting the needs of his son.	Communication with Parents Beliefs and Assumptions Educational Programming	Diane Richler Kara Walsh Angela AuCoin Catherine Montreuil Denise Silverstone	Communication with Parents Student Perspective and Voice Programming Expectations Conflict
Parent Faith in Schools	A parent looses faith in the school when her child who is non-verbal and physically challenged doe not receive opportunities for inclusion within the secondary school.	Communication with Parents Parent Involvement Challenges and Barriers to Inclusion Transition Planning	Diana Carr Inés Elvira B. de Escallon Miguel A. Verdugo Sarah Elizabeth Barrett	Individual Education Plan Communication with Parents Transition Planning and Implementation Honest communication Professional knowledge Accommodations Labeling of parents Student rights Changing thinking Parent involvement in secondary school
It was a Memorable Day in Our Family	A family is shocked on graduation day by the attitudes and actions of the educators as well as by the different understandings of inclusion held by the school. This case illustrates the level of energy, commitment and advocacy often required from parents desiring an inclusive educational experience for their child.	Advocacy Connecting to Professional Practice Communication Inclusion	Jude MacArthur Diane Richler Alicia de la Peña Rode Bernhard Schmid Maribel Alves Fierro Sevilla	Parental responsibility Frequent and open communication Meaning of inclusion Respect for diversity Raising awareness Negotiating with the school Promoting a commitment to inclusion Equity and justice Continuous planning with parents Transforming social consciousness

Theme 5. (Continued)

Educating Emily	A mother reflects on her experiences trying to promote an inclusive education for her child. The multiple exclusionary practices employed by the school are critiqued by this parent.	Inclusive Education Teacher Education Parental Involvement Values and Assumptions	Roger Slee Robin Crain Alan McWhorter Zuhy Sayeed	Vulnerability Depersonalization Pain and triumph Teacher Education Community Problem solving School Board leadership
Of Chess and Life	A parent describes the strategic practices employed to ensure his/her child was included within the school system.	Inclusive Education Collaboration Teacher Education Learning from Parents	Bruce Rivers Inés Elvira B. de Escallon Julie A. Stone Jude MacArthur	Responsibility Trust Conflict Strategic actions Communication Shared planning Student empowerment Parental courage Parental risk taking
Rosa's World	A mother shares the story of her young daughter's experiences of exclusion and inclusion within the school system.	Inclusive philosophy School Level Planning Access	Bendina Miller Lauren Hoffman Scott A. Thompson Melanie Panitch	Parental advocacy Capacity building System support Relationships Student voice Self-advocacy Transition planning Creative practices

Theme 5. (Continued)

The Personal Program Plan	This case explores the trajectory of parents' experiences with the school system in their quest for an inclusive education for their child who has cerebral palsy.	Individual Education Planning Principal Leadership Parental Knowledge	Agnes Gajuwski & Anne Jordan JoAnne Putnam Marie Schoeman Anne Kresta Isabel Killoran Kathryn Noel	Access to resources Communication Collaborative Program planning Parental advocacy Transition planning Child's right to inclusive education
Scattered Notes form a Scattered Mom	A mother reflects on the educational experiences of her eighteen year old son who has autism.	Inclusive Education Social Justice School Culture and Organization	Carla DiGiogio Marilyn Dolmage Nithi Muthukrishna Penny Milton Alex Dingwall	Social Justice Values Educational design Facilities Curriculum Pedagogy Justice Respect Community Professional learning Counter narratives Educational access Collaboration

GORDON L. PORTER AND DIANE RICHLER

1. DIVERSITY, EQUITY AND INCLUSION

A Challenge and an Opportunity

Exploring Inclusive Educational Practices Through Professional Inquiry is about
children and the adults who care about them. It tells real stories of teachers,
principals, parents and others who work to see that children with diverse needs get
to go to school with their brothers and sisters and the other children in the neighbourhood in the community school. And – yes – we should add – in the same classes
those children are in. In other words – they are "included" and this simple action is
labelled "inclusive education".

In many communities in Canada, inclusive education is taken for granted. It has
been happening here and there for a long time – but has become quite common in
the last 20 years. In fact, today every Ministry of Education in Canada would say
that inclusion is their preferred option for the education of students with disabilities.
However, that statement of principle does not mean inclusion is a lived reality in
many schools or school boards in our country. Segregated special education classes
and indeed special education schools are still alive and well in Canada. From 2003
to 2008, one large urban school board in Canada had a decline in general population
of 28,000 students while those in self contained special education classes increased
by 5,000 students. How is this possible you may well ask?

It is possible because many teachers and parents are trapped in the traditional
special education system. They don't see a path to schooling that is able to support
individuals with special needs and do it in an inclusive classroom and school. There
are many reasons for this, reasons we can list and discuss. Some of them are:
– Vision
– Policies that lead to change
– Leadership
– Knowledge and skill
– Teacher Education and Professional Learning
– Teacher Support
– Money – financing that supports inclusion
– Parents with confidence to insist on change
– Attitudes – lingering discrimination
– And more …

This book captures some of these issues in the cases presented. You will hear
from teachers and principals who are struggling to make inclusion work – often

G. L. Porter and D. Smith (eds.), Exploring Inclusive Educational Practices
Through Professional Inquiry, 15–30.

facing daunting obstacles. You will hear from parents who are struggling to get their community school and the people who work there to make inclusion work for their child. The stories are compelling. The stories are real.

You will also hear from "commentators" who give you their take on the case at hand. Some of these commentators are professionals – teachers, academics, officials; and some are parents and advocates. All bring a valuable perspective to the issues. And of course you will have your view of the situation. And that brings us to the point of this opening chapter.

We have been engaged in the work of building inclusive schools in Canada for 25 years. Our collaboration has been through our work with the Canadian Association for Community Living. Twenty years ago we edited a book on inclusive education – Changing Canadian Schools (Porter & Richler, 1991) – and we wrote a chapter where we set out factors that had led to that point in time. One of the elements of that analysis was identifying 3 critical factors that seemed to be in place where inclusive education was able to move ahead. They were:
– Law – policy framework;
– Advocacy – parents & supporters;
– Educational Innovation – in school and classroom practices.

We suggested that you need all 3 to be actively present to produce long-term change in the education system. In this chapter we want to review these factors, reflect on them in the context of today's schools and add some new elements to our analysis.
AND SO WE BEGIN ….

THE EMERGENCE OF INCLUSIVE EDUCATION IN CANADA:
FROM EXCLUSION TO A NEW VISION

It is helpful to further define what we mean by "inclusive education" and to explore why it became a priority for so many families and educators.

In the 1940's and 50's in Canada, as in much of the world, children with intellectual disabilities were not accepted into the public education system. Evaluation methods focused on labeling children as "educable", "trainable", or severely or profoundly disabled. Children with any of those labels were not accepted into school.

The Second World War produced two concepts to challenge this exclusion from school. First, the return of so many wounded veterans led to the proliferation of rehabilitation techniques which served to demonstrate that only the war-wounded, but that other people with disabilities could also overcome the impact of their impairments. Second was the awakening of the concept of human rights, and the adoption of the Universal Declaration of Human Rights in 1948 guaranteeing the right to education for all.

And so, despite the fact that in Ontario, for example, it was against the law for school authorities to accept children with I.Q.'s of less than 50 since the enactment of the Special Classes and Auxiliary Classes Acts in 1911, parents and others began demanding change.

In a letter to the Toronto Daily Star in 1948, Victoria Glover wrote:

Sir:

May I say a few words on behalf of our backward children, and their bewildered mothers. There is no school for such children, no place where they could get a little training to be of some use in the world, only Orillia (a provincial institution, eds.) which is always full. If these children can be taught something at Orillia, why cannot a day school be put at their disposal? I am sure their mothers would gladly pay for their transportation to and from school. After all, they are paying taxes for other more fortunate children's schooling. I think it is time something was done for parents who from a sense of faith and hope in a merciful providence want to keep them at home living a normal life. These are real parents, only asking a little aid and encouragement to shoulder their own heavy burden. God bless them, and may the Ontario government help them and their children who might still be made something of, living a normal life and with the perfect love, understanding and guidance of such parents.

Victoria Glover

The response to Mrs. Glover's letter and to similar calls to action across Canada resulted in, parents banding together and creating classes for their children – often in private homes or church basements. These activities were also the beginnings of the local associations which came together in 1958 to form what is now the Canadian Association for Community Living. Changes in legislation led to the take-over of these schools by Ministries of Education, mostly in the 1960s and early 1970s.

Concurrently in the late 1960s and early 1970s, those working to support people with an intellectual disability were jolted by the introduction of the principle of normalization. First developed in Scandinavia, the principle was elaborated by Wolf Wolfensberger (1972) while working in Nebraska. He was invited to Canada to the newly formed National Institute on Mental Retardation, sponsored by the Canadian Association for Community Living, to finalize and publish a text on the subject. He also developed a plan for promulgating it throughout Canada (Wolfensberger, 1972). The essence of the principle was that people with disabilities should be supported to live lives as similar as possible to those of their own age who did not have disabilities. The promotion of normalization in Canada focused on how services such as early childhood, residential, vocational and other programs could be offered in communities to replace the need for institutions and also underlined the possibility for people with disabilities to form meaningful relationships with persons who did not have disabilities.

THE CLAMOUR FOR INCLUSVE EDUCATION

Education services were funded outside of the health and social services systems that were the main target of a national plan to transform services for people with intellectual disabilities, but parents and educators were highly influenced by the implications of the principle of normalization. Parents could see that although their children might now be getting an education, and that education was even part of the public system in most cases, it was usually in the original facilities begun by the parents. Their children were being kept apart from the rest of their peers. In essence, being educated in a separate system prepared students for a life of segregation – moving from special schools to sheltered workshops and group homes – not the inclusive future they had begun to dream about. Parents began asking that the special schools be transferred into special classes in regular schools. Then they began to ask for their children to be "integrated" into regular classes. And finally, they began to clamour for inclusion – a transformation of the regular system so that their sons and daughters could be part of regular classes.

The first attempts to include children with intellectual disabilities into regular classes in Canada began in the 1970s. The normalization movement was given a boost by the publication in 1970 of the report One Million Children, the final report of the Commission on Emotional and Learning Disorders in Children (1970) which endorsed the idea that children with disabilities should go to their neighbourhood schools and called for increased integration and a greater focus on individual rather than group needs (Philpott, 2007). The inclusion of the equality rights provisions in the Charter of Rights and Freedoms (Department of Justice Canada, 1982) further entrenched the notion that people with disabilities had a right to access services without discrimination on the basis of disability.

Even before parents had witnessed inclusive education in practice, they articulated reasons why they thought it would be preferable to the segregated programs they knew. With more experience, they clarified their messages. First, they recognized that as for their children without disabilities, a good education was a key to a better life, and that segregated education was preparation for a segregated life. They knew that inclusive education would create "social capital" for their children, what Robert Putnam describes as the "the collective value of our social networks" [who people know] and our will to do things for each other [norms of reciprocity]. While social capital is essential for all, it is especially important for people with disabilities who are often isolated. Inclusive education helps to build the trust and reciprocity with others that students with disabilities can rely on in the future to help them fully participate in their communities.

Recent research by Wagner (2008) analyzing the Canada Participation and Activity Limitation Survey (PALS) demonstrates that, according to parents:

- Children who are highly included in school are in better overall health than those not included, regardless of type or severity of disability;
- Children who are highly included make more academic progress at school;
- Children who are highly included tend to look forward to going to school more than do others;
- Children who are highly included tend to get along with their peers.

WHAT IS INCLUSIVE EDUCATION?

Inclusive education means, simply, that all students, including those with dis-abilities and other special needs, are educated in regular classrooms with their age peers in their community schools. Students with disabilities go to the same schools as their brothers and sisters, are provided with access to the same learning opportunities as other children, and are engaged in both the academic and social activities of the classroom. In inclusive schools, support is directed to both the students and their teachers so they can accomplish relevant individual goals. Inclusive education implies that children and youth with special educational needs should be included in the educational arrangements made for the majority of children. According to UNESCO,

> Inclusive schools must recognize and respond to the diverse needs of students, accommodation of both different styles and rates of learning and ensuring quality education to all through appropriate curricula, organizational arrangements, teaching strategies, resource use and partnerships with their communities. (UNESCO, 1994, p. 11)

While inclusion happens at the classroom level, it usually requires a major transformation of existing systems. In the past, responsibility for educating students with disabilities has traditionally come under the auspices of departments of special education which ran their own programs. Inclusive education requires that there be one system responsible for educating all learners. All decisions about curriculum, assessment, teacher in-service education, resource allocation and financing need to be taken in a context that supports inclusion. This is a radical departure from previous systems, where decisions about the regular system often intentionally or inadvertently made inclusion difficult or impossible.

WHAT IS WRONG WITH TRADITIONAL SPECIAL EDUCATION?

Traditional special education typically carried out by specialist teachers and in isolation from other children in special classes or special schools, has failed in several ways. First, it has failed to produce results. Students who experience segregated special education are not prepared for fulfilling lives in their communities when their education is finished. Research in Canada reported by Timmons and Wagner has indicated that they do less well than similar children who go to regular classes. There is nothing surprising in this. A segregated school program does not prepare young people to be part of the community and society when they become adults. Growing up and interacting with their peers does that.

Second, a system that encourages schools and teachers to abandon children and youth who have learning challenges is not good policy. Presuming that any child with special needs must be sent to a special program erodes the professional stature of teaching as a profession. Individual teachers may need support in a number of areas but their professional and ethical responsibility is to teach all children. Defining the regular classroom as a place for "ordinary" learners and putting unrealistic pressure on school systems to develop a parallel system for all those thus abandoned also takes the focus off efforts for school improvement. It is irresponsible and unethical educational policy, and in the long term it is not financially sustainable, as the struggles over funding issues experienced in many parts of Canada demonstrate.

Finally, segregated special education is not appropriate from a moral or human rights perspective. In 2010, we still have thousands of children in Canada who are confined to segregated classes, and a few still attend segregated schools. Twenty-five years after the Charter, and in an international environment where Canada should be providing leadership in the implementation of the recent United Nations Convention (2006), we are left with many traditional educational practices. As a democratic nation we can do better.

MOVING INCLUSION FORWARD...THE FACTORS THAT PRODUCE CHANGE

Our analysis of the factors producing change up to the early 90's led us to conclude that the three critical factors were law, advocacy and innovation. A review of progress – and obstacles since the earlier publication confirm our framework for determining the preconditions of the change process, but the emphasis in each area has shifted considerably. In the case of law, we have moved from litigation to creating an international framework; in the case of advocacy, we have paid more attention to the opinions of other stakeholders; and in the case of innovation, we have...

LAW AND LEGISLATION

In *Changing Canadian Schools* we explored legislation and litigation and concluded that section by stating, "Additional litigation by parents in the coming decade will be necessary to establish clear jurisprudence in this contentious area." (Porter & Richler, 1991, p. 16)

The case of Emily Eaton was the first inclusive education case in Canada to reach the Supreme Court and the results had a mixed impact on the struggle towards inclusion (Supreme Court of Canada, 1997). When Emily was 12 years old, after she had spent three years in a regular class, her parents were told by the Brant County Board of Education that she needed to be educated in a special education setting. Her parents appealed to the Ontario Special Education Tribunal, which also confirmed the placement decision. The parents then lost in Ontario's "Divisional Court" but won in the Court of Appeal. The Court of Appeal overturned the lower court's decision but the Supreme Court reversed the Court of Appeal, essentially saying that segregated education was not equal to discrimination. Although many advocates have tried to put a positive spin on the Supreme Court decision, recognizing for example that the Court does state that inclusion is always the preferred option, the case put a chill on parents' hopes that the Charter of Rights and Freedoms would provide a legal guarantee for inclusion.

The Eaton case demonstrated the conflict that often exists between parents and educators in attempting to meet individual needs and promote inclusion. Human

Rights Commissions throughout Canada have identified special education as a critical issue. Commissions in Ontario and New Brunswick have established guidelines for accommodating students with disabilities in the education system. Other commissions have also identified this as a priority area that continues to result in many complaints each year. It will undoubtedly be the focus of future deliberations by human rights commissions.

New Brunswick, which was the first Canadian province to mandate inclusion has again set a precedent by identifying actions to be taken and efforts to be made to support inclusion and accommodation – in the regular class – BEFORE use of other alternatives is warranted as per the human rights law. This was developed because parents and teachers have still not worked out how to assure attention to individual needs and inclusion – even in New Brunswick where inclusion has been the law or default since 1986.

The New Brunswick Human Rights Commission (2007) developed a "Guideline for Accommodating Students with a Disability". The guideline explains the "duty to accommodate" (p. 5) as well as the criteria for "reasonable accommodation" (p. 8), and the limitations on the duty to accommodate (p. 27).

Such guidelines can be useful given the conflict that often surrounds such matters. A family or parent demands one thing. A school offers something else. Sometimes the demand is for more special services. Sometimes the demand is for more access to regular education or inclusion.

The key points from the "guideline" regarding the responsibility of "educational providers", that is schools and school boards are as follows:
– anticipate and plan for accessibility and inclusion;
– ensure staff have the training they need to accommodate students with a disability;
– assist with assessment and education planning with the help of experts or specialists as needed;
– deal with accommodation requests in a timely manner;
– ensure that schools are welcoming and that all students treat one another with respect;
– take immediate action in situations where bullying and harassment may be taking place.

Schools also need to ensure that unions, professional associations and others involved in providing education and support services are also part of the accommodation process and fulfill their responsibility to support accommodation measures.

The following chart demonstrates the steps prescribed by the New Brunswick Human Rights Commission.

Another legal strategy has been to move the debate to the international arena. One of the most important strategies of the past several years has been the active participation of the Canadian Association for Community Living, and the international federation to which it belongs, Inclusion International, in the negotiation of the Convention on the Rights of Persons with Disabilities which was adopted by the United Nations General Assembly on December 13, 2006.

Flow Chart A
Inclusion Process

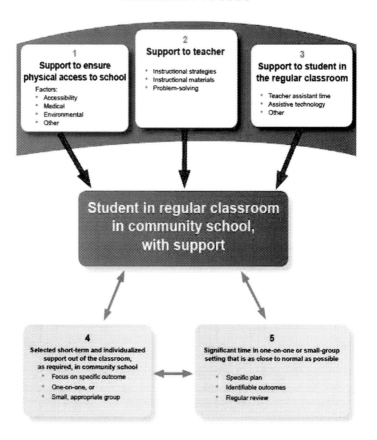

Flow Chart – New Brunswick Human Rights Commission – "Guideline on Accommodating Students with a Disability", 2007.

Article 24 of the Convention states that governments "shall ensure an inclusive education system at all levels" and that
– Reasonable accommodation of the individual's requirements is provided;
– Persons with disabilities receive the support required, within the general education system, to facilitate their effective education; and
– Effective individualized support measures are provided (United Nations, 2006)

The Convention has been ratified by Canada as well as 88 other countries. A total of 146 countries have signed the convention. This represents a commitment to action that is unprecedented and provides an international context to the issue.

Another recent development in Canada has the potential to influence the impact of the legal system on issues related to inclusive education. The Supreme Court of Canada (2010) affirmed the power of tribunals to make Charter rulings and to order appropriate remedies. In a landmark decision released on June 11, 2010, authored by Justice Rosalie Abella, the Court unanimously declared that all regulatory tribunals that are empowered to decide questions of law – which include arbitrators, labour relations boards and other tribunals in the fields of labour, employment and human rights – have the same jurisdiction as courts to apply the Canadian Charter of Rights and Freedoms and to order whatever remedies they find appropriate. The only exception is any remedies that are expressly precluded by the legislation under which the tribunal operates.

These legal advances will take some time to play out but certainly provide more leverage for the legal system to support progressive developments in achieving an inclusive school system.

ADVOCACY

In Canada we have made progress in recent years but it has been in selected schools and in selected jurisdictions. There remain obstacles and often they are greatest in the most urban and wealthy parts of the country. In part, it is a reflection of the number of people involved – parents, professionals and others. It is also a function of the institutions that are in place and the role those institutions play in the system. Some of this is as simple as the reluctance to change, but it can also reflect a genuine lack of appreciation for the value of inclusion to the children involved.

The dilemma for school systems that have not gone far with inclusive approaches is that the financial cost of maintaining the status quo is high. In February 2010, the chair of the Toronto District School Board (TDSB) lamented about the high cost of special education. In a Toronto Star article (Rushowy, 2010), Bruce Davis noted what inclusive education advocates have said for some time. Mr. Davis states that while the cost of special education has been increasing dramatically in recent years, the general population of the district's schools has been in decline.

The article notes that "In 2005, the Toronto public board served 31,600 special needs students; today, 36,800". At the same time overall enrolments have gone down. A senior administrator in charge of the special education system is quoted as follows— "Karen Forbes, senior superintendent of special education for the Toronto board, said there are several theories as to why the number of special needs cases is on the rise, including better identification and that people feel more comfortable in asking for support".

Many parents have concluded that self-contained special education is the default path for many children with special needs. Parents of children with intellectual disabilities feel it is especially true for them. Many parents in Toronto have asked for information and advice from Inclusive Education Canada when local schools tell them they cannot appropriately serve a child with a disability. They identify lack of funding and lack of school resources or capacity to put appropriate supports in place as the problem. It is not a surprise that this happens when a high proportion of the available money goes to special classes and in some school boards to special schools.

The following letter from a parent seeking help and advice helped to illuminate the issues many parents are currently faced with,

My Name is Martha and I have a fantastic 8 yr old boy who was diagnosed with autism at the age of six. Since then it has been an up-hill battle with the local school board – a big one - and trying to get my son support within an integrated classroom. He was placed in a behavioural class, which was ok at first but had a shortened day. Now, this year, the teacher has no experience with children on the autism spectrum and has filed several violence reports against my son who has been riled into such anxiety that his melt-downs were out of the teacher's scope and he lashed out. The Vice-principal has told me that the board simply does not DO one-to-one support for students like my son. The Principal simply thinks my child is "will-full" and has suggested we try keeping him in school only a half day. They are having me look at several "Autism" classes they have set up. These do nothing to service the social deficits that, typically, are the main difficulties these kids have in a classroom setting.

He is a typically happy kid. He loves artwork and creating paper versions of his favourite action figures, Spiderman and the Transformers. He is even in a 'typical' childcare setting with other kids in his school. I would like to know more about what my rights are and how to proceed with this. I am at the point where I made (may) need to hire a 3rd party to advocate for my son because too many doors are being slammed in my face.

Any advice on this situation at all would be greatly appreciated. (Martha, personal communication, February 8, 2009)

This mother's dilemma is not a unique experience. Many share her aspirations for her son and the frustrations she shares about the response of the education system to her situation.

To support inclusion, money needs to be spent on supports in local neighbourhood schools to help teachers accommodate the needs of students with disabilities. If the message to classroom teachers is to send students with learning challenges to a special program within the school, we will continue to see an increase in the demand for more dollars for special education. School leaders must look at other models and create capacity for equity and support in community schools. Putting more money into a broken system built on segregation and specialization will not solve the problem. Changing the system will!

A recent ad campaign for inclusive education conducted by Canadian Association for Community Living (2009) was based on addressing the general public's main concerns about including kids with disabilities in regular classes in neighbourhood schools. The result of focus group inquiry identified three issues uppermost in the minds of participants:

- They will be disruptive in class;
- They will hold other kids back;
- They will take up all the teachers' time.

These are clearly serious concerns but they do not have to be issues if teachers are well educated and use effective instructional strategies. Similarly, school practices must have appropriate supports for both teachers and students in place, including a strong collaborative structure and the capacity to solve problems when they occur.

This leads us to consider the final factor needed to make inclusive schools a reality, the development of dynamic and innovative school and classroom practices by teachers and educational specialists.

EDUCATIONAL INNOVATION

In the last twenty years, teachers, school leaders and educational researchers have developed many strategies and approaches to support inclusive schools and class-rooms. In the "cases" that follow, the presence – or absence – of these practices can be observed. Effective practice leads to success with inclusion. We want to share just a few of these with you. It is not intended to be an exhaustive or complete list, but it illustrates some patterns we have observed in recent years.

We need strategies to move ahead based on sound policy, effective practices, and funding policies that ensure support for schools, teachers and students. We need to ensure that clinically based labels do not result in programming that is exclusionary.

It is past time for educational leaders and policy makers to purge our educational system of segregation and discrimination based on a diagnosis or clinically based label. Exceptions to inclusion will occur from time to time, but they are currently much too common in many parts of Canada. We need to make these "exceptions" truly exceptional, and they need to be restricted to "individuals" in the local school, not to groups based on clinical labels. We need a new wave of principled school reform that will contribute to accommodating the diversity of our student population, to inclusion as a guiding principle, and to school improvement on a broad basis for all our students.

First, we have to RAISE THE BAR of expectations for schools, for teachers, for school leaders, for education officials, for our political leaders and for our fellow citizens – the public in our communities – including parents. We need to insist on schools for all our children that are inclusive. The European Agency for Development in Special Needs Education described it this way:

Widening participation to increase educational opportunity for all learners:
The goal for inclusive education is to widen access to education and to promote full participation and opportunities for all learners vulnerable to exclusion to realise their potential. (European Agency for Development in Special Needs Education, 2009)

We need to share the research evidence about inclusion and the benefits it has for children. As noted above, for some time inclusion has been criticized as setting up conditions where teachers are spending all their time with students with special needs and neglect other students. It has been suggested that inclusion holds other children back.

Two Canadian research reports issued in 2009 show that this is not the case. In a document prepared for the Ontario Ministry of Education in their "What works? Research into Practice" series, Sheila Bennett (2009) shares the following findings:
– Including students with exceptionalities in the regular classroom does not have a negative impact on the academic achievement of other students.
– Social benefits accrue to both regular and exceptional students in inclusive settings, among them an increase in advocacy and more tolerant attitudes. (p. 1)

This is supported by another 2009 report from The Centre for Education Research and Policy (CERP) at Simon Fraser University. The report *Disabled peers and academic achievement* (Friesen, Hickey, & Krauth, 2009) stated that inclusion of special education students doesn't affect classmates' education:

"...attending school with a higher percentage of students with learning dis-abilities or behavioral disorders has a small impact on the reading and numeracy test scores of non-disabled students. The relevant parameter estimates are generally negative but are statistically insignificant and small in magnitude given the range of peer group composition seen in the data." (p. 3)

WHAT DO WE NEED TO MAKE OUR SCHOOLS INCLUSIVE?

First we need to state clearly that our goal is to have "inclusive, effective, community schools" that are both committed to inclusion and able to effectively carry it out. Once the goal is set and before us, we can make plans to move ahead. It is a challenging goal that will take a significant investment in leadership at all levels – at the policy level; the education system level; and the school and classroom levels.

A few critical steps to consider in implementing this approach include the following:

1. *Transition plan*
A plan for transition needs to occur over a period of 3–5 years to do it properly.

2. *Support to Teachers*
Understanding that teachers need support to accept and meet the challenges inherent within inclusive education. We need to work with them and their associations to develop the supports they need. A discussion document, addressing this need – *Supporting Teachers: A Foundation for Advancing Inclusive Education* (Crawford & Porter), was developed in 2004. A graphic of the range of supports needed for teachers to be successful with inclusion are outlined below.

3. *School-based Support Team*
Schools need to develop a "School-based Support Team". Support teachers, school administrators, para-professionals and other professionals must work closely together to develop ways to help classroom teachers with the challenges they face. They need to share information on the needs of students, news from contacts with parents and teachers, and most importantly, the nature of support teachers may need to meet the instructional challenges of an inclusive classroom. A "team" will meet often,

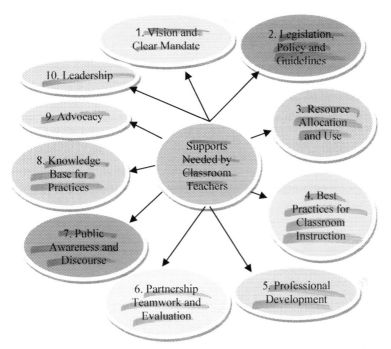

but a formal meeting at least one per week is required to keep on top of the various issues faced by teachers. Minutes are taken, and the team reviews actions taken on issues raised at previous meetings. New concerns and issues are added to the list and the team sets priorities for use of time and resources to assist teachers, and thus students. An efficient school-based team can help resolve many of the difficulties teachers encounter. They can also seek the assistance of outside personnel if that is necessary.

4. *The Support Teacher Model*

School systems need to define a new role for the special education teacher as a "support teacher" providing assistance and collaboration for classroom teachers. Inclusion eliminates the need for special education teachers to provide direct instruction to exceptional students. This is not an opportunity to save money in hard pressed school budgets, but an opportunity to provide a different kind of service. The teacher resources traditionally used for segregated instruction or pull-out resource instruction must be used to support teachers and students in regular classrooms. In this role, the support teachers collaborate with the regular class teachers and provide them with advice, assistance, and encouragement with their instructional strategies. This support is particularly important for teachers at the start of their careers and in cases where the teacher has a student whose needs are quite new to them. It may be that co-teaching will also be a strategy used, but however it is organized and delivered, having a highly effective support teacher can be a critical element in an inclusive education program.

5. *Effective and Appropriate Use of Other Staff to Support Inclusion*

School-based staff also play a key role in making inclusion a success. These resources are given various titles - teacher assistants, education assistants, student aides, teacher aides, and educational technicians – but whatever they are called, they need to be truly incorporated into the instructional team and given the opportunity to make a difference for students.

The same is true of other professionals who may be school based or who may come to the school when they are needed. This includes staff such as behavior consultants, mentors, school psychologists, speech/language pathologists, physio-therapists, occupational therapists and more.

6. *Focus on Instruction for Diversity – "Differentiated Instruction", "Multi-level Instruction" and "Universal Design"*

Teachers working in inclusive settings need to use instructional techniques that recognize students differing skills, abilities and interests. Teachers need access to ongoing in-service and planning time to develop and utilize effective approaches. In her monogram *Including students with exceptionalities*, Sheila Bennett (2009) puts it this way:

> **Use a variety of instructional methods, including differentiated instruction and universal design.** When programming for students with exceptionalities use a variety of instructional methodologies that incorporate differentiated instruction and universal design for learning (Ontario Ministry of Education, 2005). Be sensitive to external stimuli (hearing, sight), physical space (mobility) and general layout of your classroom. Try to see the environment from a number of perspectives.

The European Agency for Development in Special Needs Education (2009) describes the instructional challenge in similar ways. They suggest that an approach to learning that aims to meet the diverse needs of all learners without labelling/categorising is consistent with inclusive principles and requires the implementation of educational strategies and approaches that will be beneficial to all learners:

- Co-operative teaching where teachers take a team approach involving learners themselves, parents, peers, other school teachers and support staff, as well as multi-disciplinary team members as appropriate;
- Co-operative learning where learners help each other in different ways – including peer tutoring – within flexible and well-thought out learner groupings;
- Collaborative problem solving involving systematic approaches to positive class-room management;
- Heterogeneous grouping of learners and a differentiated approach to dealing with a diversity of learners' needs in the classroom. Such an approach involves structured goal setting, reviewing and recording, alternative routes for learning, flexible instruction and different ways of grouping for all learners;
- Effective teaching approaches based on targeted goals, alternative routes for learning, flexible instruction and the use of clear feedback to learners;

– Teacher assessment that supports learning and does not label or lead to negative consequences for learners. Assessment should take a holistic/ecological view that considers academic, behavioural, social and emotional aspects of learning and clearly informs next steps in the learning process.

7. *Problem Solving*

Effective teaching and support strategies need to be proactively put in place but there will always be unanticipated issues involving students, teachers or parents – and in many instances – all of them. As a consequence it is necessary to develop a variety of approaches to solving problems. Collaborative problem solving processes at the school and district level supports all students. The diversity of students in an inclusive classroom makes effective and collaborative problem solving even more of a priority. Classroom teachers need to ask for and accept assistance when needed and the school needs to assure them they will have the support required.

8. *Partnerships with Parents*

Parents and teachers as well as other school staff have to forge real partnerships to meet the needs of students. Mutual respect and effective collaboration can make the difference between success and failure. Parents often feel their knowledge and insights about their children are not respected. They need to be. In turn, teachers often feel parents do not understand the challenges they face or the limitations on what they can do with the support available. Open communication and an unwavering commitment to work through challenges is essential.

9. *Connecting Inclusion to School Improvement*

Having effective and inclusive schools is not a choice to be made. We can do both. Many schools in Canada have done this. Many argue that a high quality school can be a high quality inclusive school. Some support strategies and new approaches may be needed but they can be accomplished rather quickly if there is a commitment and will to do so.

What about the financial questions related to making inclusion a reality?

Money is not the issue in moving from segregation to inclusion. In fact some of the smaller and less wealthy communities and provinces of Canada are leading the way. Many of Canada's wealthiest provinces and communities spend a great deal of money on segregated special education programs, but little on making regular classrooms places where students with special needs can be welcomed and successfully included. Money spent on segregated special education needs to be re-directed to support teachers in inclusive regular schools (Crawford & Porter, 2004). In some situations the investment may need to be increased, especially during the transition period. However, because the investment to support inclusion is principally directed toward supporting classroom teachers, it has spill-over positive benefits for other students and for the classroom environment as a whole. This investment is critical if we are to make our schools instruments for creating an equitable and democratic society. (Porter, 2008, p. 5)

We see inclusion as one of the "sustaining pillars" of education as we move forward in an ever more diverse Canada in the 21st century. Our schools need to reflect our commitment to diversity and inclusion. If they do we will have a better future as a democratic country and Canada can be a beacon to other nations in this effort.

We hope this book of cases helps guide the way ahead towards achieving inclusive education for all students.

2. COMMITMENT TO INCLUSION

Inclusive education becomes a reality when all those involved in supporting teaching and learning are deeply committed to embodying philosophies and practices that promotes access and inclusion. Faithfulness to ensuring that all voices and perspectives are authentically invited and included is a hallmark of a commitment to inclusive education. Educators and educational systems that genuinely believe in inclusion ensure that policies, practices and processes are equitable, just and fair for all.

A dedication to fostering educational communities that enhance and involve all members is a necessary requirement for inclusive education. Promoting and sustaining an educational vision of inclusion is challenging and difficult shared work. Collaboratively achieving this vision requires unwavering belief in human rights and social justice. These beliefs are based on a deep respect for the dignity and sacredness of the individual. These convictions and dispositions provide the foundational strength; energy and integrity that inclusive educators will require in the joint quest to ensure educational opportunities are truly accessible for all. The promotion of inclusive educational practices and policies is inherent within teaching and learning that is deeply rooted in a democratic stance.

Overview of Cases

The cases and commentaries in this section of the text reveal the many visible and invisible dimensions associated with individual and institutional commitments towards inclusion. The diversity of ways a commitment to inclusion can be communicated is unveiled in these written narratives.

Educational structures, systems, practices, policies and decisions reveal the extent to which a commitment to inclusion exists and is embraced by the individuals occupying various roles within the educational setting. The cases also illuminate how a lack of such a commitment can also be communicated through educational structures, policies and decisions. The individual judgments and actions of professionals can also explicitly reveal a lack of commitment towards inclusion.

The five cases in this section invite deep and critical reflection into how both individual and institutional educational practices, decisions, processes and policies reflect a commitment to inclusion. The implications of the existence or absence of this commitment to inclusion is further explored through the written commentaries and professional inquiry processes that follow the cases.

G. L. Porter and D. Smith (eds.), Exploring Inclusive Educational Practices
Through Professional Inquiry, 31–69.
© 2011 Sense Publishers. All rights reserved.

CASE ONE: CRAFT A QUILT

"Look he's shivering. His hands and arms are freezing," our grade two teacher exclaims. The teaching assistant scoots past me in the hallway. "He needs a quilt," she calls out. I followed closely on her heels. I wondered why Josh needed a quilt. Is he in shock? We had this happen once before earlier in the school year and had to call an ambulance. Josh was in hospital for three days.

Mrs. Hooper wraps Josh in a blanket that she keeps in the classroom just for this purpose. He looks much better now and is even trying to grin at us. I stayed in the classroom for several minutes making sure that Josh was all right. Looking at the freckled, but pale-faced, boy I thought about the time before when he had been hospitalized. We were all so concerned.

As I walked back to the school office, I reflect on Mrs. Hopper's comment about getting a quilt for Josh. Her choice of the word "quilt" seemed a little strange to me. In a way maybe it was a good choice. Quilts take time to sew and there are so many pieces to them. Come to think of it, planning for Josh, our new student, was in many ways like crafting a quilt. There are so many pieces of the educational plan that need to be developed for a child with medically fragile needs. The development of the plan takes a great deal of time and a variety of resource staff are involved.

Each medical issue surrounding Josh has raised so many questions. My thoughts return to the little boy shivering beneath a rough blanket. Josh moved here on such short notice. It had left me with a very narrow window of time to collaborate with his family, other caregivers and his medical and educational support team. For the first few days, I didn't even have his cumulative school record from his previous school placement. I had to arrange educational sessions for our teachers and the teacher assistant who would work directly with Josh. Even now there are so many unanswered questions and concerns about Josh. I've done my best to try to see that Josh is safe and happy at our school. There are daily challenges but, as, principal, I've tried to do my best for him and for the school staff who work with him.

One of the school's parent volunteers interrupts my thoughts by knocking on the frame of my office door. She startles me. I must have been daydreaming. "I know how to make a quilt. Let's all make one for Josh," she exclaims.

What a great idea. I immediately accept her offer to help us create a special quilt for Josh. The next morning I find myself in the centre aisle of our local fabric store. My hands grip a detailed list of material and sewing items. I am sure that it must be obvious from the perplexed look on my face that I don't know how to sew and that I am totally out of my element.

My eyes scan each bolt of cloth. There are so many colours, patterns and textures. The possible permutations and combinations seem endless. Trying to imagine the swatches of fabric together was like trying to prepare for the uncertainty of Josh's behaviour. He, too, could certainly demonstrate a variety of patterns and colours. His behaviour could vary widely throughout the school day. It could range from quiet concentration in math class to uncontrollable screaming in the playground. Even his eye and skin colour changed when he was upset.

Josh's mind, like a bolt of cloth, holds potential. I'm thinking of how it might unfold if I create an environment that will foster his true abilities. Right now his abilities seem hidden in the folds of his cognitive and physical challenges.

I remember our first case conference when approximately twenty resource staff sat in cramped student desks that had been pulled together to create a long boardroom table. I started the June meeting by explaining that Josh was entering grade two in the fall and that he would be coming to our school. Our kindergarten to grade five school has an enrolment of three hundred and fifty students. Students with special needs make up about ten percent of our population.

Mr. Marino, the school district's special education supervisor introduces Josh's parents and each of the resource staff around the table who will be part of Josh's support network. He also briefly explains to us how each of the resource staff would contribute to Josh's programming and care.

The room falls silent. Josh's father begins to speak. "We're not sure we want Josh to come to this school." The faces around the table look surprised. Josh's father explains that he is not sure that our school will be able to cope with Josh and his needs. He tells us that Josh's epileptic seizures cause him to regularly aspirate his liquid food. He indicates that Josh is non-verbal and will need help with his feeding and toileting. Josh has limited vision and other sensory needs. He'll require a wheelchair, change table, lift and assistive technology including a voice output system.

We are all making notes furiously. My mind begins to spin. How will we obtain all these resources before Josh arrives at our school in September? How will we learn how to deal with Josh's many challenges?

Josh's dad asks, "Do you have a private change room?" "No." I reply. "Our school doesn't have a special room to change students." I know that modifying the infrastructure of the washroom area to include a bathtub, lift, change table and sink will be a very time consuming and expensive endeavour. I try to maintain my composure but the implications of meeting this student's needs are overwhelming. I look at the shocked faces of the teachers sitting around the table. How should I respond?

"I'll begin immediately to investigate what arrangements can be made." My eyes meet the concerned eyes of Josh's parents. It is then that I realize that I am not the only anxious participant at this case conference.

During the summer months I met with district resource staff, a construction renovation team, teachers, the teaching assistant, Josh's parents and his doctor. We tried to put all the pieces together for September.

Josh's first few months at the school were challenging for all of us. All of the pieces were not fitting neatly together. We have all learned so much and have tried to ensure that each piece of his individualized education plan eventually fits together to create a blanket of support and security for Josh.

By December, Josh begins to be included by his peers. He enjoys story time and music. He grins at jokes, acknowledges others with a nod and motions toward the teaching assistant when he wants her to move him into the reading circle.

We continue to try to accommodate Josh's needs. Everyday remains a challenge for the school team. I try to support the staff and to ensure Josh is happy and gets the best care that we can provide. Some days I leave the school feeling so overwhelmed by the demands of the day.

Now it is February and I am standing amid bolts of fabric engulfed in thoughts of Josh. A sales clerk approaches and asks, "Can I help you?"

If only she only knew how much help I really needed.

PROFESSIONAL INQUIRY

Assumptions and Beliefs

- Discuss how the assumptions and beliefs of each of the educators in this case influenced their decisions and actions.
- Discuss the level of professional responsibility each educator demonstrated towards Josh's success.

School Culture

- Describe the culture and ethos of this school.
- Identify the actions and decisions that contributed to the development of a shared vision towards inclusion in this school.
- Explore the significance of a shared vision of inclusion for a school community.

Leadership Practices

- Identify the possible impact of the principal's actions and modeling upon the staff, volunteers and students in this school in regards to Josh.
- Discuss the principal's perspective and attitude towards fully including Josh in the school.
- Analyze the strategies employed by the principal to fully include Josh in this school.
- Discuss the principal's approach to collaborating with Josh's parents.

Inclusive Practices

- Discuss the impact a school's culture can have upon fully including all students.
- Identify the resources necessary to fully include Josh within this school.
- Critique the actions of the district's special education supervisor in supporting the inclusion of Josh within the school.
- List additional strategies to support Josh in this school.

Ethical Practice

- Identify the ethical dimensions associated with this case.

CASE COMMENTARY REFLECTIONS

After reading the commentaries reflect on the following:

New Insights
Identify new insights gained from reading the commentaries.

Understandings
Discuss the impact of the commentaries on your understandings of inclusive education.

Questions
Identify questions that emerge for you from reading the commentaries.

CASE COMMENTARY 1

Heather Hogan

True inclusion means meeting the educational, physical and emotional needs of all students without exception. Although some students are more easily "included" into the regular system, from time to time, there are students who challenge our beliefs and abilities. Such is the student in this case study. I have had this student in my school in the past. He wasn't named Josh but he had extensive medical, physical and cognitive needs. When he was entering Kindergarten, we had a similar meeting with the parent and our team to discuss how we were going to accommodate all of his needs. This seemed like a daunting task at the time but there was never a doubt that this little boy had every right to attend his local school alongside his peers.

In this case, the parents appeared to be somewhat apprehensive and the school did not have all of the answers at the initial meeting, but they believed Josh had a right to be there. They may have questioned how and where they could provide for his needs but that did not stop them from beginning the process.

It would take a lot of time, education, communication, problem solving and patience to ensure that Josh would be welcomed and have a place at the school where both his physical and educational needs would be met.

Many schools will use a team approach to develop a plan for students who have extensive physical and cognitive needs. The work of this team, which includes the parents, is to create an individualized plan that will address all of Josh's needs while moving him forward.

The school chose to look at Josh's positive qualities rather than letting his challenges get in the way. Children are very accepting. This openness leads to increased interaction with classmates. A true indicator of successful inclusion for me is acceptance by peers. It is essential that Josh be included in an age appropriate class with his peers since they are the ones who will be with him during his many years in the school system.

As mentioned in the case study, some days are more difficult than others. However, when educators have a core belief and deep commitment to inclusion they are more likely to be able to weather the difficult times and move forward towards the attainment of this goal.

CASE COMMENTARY 2

Amanda Watkins and Cor Meijer

I was impressed with the reflective approach taken by the author – the use of the metaphor and imagery of the quilt is a good tool for sharing reflections with wider audiences (maybe including those who also work with Josh?) I wonder how further reflection on other aspects of the experience of working with Josh can be applied in other contexts?

The author doesn't reflect on this issue, but it seems clear that there must be something about the school and the staff team that Josh's parents understood and trusted enough to agree their son should be educated there, despite everyone's initial reservations. What was that? How can it be explored and understood more overtly? How can it be built on? Perhaps this attitude or feeling that resulted in Josh's parents trusting the team is more important for ensuring the successful inclusion of a boy like Josh than resources and equipment?

Within the work of the European Agency for Development in Special Needs Education, we hear, see and find that positive attitudes and a school ethos and culture of meeting diverse needs are the foundations of successful inclusion. Without positive attitudes amongst all school stakeholders, inclusion is an uphill battle. The leadership within a school and the ability to communicate and engender a shared vision for an inclusive school culture is central to shaping and promoting positive attitudes.

The author days: 'Some days I leave the school feeling so overwhelmed by the demands of the day ... If only she knew how much help I really needed.' I can understand this. I imagine dealing with the complex needs of such a student has been a steep learning curve, but has resulted in the development of confidence as well as skills in the team. How can this increased confidence, commitment and knowledge be applied in other areas? Is it possible to see any transferability?

Perhaps making some of the 'informal' and tacit knowledge within the team in dealing with Josh more 'formal' and explicit is a way of recording learning for future situations?

CASE COMMENTARY 3

Zana Lutfiyya

The principal at Josh's school typifies how many school principals feel about supporting and educating students with special needs. They truly want to 'do the right thing'. They want to take into account the needs and desires of all of the students, the teachers, teaching assistants, consultants, and families. However, pulling it all together can be an ongoing struggle. We expect principals to be school leaders, and they usually are. Principals need to hold positive expectations about the capabilities of students and staff. They need to provide guidance, reassurance and support to all members of the school community. In turn, principals need the training, support and resources that will enable them to fulfill their leadership role in an effective way. When principals have not had the opportunity to teach students with diverse needs themselves, they may experience difficulty fostering the attitudes and skills that they need to promote in others.

The analogy of crafting a quilt is an apt one for the work that educators do. While individuals may prepare certain pieces themselves, it takes a group of people, working as a team, to bring all of the pieces together into a coherent and beautiful whole. Each quilt block is made, sewn to the others, and then attached to the quilt's backing or foundation for the entire structure. Finally, small, neat stitches, done in intricate patterns are added to bring depth to the quilt. Quilters are guided by the pattern they have chosen to follow, but inevitably make changes and adaptations along the way.

I will suggest that the actual thought and effort that goes into crafting a unique quilt for a student like Josh will ultimately be as significant as the finished quilt itself. Successfully educating all of our children well is a perennially engaging, challenging and unfinished journey. And like all journeys, our traveling companions make all the difference in the world.

CASE COMMENTARY 4

John Loughran

This case builds up in an interesting and engaging way. As Josh's needs become apparent, the title of the case takes on added significance. The way the story line is constructed draws the reader in to begin to recognize that it is not just Josh that is important to this case; it is also his caregivers, teachers, the principal and Josh's parents. All of these individuals form a support system for Josh yet, as becomes increasingly apparent, each of these participants really require support and under-standing as well – perhaps that is something that is too easily overlooked in a situation such as this.

Stereotypes of "special needs" are challenged through this case as that which Josh requires slowly unfolds in a thoughtful way that perhaps mirrors what the situation was initially like for the author. At first, the idea of enrolling a student with special needs might not appear to be all that demanding. However, as the implications in so doing become apparent, so the level of support and the necessary adjustment to the 'normal' things in a school environment begin to bite. Initially there may be issues around the physical nature of the environment, but of course, it does not take too long before the well being of the student moves beyond the physical alone. As those shifts in understanding arise, the nature of support then takes on new meaning not only in terms of what needs to be done, but also whose needs require attention – when and how.

The parents' concerns in the case regarding the school's ability to support Josh reveals the complexity involved in fully including all students: "We're not sure we want Josh to come to this school." This shift in perspective gives the case real strength and causes the reader to think again about the anxiety associated with caring for students with special needs from a range of perspectives "My eyes meet Josh's parent's concerned eyes. It is then that I realize I am not the only anxious participant at this case conference."

The reality of what it really means to work with students with diverse needs is well demonstrated through this case; it highlights a number of salient issues in ways that invite the reader to think again. And that is a good thing.

CONNECTING TO PROFESSIONAL PRACTICE

The case commentary writers identify the importance of school culture, leadership practices, shared vision, joint commitment, core beliefs, shared responsibility and collaborative team work as essential elements in supporting inclusion. Consider how these elements, dispositions and practices have been reflected in your practice within the various professional contexts in which you have worked. Identify how this case might impact upon your own professional judgment and actions.

CASE TWO: BUILDING BRIDGES

"Steve. Steve," I called out to him. His eyes are fearful. I feel his anger. His anger borders on rage.

Fitting in is so very challenging for Steve. Often his own inappropriate actions and words cause his peers to persecute him. Even with his outbursts, however, I felt that he wanted to be accepted. His eyes were so bright and bold – but his very existence was so tarnished from the poisoned environment of his early life.

Steve has experienced a dysfunctional home, parental divorce, neglect and physical abuse. These experiences have left deep wounds. I realized that, with his basic needs unmet, academic success and social skills would not figure as priorities. How could they be for this grade eight student? From the perspective of my own secure and ordinary life, was it possible for me to ever comprehend the weight of the baggage that he carries each day?

Steve is like a caged bear. He is curious yet reluctant. He is strong yet afraid. He is aggressive yet fearful when challenged. Trust is not an option. Trust requires faith. His faith is like a pane of glass – transparent, brittle and often left shattered.

The reports from his social worker describe the number of times he returned from school to find home doors locked and no one willing to let him in. These reports depicted Steve as a lonely, skinny, under-dressed kid, just hanging around and waiting.

I know that I need to make a connection with Steve to foster a relationship. I know that I need to confront him about his current reality and to provide a continuum of support and hope. How can I develop a rapport with this student? How can I prove to Steve that I can be trusted? How could he trust any adult? I go over and over the issues that are part of Steve and his life. I ask myself, "What strategies might work? How should I try to begin a conversation with him? How could I build up some sense of trust?"

I am the new principal at Steve's school, Forest Ridge. I have only known him for few months. When he sees me, he nods vaguely in my direction. He never makes eye contact. His response is minimal. It is like he wants to be invisible.

Test scores reveal that academically he is below grade level. His academic deficits have accumulated over time along with his years of neglect, lost opportunities and his rapidly dissipating sense of hope. I can tell that school is a chore for Steve and that he knows that he doesn't fit in with the other students. He seeks attention through his sly wisecracking, his mimicking of teachers, overturning his classmates' books and tripping them in the playground.

His academic curriculum has been modified in an attempt to meet his needs. Our student services team has drafted a special education plan centred on the development of appropriate anger management techniques. Steve's anger can frequently be seen in his face and in his walk. Steve grabs attention from his peers by his aggressive defiance and argumentative nature. It is easy for him to gain power over the other students. All it takes is one of his threatening gestures or the sound of the eerie whistling noise that he makes before striking out at someone.

In Steve's world trust does not exist. There is no value in honesty. Rarely can I believe what he says. Trust is not a word I use in his presence. It is meaningless for him. At times I truly wonder if he really knows the difference between right and wrong.

I have read and reread his cumulative record and his student services file. I have consulted with the teachers who have worked hard to unlock the tight box that is called Steve. Little insight flows from these records and experiences. I do recognize both strength and pride in his nature and posture. I fear his pride will stifle any desire to ever ask for help.

I secretly pledge to make life better for Steve. I don't know yet how this will happen.

Where should I start? How do I address academic needs when his basic needs at home are so evidently lacking? How do I address the bullying he experiences from peers when they are fed up and are only turning his tactics back on him? I'm not surprised at the giggles and held noses. Steve's hygiene habits are poor. No wonder Steve's has such a poor self-concept of himself. I ask myself, "Do social skills trump academics? How can I make this school a safe environment where Steve is valued and accepted by his peers?" With so few positive experiences and good role models in Steve's life, I wonder how I can ever convince him that there is value in coming to school.

Mr. Jones, Steve's classroom teacher, approaches me. He is also greatly concerned with Steve's lack of effort and has identified many dates where homework has not been completed. Mr. Jones' face says it all. He is experiencing conflict between compassion for Steve and his duty as a teacher to impart knowledge. Other teachers at Forest Ridge believe that Steve is capable of meeting their expectations but that their repeated efforts to enforce satisfactory completion have failed. Mr. Jones and other teachers have expressed their concerns that trouble is ahead for this child.

My frustration is mounting. The barriers to making genuine contact with Steve seem insurmountable. I am desperately seeking a weakness in Steve's resolve. I need to find a way to enter his world and lead him out of his tight box.

One Friday in late January, I glance into Steve's classroom on my morning walkabout. I notice that Steve in not there. I continue down the hall past a room that holds the school kitchen. There stood Steve working with his head bent over the kitchen counter beside the teaching assistant. Steve's face shines. It is lit up with excitement. He even has an enthusiastic air about him as he moves from the counter to the stove. I stop and continue to watch mesmerized by the scene.

A math lesson in our school kitchen has provided an opportunity for Steve to cook. Measuring ingredients, mixing and baking seem to provide a joy for Steve that transforms him. This is the first time I have ever observed Steve enjoying anything. He is involved, happy and engaged. Can this be the opening that I have been trying to find?

I acknowledge Steve and remark about how happy he looks in math class. "Hello Steve. You sure look like you are enjoying your school work today."

I leave the kitchen and return to my office. Thirty minutes later, I hear a knock at my door. I turn in my chair and see a face shining with happiness and pride.

Steve's smile warms my heart. He grins and asks me "Would you like a brownie, Mr. Adams? I have never baked anything before and Mrs. Hamilton says they are the best." We share a grin. I realize that he has taken a first step to beginning a conversation. Steve extends his hand like a drawing bridge as he offers me a brownie. I know that we have made a connection.

I accept his generous offering and eat the brownie. It is the best brownie that I have ever eaten.

PROFESSIONAL INQUIRY

Professional Knowledge

– Identify the professional knowledge demonstrated by the principal in this case.
– Explain the significance of the principal's professional knowledge for supporting inclusion of all students.

Commitment to Inclusion

– Discuss the importance of the principal's commitment to fully include Steve within the school.
– Speculate on the impact the principal's commitment to inclusion may have on the staff and students in this school.

Educational Practices

– Identify the educational value associated with Steve's engagement in a math lesson facilitated in the school kitchen.
– Discuss methods to enhance the educational programming provided to Steve.

Inclusive Practices

– Identify the value and challenges associated with creating innovative educational programs that honor student strengths, interests and incorporate holistic learning approaches.
– Discuss the impact resources can have on the inclusion of students within schools.
– Analyze the school's plan for meeting Steve's needs.
– Identify additional strategies for supporting Steve in the school.

CASE COMMENTARY REFLECTIONS

After reading the commentaries reflect on the following:

New Insights
Identify new insights gained from reading the commentaries.

Understandings
Discuss the impact of the commentaries on your understandings of inclusive education.

Questions
Identify questions that emerge from reading the commentaries.

CASE COMMENTARY 1

Bendina Miller

When I think of Steve I have two clear questions. How can Steve demonstrate his learning and how can that learning be translated into credits toward recognized success? It is clear that Steve's background is unique, however, when the principal saw Steve achieving success in the home economics lab how would that success be translated into the traditional recognition of success. Clearly, mathematics was applied in the baking of the brownies — fractions, measurement, temperature, etc. Social responsibility is an aspect of cooking in the lab — team work, sharing, and communication. If Steve had to read the recipe there would be an application of literacy skills. So, a truly honouring and inspiring school would assess the unique learning outcomes and celebrate the demonstration of knowledge and skill. While Steve demonstrated a significant lack of self-confidence I cannot help but believe that if he received authentic recognition for the learning he demonstrated in making the brownies it would build significant confidence for him, as a learner. If he could be reassured that making brownies was about more than baking — it was about reading, numeracy, social responsibility — that would be an authentic way of providing learning feedback to Steve, of building his confidence and of assessing his learning.

The piece that is missing for me in this scenario is the inclusive nature of learning. Had the principal seen Steve in the home economic lab working with a group of age-grade appropriate peers, applying literacy and numeracy skills to preparing and baking brownies then I would see this as an authentic and inclusive learning experience for all students. Steve working alone in a lab with an adult is a segregated learning experience which lacks the authentic natural experience. There is much to learn from this case study. There are many practical and authentic applications which could move this case study into a viable inclusive education scenario — applied mathematics and applied literacy which would be powerful learning environments for all students.

CASE COMMENTARY 2

Marie Schoeman

Many schools today have to deal with challenging behavior such as that of Steve. Teachers feel frustrated and helpless to address the educational needs of students who have so many problems at home which find expression in disruptive and anti-social behavior at school. Cases such as these often make them doubt that inclusion can ever work. They would prefer that the child is taken off their hands and dealt with by a professional who is trained for this. We know however, that it would be impossible and inappropriate to send away every child like Steve. Every school is a micro-cosmos of society and needs to find responses to the challenges that society offers if it truly wants to become an inclusive centre of learning, care and support. The first step towards solving Steve's problem is being sensitive and responsive towards his needs and home circumstances.

At first, his teachers were at a loss to making a breakthrough in turning around his learning breakdown which had become cumulative over time. It was only when an alternative approach to teaching mathematics was explored, by linking it to practical and real life experiences, that the key could be found to how Steve learns best. The lesson clearly appealed to his learning style and interests and allowed him the opportunity to succeed rather than fail. Adapting the teaching method is the first step in curriculum differentiation.

The head teacher, through his persistence and commitment to addressing Steve's needs, was the one who observed Steve's breakthrough in learning and seeing it as a key to supporting him further. Inclusion cannot be realized without the support of the school principal and whole staff. Observing a child in his learning context by a critical and reflexive outside person is one of the most important first steps in finding a way to effectively plan the support of an individual student.

In my context in South Africa, socio-economic challenges are considered one of the most critical barriers to learning and development. In communities where many parents are unemployed, disrupted family life and violence affect the lives of many children. Our education system wants to ensure that all schools become inclusive centers of care and support. There needs to be a component of social support and counselling, involving collaboration between health, social welfare services and education, in all education support. But curriculum still remains the key to successful inclusion. That is why we emphasize building the capacity of teachers and schools to differentiate the curriculum and adapt their classroom methodologies in accordance with a child centered approach.

CASE COMMENTARY 3

Tanya Whitney

This case highlights that addressing the social development issues of an exceptional student are as important or perhaps "more" important than identifying an instructional/academic response. Basic human needs of belonging to the community must be met before we can assume that there will be any meaningful engagement in learning.

However, schools are largely academic institutions, and proper assessments of student ability should always be a factor that is considered and clinically assessed from the beginning. Resource teachers must be vigilant in administering assessments that are accurate and not make program decisions based on assumptions and class performance alone. If we work at intentionally building up this student's sense of worth, then the outcome would be that he will find more reason to engage in further learning. Building up a "sense of worth" is usually not achieved through sterile and targeted teaching or small group sessions on "self-esteem" or "anger-management", it is achieved through real opportunities for inclusion.

In my experience, opportunities that cultivate real-life community involvement have a greater impact on changing a student's behavior and ultimately his/her sense of self. These opportunities require more creativity, collaboration and commitment. They also require teachers and school administrators to commit to this type of intervention.

It is important for the school to have developed a plan that includes these forms of support. For example, "interest inventories", "goal setting", "meaningful work experiences", and "service clubs" must all be clearly identified as tier 2 and 3 interventions on the school's Pyramid of Intervention. Also, the school must actively work at building an "inventory" of work/service experiences for students. Inviting the cooperation of school staff as well as community volunteers is vital. School staff can indicate their willingness to be an adult mentor who would be able to "connect" or supervise a learning experience. Community agencies can provide opportunities within and without the building for targeted students (food kitchen, race track maintenance, and daycare).

Such services all require coordination from the school level: a time-consuming investment for sure, an investment that can make a positive difference for students such as the one in this case.

CASE COMMENTARY 4

Seamus Hagerty

The trouble with teachers is that they want to teach! What's the matter with that, you say. Isn't that their job? Well, yes and no. The task for those who work in schools – as it is for parents and caregivers – is to help children learn. This is not quite the same thing.

Teaching does not guarantee learning. Insisting on the difference between the two may sound like playing with words, but it is not. When we stop looking at schools as places where teaching is done and start seeing them as venues where learning happens, we get a very different set of perspectives – as schools which have made the transition can testify.

Steve is the victim of the traditional school focus on a specific form of teaching. His classroom teacher struggles with his 'duty…to impart knowledge'. No doubt Mr. Jones is a good teacher in the traditional sense and, clearly, a caring one. But his 'teaching' did not lead to much learning on Steve's part. This only came when Steve was placed in a different, *non-didactic* environment. Suddenly, Steve blossoms, behaving well, relating well to people and learning.

This wining tale raises lots of issues. Let me focus on just two. First, how did the breakthrough happen? Was it the teaching assistant and the rapport she had with Steve? Or the fact that he was out of the everyday classroom? Or was it the task itself? Did Steve discover a particular affinity for food preparation and cooking?

We don't actually know what triggered his positive reaction, so we don't have a recipe for repeating at Forest Ridge or elsewhere.

What we do have is an affirmation that progress in possible, that youngsters with the most unlikely learning trajectories can 'switch on' and become competent, even avid, learners. For school staff, who struggle with disengaged learners, this affirmation can be helpful in sustaining the commitment to and belief in all learners by educators.

A second issue to reflect upon is how broad Steve's learning is going to be now that he is enthusiastic about work in the kitchen. Important though cooking is – and unduly neglected maybe in most schooling – it cannot be the basis for an entire curriculum. Steve's school now faces the challenge of nurturing his new-found interest in learning and channeling it into other areas so that he becomes a successful learner across a range of topics.

CONNECTING TO PROFESSIONAL PRACTICE

The commentary writers raise questions related to the meaning of full and authentic inclusion; the significance and role of community supports and the recognition of unique learning experiences within school systems. What is your response to the questions and suggestions offered by the commentary writers? Which perspectives identified in the commentaries resonate strongly with you? Which perspectives identified in the commentaries do not resonate with you?

The commentary writers also suggest that building teacher capacity to differentiate instruction and foster the development of inclusive communities requires creativity, motivation and commitment. Consider the ways in which you have supported teacher capacity and efficacy in your own professional practice.

CASE THREE: I JUST WANT TO GO TO SCHOOL LIKE A NORMAL KID

She looked directly in my eyes and blurted out, "I am tired of this life. I want to go to school like a normal kid. I am not going back to that house."

I was stunned. Sarah had looked timid and lonely when she had walked into the guidance office. I had felt that it was likely going to be difficult to pry any information out of this adolescent.

Sarah was brought to my office by the community agency that works with kids whose parents receive social assistance. She had been out of school for most of the year because she had been bullied and teased about the fact that her parents were well known drug dealers in the community. I had also heard the gossip about the Franklin family.

Sarah went on to explain that she had dropped out of school last year. She had also started using drugs herself. Apparently her own parents made them available to her. "Hey," she said with her shaggy hair eclipsing her eyes. "This is not the life I wanted. I've decided to quit. I'm afraid I'll wind up like my parents."

Sarah paused and brushed the hair away. She continued, "I want to get back into school and make something of myself." She had come to the right school. Sarah would be able to access the resources and individualized programs that were coordinated by our resource teacher. In my role as her guidance counselor, I could help Sarah access community agencies that were part of our specialized school resource team. It felt good to be able to offer Sarah that kind of support.

Sarah had not made it through a full semester of grade nine. The resource teacher and I set out a plan for her consideration. I explained to her that she could attend our program in the afternoon and concentrate on her English and math skills. Her quick smile told me that she was happy about this proposal. Sarah grabbed my hand and shook it.

"I'll be here on Monday afternoon - for sure, Sir!" I believed her.

I immediately called Sarah's social worker. She had been directly involved with the Family and Community Services agency representative who had brought Sarah to our school this morning. We arranged an early morning meeting the next day.

During that meeting, the resource teacher and I learned that it was Sarah, herself, who had called the Family and Community Services and asked to be removed from her home. Sarah said that she wanted to lead a normal life and go to school. That call must have taken so much courage.

The social worker went on to explain that the Family and Community Service agency quickly became involved and began the processes required to remove Sarah from her family home. I indicated that school services would provide whatever support necessary for Sarah. I was impressed at the huge step this girl had taken and what strength of character must reside with her.

We obtained her cumulative school record. It revealed that her attendance and marks were above average until she had reached grade eight. Early in grade eight her marks began to drop dramatically and her attendance became sporadic. She had started grade nine at a different high school but stopped attending school before the end of the first semester.

Her attendance at our school over the next few months was inconsistent. She was still living at home. She was open about her struggles. "We have loud screaming fights that end in broken dishes. There are weird strangers sleeping on the floor in the house. I'm tired of eating fast food. The place is a mess."

I assured Sarah that the school and her social worker would continue to support her in all the ways that we could. "No worries about your school. You will not be suspended or kicked out because of attendance. We know that you are doing the best that you can right now. We are happy to have you here and happy that you are motivated to learn." Sarah exhaled a sigh of relief. "Thank you," she said before walking out the door.

I checked with Sarah's resource teacher. Mrs. James reported, "Sarah is showing strong reading and writing skills, but she has gaps in her learning when it comes to math."We discussed a number of ways to support Sarah in accumulating those lost pieces that she would need to progress.

The court date to determine if Sarah would be moved to a temporary foster home approached. Sarah became increasingly agitated and unresponsive. She said repeatedly, "I want to leave that house." She constantly asked, "Will I be able to talk to the judge myself? Is there anything I can do to improve my chances of leaving that rattrap? Why would anyone make me stay there?"

I wanted to agree with her and to tell her that she was right and that surely things would work. The school staff could only advise her to tell the truth and try to assure her that she could attend our school as long as she needed. We really felt helpless. We felt that we were outside the system that would make this important decision for Sarah. We were so worried that the judge might decide that she had to stay with her family.

The week before the court date I was asked to prepare a report for the court. The school report commented on Sarah's attendance and academic program. We also shared some of the observations that we had made about her attitude toward school and about her behaviour. It was difficult to write the document and stick only to the facts. There were so many emotions involved. All the staff members who worked with Sarah wanted the best for her.

I wanted to go to the court and speak to the judge and to plead Sarah's case. I wanted to say, "If you do not remove this girl from her home then you should be embarrassed to call yourself a judge." Of course, I could not reveal how deeply we all felt about Sarah and her well-being.

During the four school days prior to her court date, we did not see Sarah. She would later tell us that her anxiety prevented her from being able to concentrate on anything. How could math instruction or language instruction compete with the burden of her court date and her decision to ask to be removed from the care of her parents.

Finally, we heard the judge's decision. The court did remove her from her home and placed her with a foster family on a temporary basis. I knew of the foster family. Mr. Jessop was a mechanic and his wife was a nurse at the local hospital. Our community knew both of them as solid and caring folks. They had four kids of their own so Sarah would have an instant family.

Sarah's attendance immediately improved to the point where she was present even when she was ill. After two weeks of perfect attendance, we approached Sarah and asked her about her desire to attend school for full days. The challenge would be to find courses that she could be successfully integrated into half way through the semester. We did not want Sarah to end up being overwhelmed and unsuccessful.

Our high school administration was extremely helpful in determining who might be the right teachers to provide opportunities for Sarah to learn and who would not dwell on the fact that she had missed half the year. Our staff also enlisted the enrichment-learning specialist to work with Sarah on her writing skills. Sarah loved creative writing. She was given the opportunity to participate in a school district enrichment group that focused on creative writing. To our delight, Sarah quickly accepted the opportunity to work with this group. Sarah excelled. Her skills flourished and her above average grades soared to excellence.

Her day now included attending the regular classes in the morning and coming to the resource teaching area for remedial skills in math and English in the afternoon. Sarah was still overwhelmed with the math despite having a second hour to work on her skills with us in the afternoon. After a few weeks her teachers told the resource team that Sarah was gazing out of the windows, distracted, fumbling with her pencil case and continually dropping it over the edge of her desk. She responded appropriately when spoken to but quickly returned to her daydreaming. Were we expecting too much from Sarah too quickly?

We asked Sarah if she would like to return to an individualized program in math again. She said, "No. Please, I really want to do everything the rest of the class is doing." But was this possible? Sarah had missed half of the year in math and that had made the gaps in her learning difficult to close. I was becoming concerned and approached the school district office student services team. I asked, "Could the student services department make provision for after hours tutoring to help support Sarah in math?" I described Sarah's accomplishments and struggles to the student services officer.

"Sure," he replied. We can manage tutoring three times per week. We will try and locate a recent Bachelor of Education graduate from the university to tutor Sarah. We will try to select a female graduate so Sarah can have a positive role model. Three days later Jacqueline joined the support group working with Sarah.

Jacqueline's tutoring assistance helped to close Sarah's math gaps quickly. Her anxiety level over the subject dropped. Her test results improved dramatically. A very different Sarah would come bouncing down to the resource area or my office and explode with news of her friends and her interesting classes.

I am proud of Sarah. She is a survivor. Sarah is now finishing the school year with excellent marks in math, English and science. She also recently presented a collection of her short stories at the district Enrichment Showcase.

The change in Sarah is absolutely amazing. I felt we had resolved some of Sarah's major issues and that perhaps we could relax a bit.

However, at the end of a great week for Sarah, I noticed her waiting outside, walking in circles and kicking the dirt roadway. It was about the time when her foster family normally picked her up. "Sarah, why are you still here?" She looked so sad and concerned.

In a barely audible voice, she whispered, "I have to go to my parent's house for the weekend."

Later that week, we learned that there is another court date approaching that will determine permanent custody arrangements for Sarah. Her parents have filed papers with the court asking for custody back. Once more, I worry about the judge's decision and Sarah's day in court.

I believe that her life hangs in the balance.

PROFESSIONAL INQUIRY

Professional Knowledge and Commitment

– Discuss the forms of professional knowledge and commitment that are necessary for educators to possess in their support of disengaged learners.
– Identify the actions and strategies that enabled Sarah to be included into her new school.

Instructional Practice

– Identify the instructional practices that enabled Sarah to achieve success.
– Explore the impact the learning environment had upon Sarah's emotional, physical, social and cognitive well-being.
– Generate additional supports that may have been offered to this learner.

Professional Responsibility

– Explore how the educators in this case understood their professional responsibilities.
– Discuss the possible impact of the educators' interpretations of their professional responsibilities upon their professional practice, actions and decisions in this case.

School and Community Supports

– Reflect on the school and community supports provided to Sarah and generate a list of recommendations for working with students who are disengaged from school based on this case.
– Identify the issues in this case and brainstorm collaborative strategies to respond to each one.

CASE COMMENTARY REFLECTIONS

After reading the commentaries reflect on the following:

New Insights
Identify new insights gained from reading the commentaries.

Understandings
Discuss the impact of the commentaries on your understandings of inclusive education.

Questions
Identify questions that emerge for you from reading the commentaries.

CASE COMMENTARY 1

Kendra MacLaren

The two things that stand out immediately in this case is that Sarah is certainly a strong, intelligent and capable young woman. The second is that she has been lucky to access a lot of support from the school, social services and the community. So often we hear of cases where funding is denied and students are left helpless with no way out. I was so pleased to see that every obstacle that has arisen has been overcome, or at least managed. The entire system appears to have wrapped its arms around Sarah to help ensure she has a healthy lifestyle and a successful experience in school. It is disheartening to think that there is even a possibility that this young girl could be returned to her family so soon. Her personal and academic success will hopefully be a factor the judge looks at seriously when the case returns to court.

In addition to speaking with the guidance counselor, I think it is important for Sarah to talk to a counselor on a regular basis outside of the school. It does not appear that Sarah's use of drugs has really been dealt with. I think it is important that her drug use is addressed professionally so she can learn to deal with stress in an alternate way. There is still the possibility of Sarah having to face another huge disappointment: moving back home. Sarah will need to learn alternate ways of dealing with her emotions in order for her to remain successful.

I also think it would be valuable for Sarah to join a support group such as Alateen. I realize she feels different than the other kids at her school. Going to a program like this would let her see that she is not alone and there are a lot of families that deal with substance abuse. This could be another support network for Sarah that will help her throughout her teen years. It is also another avenue for her to meet teens dealing with similar issues. Peer support is important and it may also help restore her self-esteem.

The Jessop's appear to be providing a very stable, supportive and healthy environment for Sarah. I certainly think good communication with them and the school is important. It would also be great for the Jessop's to receive information about the issues Sarah will be dealing with. The more informed they are about the effects young people encounter from living in homes with drug use, the more they will understand any changes they may see in Sarah's behavior. They may also be able to relate better to her and form a better relationship with her. Sarah needs people she can trust. She needs to know people are in her corner.

To deal with the stress of the upcoming trial, Sarah may need additional supports. A peer- helper, handouts for notes and other resources may be necessary for her to stay on top of her work and not fall behind in school. It may also be effective for the guidance counselor, perhaps in conjunction with a school youth worker, to have an open door policy so that the weeks prior to the case, Sarah can go to them at any point through the school day if she needs to talk. Just knowing there is someone there to talk to may relieve a lot of her anxiety. In addition to this, the Principal should call a case conference involving all staff working with Sarah. At this meeting, staff can be informed of the situation and also made aware of any adjustments, or supports that have been put in place. It may also be a good time to brainstorm possibilities for safeguards in the event Sarah does return home to her family. Should this happen, Sarah will need additional supports. Staff should prepare an action plan to help Sarah deal with this living situation.

It is important that Sarah is supported by the school regardless of the outcome of the trial. The trial alone will be a traumatic experience and it is crucial that supports and allowances are made to ensure Sarah's stability and success.

CASE COMMENTARY 2

Audrey Lampert

More must be done to alleviate the fear that accompanies the Family Court process. Perhaps in cases such as Sarah's, school authorities need to include more than "just the facts" in reports they are asked to submit to court. They need to be comfortable in revealing how deeply they feel about Sarah and her well-being. In custody cases, a guidance counselor, acting *in loco parentis*, especially one in whom the youth has confided, should be considered the youth's advocate, and should be encouraged to participate, not only by providing a written submission to the Court, but also by presenting an oral report that the Judge can discuss with the youth advocate. All facets of the child must be given a voice in court: those representing Education, Justice, Social Development, Income Assistance and Mental Health.

Frequently, government departments have their own sets of policies, procedures and protocols that differ from one another, thus, posing obstacles when they should be working together to alleviate the mental and emotional stresses and strains upon the individual. Often, the nature of the case does not hold the same priority ranking from one department to another. The obvious result in many similar cases is that the child is ill-served by the very people whose job it is to protect him/her. The student loses faith in adult role models, loses opportunities for academic success alongside peers and, in the long term, destroys potential for employability because skill-building has been interrupted by long periods of absenteeism.

As a school administrator, I have seen this scenario too many times. Ironically, it became necessary to request that a Grade 8 student, with a 5-year history of excessive absenteeism, be suspended from school. This strategy was the only means available to get the attention of the delinquent parent and force a meeting with the parent and District officials. The Department of Social Development does not seem to equate chronic absenteeism year after year as an abdication of parental responsibilities, that is, child neglect. From an educator's perspective, this is child neglect in that it denies the child's intellectual and social development. To compensate, the education system "socially promotes" the child to keep the student with her peer group. This strategy is a double-edged sword for it compels the student to feel intellectually inadequate when she compares her academic achievement with that of her peers. An "alternate school" placement can, in some cases, address this problem success-fully, but there needs to be congruency in the definitions of "neglect" that includes all domains of wellness: intellectual, emotional, social as well as physical.

This writer is of the opinion that it is absolutely essential that the child should have the right to speak in court to the judge directly, rather than indirectly through filters. As well, the justice system could be made less intimidating for students if teachers and counselors could meet judges via professional development oppor-tunities or as guest speakers in their classrooms to talk to students about the justice system, or on field trips to court…strategies that have been used successfully in my career. Making these connections can remove the mystique and fear surrounding our courts such as that expressed by Sarah and her supporters at school.

CASE COMMENTARY 3

Tracy Beck

Most teachers come to their careers out of a genuine desire to help students. They want to educate and empower the children in their care, to be motivational and inspirational, to help students learn, grow, and develop. With the constant demands of administrative paperwork, reporting timelines, classroom management, and parental communication, some teachers however, find themselves losing their passion. They still want the best for their students, but in many regards, it feels like some situations are out of their control, or as the guidance counselor in the case study indicated, they are "outside the system," making vital decisions.

Sarah was experiencing tremendous challenges at home, which transferred into her life as a student. Despite a drastic change in her academic performance in grade eight, and significant attendance issues, it doesn't appear that the school intervened in any way. Further to that, at a new school in grade nine, her attendance continued to slip, eventually leading to her dropping out before the end of the first semester. Although the guidance counselor had heard rumors about her family life, there isn't anything to indicate that any steps were taken to support her in school during grade nine.

Educators have both a legal and moral responsibility to report child abuse to their local child protection agency. Once Family and Community Services and the school became involved, they heard Sarah report clear examples of emotional abuse and neglect, yet this didn't seem to spur any formal reporting or any further action. If she were being physically or sexually abused, surely she would have been taken out of the home immediately, with a full investigation launched. Why does society seem to view emotional abuse and neglect as less significant or impactful than the more physical forms of abuse? A school social worker or community counselor of some kind may have also been able to help Sarah work through some of the scars left by the abuse. She was certainly demonstrating signs of significant stress and concern that she may be placed with her family again. Nothing in the case study indicates that this form of support was offered.

How is it that some students can manage to slip through the cracks, as Sarah did? In high schools there are Student Success initiatives in place to ensure that situations like this never happen. Do they work though? Are they enough to ensure that each student has the supports necessary to succeed? In what way was the School Resource Team involved in Sarah's situation? What resources are provided to school departments? While Family and Community Services, as well as the school, are clearly working with Sarah's best interests in mind, it seems like there are a lot of others lines of intervention and support that could be available to her.

CASE COMMENTARY 4

Anke Grafe

What are Sarah's options to continue with her new life (school and foster family) without completely losing her natural bonds with her original family? The solution can't be black or white–meaning either parents or school–ideally it will include both the parents and the school.

In order to reach this aim she needs to receive further counseling to boost her self-esteem and confidence in making the right decision. It's the great step away from her original statement, "I'm tired of this life..." towards "That's me; That's my vision of my own future; Yes, I'm the daughter of my parents, however, I am not their victim."

Even at this stage, she can proudly look back to what she has already achieved. She benefited highly from previous counseling, what she needs to learn now is to get independent of this counseling and start her own self-instruction because her life hangs in the balance if she does not realize her own strengths as well as weaknesses.

In practice, the counselor could set the task that Sarah describes her own personal profile. On the one hand they need to continue with the original support in order not to risk a setback, and on the other hand she needs to work on her personal profile and her self-esteem. For the best interest of this student, her voice and perspectives need to be heard by the courts that ultimately have the power to make the final decision regarding her living arrangements.

CONNECTING TO PROFESSIONAL PRACTICE

The commentary writers identify the complex needs of this adolescent student and raise some questions related to the past interventions employed by the school.

They also make recommendations for future actions that may help support this student.

Consider a student from your own experience that was able to "slip through the cracks" within the school system. What could have the local school, school system and community done to better serve this student? What recommendations would you offer to schools, families and community agencies to help ensure that all students are fully included in schools and have access to safe growth promoting environments?

CASE FOUR: ONE OF MY GREATEST CHALLENGES

"How will the morning be?" I wonder. "Will Ilija come off the bus with a big smile that covers his entire freckled face and tell me a story about his cat or dog? Or has it been one of those struggling mornings for his parents to get him ready for school, and he will arrive like a thundercloud ready to burst? Will he be cradling his drawing book with pictures to share with his friends or will he be clutching the video game that Mrs. Jones, my principal, tells his parents that he is not allowed to have at school?"

These are the questions and concerns that weigh on my mind this morning as I wait for Ilija in the school corridor. Ilija is a wonderful boy who has a smile that radiates like sunshine. However, his behaviour is like the wind. It can be so unpredictable. At school most days he is like the warm breeze that goes through a window and touches your face gently. On the other hand, sometimes when a task is difficult, or he simply doesn't want to do his work, or he has had a bad start at home, then he becomes a strong wintry torrent that can chill one to the bone. When his behaviour is stormy, he bolts and wants to go home. Home is the place that he can do as he pleases with no tasks or responsibilities.

Not surprisingly, time at school is difficult for him. Luckily, these difficult times occur less often now, but I worry how it will be for him when he leaves our school. What will the outside world be like for him? Addressing Ilija's needs is going to be one of the greatest challenges in my teaching career.

Ilija is a ten-year-old student who is diagnosed with a global delay. He is at a primary level academically. Ilija often displays resistant behaviour when he is expected to complete tasks or to move from one class to another. He is on a modified individual educational plan in mathematics and language with accommodations in all other subjects. A teaching assistant supports Ilija along with other students in the school.

His peers are so important to him and he is able to socialize with them at recess and lunchtime. I sometimes see him, playing games, scooting around with Matt - both of them laughing and jostling with one another. I'm glad for this friendship but worry that the rough and tumble may become too rough.

At the beginning of the school year, I remember the first case conference with his parents. His mother, Mrs. Martinez pleaded with tears in her eyes, "I just want my son to be happy at school." Near the end of the conference his father demanded, "How do you plan to include my son in the classroom settings? I don't want him isolated. He is happiest when he is with his friends."

I assured them that it is important for me to see that Ilija will be with his peers for most of the day. I think of his relationship with Matt and consider how I can involve other classmates in their play. Before I can make any suggestions the science teacher, Mrs. Frank, explains that she intends to have him involved in nature walks, projects and group labs. Ilija's parents nod in agreement to this suggestion. Other classroom teachers also promise that Ilija will be included in their classes. I explain to Mr. And Mrs. Martinez that Ilija will be in the resource room for only his basic math and language instruction.

I am relieved when the expressions on his parents' faces turn from troubled looks to expressions of contentment. I think to myself, "Stop worrying. Things are going well."

I share many ideas for the academic part of his individual educational plan. I show his parents the match, select, and name method to increase his vocabulary, literacy books to use at his level in reading, and a functional skilled based math program. I even have a plan for his resistance to complete work.

My confidence is growing as I sense that Ilija's parents will support the behavioural plan that I have developed. I tell them, "The key will be to alternate easy tasks for more difficult tasks for which he needs assistance. Since he wants adult attention, we will avoid getting into discussions and negotiations with him. We will simply state the request and let him know what activity will follow once he complies. He will learn that he must complete the job first and then the reward will come."

I am confident that we can meet his educational needs. During the case conference, I believe everyone is on board with the plan that I have so carefully constructed, discussed with my colleagues and researched from recent journals. After I present my goals for Ilija, his parents appear agreeable and actually are accepting of the educational plan. They really want him to learn to read, and they seem to understand his need for a behavioural plan. As I leave the meeting, my spirits are buoyed. I really believe that Ilija can succeed if we all work together.

His parents appeared to feel positive about the meeting and were committed to Ilija's success. However, it wasn't long before I learned that they were not following through with the plan at home. I realized that Ilija still had no expectations or responsibilities at home and that life at home still centred on his wishes. Whether it's a demand that supper not be put on the table until nine o'clock or the purchase of a new video game he is in control of Mom, Dad, and his two older sisters. Each and every one of them caters to his demands so life at home will be peaceful. They believe that Ilija's world at home is a happy one.

I recognize that the influences from home will make learning an extremely difficult task for Ilija at school. Mr. Chin, the school social worker, meets with the family and gives them ideas about how to increase Ilija's responsibilities at home and shows them how to set up a tracking method to encourage consistent behaviour. Ilija's parents seem unable to carry out the plans. Their perspective of happiness for Ilija overrides their ability to clearly see Ilija's future. At school, Ilija does not understand why things have to run differently. Ilija cannot comprehend why rules need to be followed and tasks need to be completed.

So, today I wait with anticipation. The bus arrives, and I see him slowly walking off the bus and just by the look on his face I know this is going to be one of those days. The video game is clutched tightly in his hand. With a plan in mind, I greet him. "Good morning Ilija. Good to see you." No response. I prepare myself for a challenging day.

I remind his teaching assistant to start with a task that he likes and can do with success. She will then take him to his grade five reading class and let him join in with his group for silent reading. We will address the issue about his video game later in the morning by using the Circle of Friends approach. These are students who volunteer and who are coached to help Ilija when he is upset. The student might say, "Mrs. Jones will take care of your video game. She did it for me the day I forgot and brought mine. She is good about returning it at the end of the day." Then Ilija and the student go to the office together to deposit the game. Hopefully, this will work and then the day will proceed positively.

Again we will have to call the Mr. and Mrs. Martinez. I know they try with Ilija, but until they see the big picture it is going to be tough here at school. Thank goodness I have the support from my principal. She will call the Martinez family as she thinks it is better that they do not see me as the only one making decisions for Ilija. I wonder if they will understand Ilija's need for consistency at home and at school.

It is good for me to remember that we have come a long way with Ilija and I contemplate the gains he has made as we set new goals for him. He is reading, writing one or two sentences in his journal, following his math program with success, willing to express his thoughts and feelings when he is angry, joining in group work with his peers and engaging in conversation with his teachers.

However, I continue to wonder. What will it be like for him in five or ten years? What can we do as a school to prepare him for his future steps in life? How can we foster parental understanding regarding the importance of structure at home as an essential element for further growth? As Ilija gets older it will be important that he understands the need for compromise and delaying gratification.

It will be a long journey with many challenges.

PROFESSIONAL INQUIRY

Inclusive Pedagogies

- Explore the importance of inclusive education and its wider influence on society.
- Explore the goals associated with inclusive pedagogies from the perspective of Ilija, his parents and the school.
- Identify the strengths and limitations of using a "Circle of Friends" approach to supporting the social life of Ilija.
- Discuss the exclusion of Ilija from the case conference and the implications of this action for inclusive education.

Working with Parents

- Generate strategies for working with and supporting parents who appear to agree with educational programmatic decisions about their child but whose actions seem inconsistent with the same agreement.
- Consider approaches that may assist educators in fully understanding the parents' perspectives regarding Ilija's educational and social life.
- Critique the school's decision not to involve the parents in the development of the behaviour plan.

Educational Programming

- Identify strategies that educational personnel can employ to assess the impact of settings, events and/or contexts in which a student operates for the purpose of enhancing educational planning.
- Generate long term goals for Ilija based upon the information in this case.
- Generate additional strategies for the inclusion of peers and the resource teacher in the educational programming for Ilija.
- Analyze the educational programming presently being offered to Ilija from an inclusive education perspective.

Inclusive Philosophy

- Explore how understanding the nature of an inclusive ideology may help teachers meet the emancipatory rights of all students within school environments? Consider how these rights ensure self-efficacy and self-esteem for a learner as well as for teachers and parents?
- Discuss how teachers, parents, and students can be supported to gain an inclusive philosophical understanding of education and the right to belong?
- Reflect on how each of these partners can collectively access and embrace actions that are necessary to support the holistic needs of all children within the classroom?
- Explore how teachers can address systemic barriers within schools that may interfere with the inclusion of students? Consider the types of initiatives that will help teachers to access alternative and inclusive pedagogies?
- Reflect on the nature of education—whether it is to open the world to children and empower them to meet their intellectual, physical, emotional and spiritual needs or if it is to ensure an avenue for the state to meet quotas of productive, socialized and uniform citizens.
- Explore how school cultures seldom define inclusive education as a fundamental human right for all children and peoples.
- Discuss how traditional methodologies found within educational pedagogies for children/youth with diverse needs may not reflect emancipatory approaches to learning nor make way for alternative and inclusive initiatives.

CASE COMMENTARY REFLECTIONS

After reading the commentaries reflect on the following:

New Insights
Identify new insights gained from reading the commentaries.

Understandings
Discuss the impact of the commentaries on your understandings of inclusive education.

Questions
Identify questions that emerge for you from reading the commentaries.

CASE COMMENTARY 1

Margaret Kress White

Ilija Martinez is a ten-year-old student with a global delay. This delay simultaneously influences his intellectual, physical, and emotional developmental. Although he has academic success within a modified educational program, and he experiences significant social benefits from inclusion with peers, he often has difficulty with the completion of complex tasks and in transitioning from one activity to another. His peers are very important to him and he socializes with them at recess and lunchtime, however, he seems to spend a great deal of class time working alone.

Ilija's successes in reading, writing and math, and his willingness to join peers in group work needs careful assessment and consideration when looking at his resistance in completing tasks and transitioning. There is an indication that teaching and support staff believe Ilija's parents are not consistently engaged with advised school techniques to manage Ilija's behavior at home, perhaps creating confusion for Ilija once he arrives at school and, thus, limiting his potential to engage productively in school work.

Teachers and parents must think about the goal of inclusive pedagogy and the factors influencing student emancipation within schools. This should be established prior to assuming that behavior assessment and modification is one of the most important, if not the most important consideration in Ilija's educational plan. Along with logistical variables found in the culture of schools, teachers' personal experiences, backgrounds, and attitudes significantly influence their actions and their understandings of how to support diverse students. These factors and the variances in learning styles, academic abilities, emotional stances, physical endurances, and cultural backgrounds of similarly-aged students that exist within every classroom must be examined. Educational researchers (Bunch and Valeo, 1998) show that student diversity and learning variance is the reality within many public schools in Canada, and yet many students experience increasing frustration and detachment (Kunc, 2000). The frustrations experienced by a student with a global delay may be caused by much more than home-school changes. The literature indicates challenging student behaviors are often manifested by default through traditional teaching methodologies and competitive societal influences (Kunc, 2000). Inclusive pedagogies including differentiated instructional design and creative programs to help students acquire self-efficacy should be used in conjunction with external reward systems often found within behavior modification programs. Alternatively, teachers can explore such ideologies found in Gentle teaching (McGee & Menolascino, 1991), Montessori methodology (Hainstock, 1997), Choice theory (Glasser, 1998) and Indigenous knowledge (Brendtro, Brokenleg & Van Bockern, 1990) to move to an understanding of the psychological complexities found within student behaviors and to create pedagogies to help students internalize positive behavioral changes to enhance learning and wellness.

Understanding the importance of inclusive education, and its wider influence on society, helps teachers embrace pedagogies that support students with diverse learning needs. Peer tutoring has a strong influence in the acquisition of all students' academic and social skills. This influence is shown to be as important as or more important than adult-led teaching or role modeling, and it opens the door for teachers to explore avenues of cooperative learning and peer-led instruction and support in their own classrooms (Allan, 2005).

CASE COMMENTARY 2

Alice Bender

Great gains have been made in this case, so many of the strategies need to be maintained. It is important to build on those successes. A revision of the Individual Education Plan with all members present is in order and the active participation of the student is recommended. The suggestions I have for the revision of the Individual Education Plan include:
- Re-assess the needs of the child with his input. Based on the statement "he is happiest when he is with his friends" would lead me to recommend working towards full inclusion with the support of the resource teacher in the classroom, maximizing the use of the resource teacher time to the benefit of more children while allowing Ilija to spend more time with his peers and allowing his peers to recognize that everyone needs help from time to time.
- Meet with the parents. It is important that the child also be present at the meeting in order for him to hear and see that the school and his parents are partners and that although his parents do not necessarily always follow through at home, they do approve and support the actions taken at and by the school.
- Reinforce the distinction between home and school. Make it clear to Ilija that home is home BUT school is school. As is often the case, parents do not or simply cannot follow through at home (for a multitude of reasons). It is therefore important that the success of the plan not depend on actions over which the school has no control.
- Support the parents. It may be useful to pin point only one action at a time to be carried out at home. For instance, assigning a specific bed time or a finding a specific place for Ilija to store his video game before leaving for school may be an initial goal. Once this has been achieved a second goal can be added.
- Success breeds success. Keep up the actions that are working well and expanding on them (for example: the use of the circle of friends). Add new goals one at a time. Make the plan manageable, measurable and do-able.

CASE COMMENTARY 3

Darlene Perner

It appears that Ilija has strengths as well as needs. Ilija's family and his teacher have the ability to establish a plan for Ilija's immediate and future needs. An education and behaviour plan for Ilija should be developed and implemented collaboratively between home and school. However, before establishing an education and behaviour plan for Ilija, it would be most helpful to first have Ilija, his peers, family and teacher participate in a person centred planning process such as MAPS. By using person centred planning, Ilija's strengths and needs can be shared in a collaborative, non-threatening way. Everyone will need to contribute in identifying what Ilija, and those closest to him (e.g., his teacher, his family, and his peers) need in order to make Ilija's immediate and future plan successful. An experienced facilitator of person centered planning should be employed to ensure the success of the process and the outcome.

After facilitating many MAPS, I can readily state that the barriers and tension between the teacher and the parents/family seemed to dissipate in a relatively short period of time (e.g., within the first hour of MAPS) because the focus was on the student, not on the teacher or the family. The meetings became interactive instead of one-sided. For example, Lisa who was included in fifth grade was exhibiting defiant behaviour in school. Lisa's mom felt that the "school" was blaming her for Lisa's behaviour. As a result, she and the principal would always get into a "heated" argument and mom would leave the school before meeting with Lisa's teacher. A MAPS for Lisa was implemented, and many of the barriers, primarily the hostility between the principal and the mom, became a non issue. Lisa's mom saw that Lisa's teacher, teaching assistant and peers saw Lisa as a positive, contributing member of their class, and the principal saw Lisa's mom as one who was close to and very supportive of her daughter.

Another suggestion would be to have Ilija's family observe him in school to demonstrate his ability to perform tasks and to conform to school life while having fun and being happy there. It may be helpful to video tape Ilija in school and use this for the family to view instead of direct observation. In this case, Ilija and his teacher could point out his strengths and successes as well as some of the strategies used to help Ilija through difficult tasks and times (for example: transition times).

A third recommendation, if needed, would be for the teacher and family to access professional development related to working collaboratively on instructional strategies such as positive behaviour supports. In this way, both the teacher and family may be able to support each other and ensure that approaches agreed upon are being implemented consistently. The teacher and family should be helped to follow through with such strategies.

CASE COMMENTARY 4

Dr. Scott A. Thompson

Functional Assessment and Positive Behavior Support

The first issue that this case study promoted me to think about was the role of *Setting Events*, and *Setting Event Strategies*; these issues are from the functional assessment and positive behavior support literature. Sometimes, if teachers keep data on the relationship between possible setting events in the home environment and events that occur at school (I am thinking of the *Setting Events Checklist*, or more recently what is being referred to as the *Contextual Assessment Inventory*) then such tools may help the school-based team (including the parents) make some decisions about home-school strategies. Students could also think through how such tools and data could help them support parents/guardians

This case study also got me thinking about Yssedyke & Christenson's (2002) work in the area of academic behavior. They proposed a very holistic approach to understanding academic success, including an assessment of what they term, the *Total Learning Environment (TLE)*. The TLE includes consideration of the some-what expected, *Instructional Support for Learning Components, Home Support for Learning Components*, and the degree to which home and school support each other, through an assessment of the *Home-School Support for Learning Components*. This latter assessment is not always considered and certainly rounds out the overall process.

I guess the other area in which this case study really speaks to me is how do we, as educational personnel really support parents, and most especially parents/guardians whom hold different values and/or goals for their son/daughter than those in the educational setting. This is a significant area for student teachers to think through deeply.

Finally, I feel compelled to talk about Circles of Friends (CoFs). In this case study, the CoF is a group of peers that coach Ilija "when he is upset." I am not the first to recognize that there are difficulties with such an approach. In CoFs there is a distinct lack of reciprocity—that is the student with a disability seems always to have their behavior subject of monitoring by other peers, and almost never is in the position of being a monitor. I think it sends a very debilitating message to students with disabilities. Perhaps student teachers or others could think through the implica-tions of CoFs as a social engineering strategy. Indeed, Sapon-Shevin, Dobbelaere, Corrigan, Goodman, & Mastin (1998) identified the conspicuous lack of reciprocity inherent in CoFs—target children are always recipients of help and never helpers. Furthermore, some researchers claim that CoFs do not address issues of equality in light of lack of reciprocity.

CONNECTING TO PROFESSIONAL PRACTICE

The commentary writers recognize the school's commitment to inclusive education. They also raise serious questions regarding the use of the pedagogies used by the school to support the inclusion of Ilija. Issues related to equity, emancipation and social engineering emerge in the reflections offered by these case commentary writers.

Explore how theories related to equity, emancipation and social engineering are lived out in your own professional practice. Consider how this case and the associa-ted commentaries may enhance your own professional thinking and action in the future.

CASE FIVE: SAM

Sam disembarks the special needs bus and, with a downward gaze, shuffles into the school. He makes his way directly to his locker and opens it. He removes his coat and hangs it up. He takes his agenda out of his backpack, places the backpack in the locker, and goes to his teaching assistant, who has been waiting and watching him from a distance since the moment he arrived. Independence is the goal here.

Sam has a disorder that causes severe cognitive delays. Nearsightedness, obesity, and gross motor deficiencies come with this disorder. Sam often doesn't make eye contact and has a speech impediment. When I speak to him he twists away, mumbling to himself. Other characteristics of the disorder are a cheerful nature and a friendly disposition. Sam has a toothy grin and galloping strides. He bounds across the classroom in four happy leaps. Sam's open, trusting hand will grab on to any passer-by. He would go with anyone. His classmates, particularly Jerrod and Jose, always include him in rough and tumble sports and games. They like him. Sam continually wraps his arms around Jerrod and Jose and his other classmates.

Sam is in grade six. He is one of 32 students in his class. The needs of the class are many. There are several students with Attention Deficit Hyperactivity Disorder, a girl with Asperger's Syndrome, a boy with Obsessive Compulsive Disorder, a student with serious environmental sensitivities, two students on modified educational programs and a number of students with behaviour needs. Fortunately, the class has the support of a teaching assistant.

I am Sam's resource teacher. At the recent school team meeting, I explain my plan for Sam. "My goals for Sam this school year are to integrate him into the classroom as much as possible, while still meeting his educational needs. I want to provide appropriate social opportunities for him to build and maintain personal connections. I want to begin instruction in essential life skills."

Focusing on these specific outcomes, I have laid out several routines. I already know the benefits of repetitive, organized and safe activities. Daily, Sam attends music or art class. I've observed him, concentrating on painting bowls of fruit or singing, albeit off key, in the choir. The music teacher and the art teacher modify his programming, work with the teaching assistant and grade his work. Three times weekly, Sam participates in physical education. I note Sam is putting on weight and he is moving more slowly when playing sports. I overheard Jose's comment about "fatso and slowpoke" just yesterday. I also saw Sam's face when he overheard this comment.

Sam's teaching assistant works closely with him. Every day, Sam has a volunteer buddy who helps him with his duties as a member of the school's composting group. His buddy then accompanies him to the gym or outside for activities designed to improve his gross motor capabilities. Twice weekly, Sam helps parent volunteers prepare snacks for one hundred students. Weekly, Sam creates a menu, shops for food items, prepares a small meal, and cleans up. Lastly, Sam goes bowling with a small group of students with developmental delays from several local schools. I'm proud of the range of activities Sam completes on a daily and weekly basis. I see hope in his future as an assistant to a chef or perhaps a sport facility attendant.

While these activities address some of the goals I set for Sam's social growth, he remains somewhat isolated. There are no other students in the school with similar needs and abilities as Sam. I do admit that his social opportunities are limited and artificial. No one invites Sam to participate in after school activities or weekend birthday parties. They wave goodbye and Sam is left standing alone waiting for his special bus.

There are other challenges with Sam's academic inclusion. I currently design his language arts and math activities. His teaching assistant implements them. The classroom teacher has no hand in preparing lessons for Sam. Sam doesn't attend science and social studies classes. The teaching assistant and I deliver life skills activities for him in place of science and social studies.

It's not that the teachers don't care about Sam. One of them, Mr. Jamieson sums up the feeling of the staff by saying, "We are daunted by the diversity of needs in the classroom. It's best for Sam to have someone else take care of his academic requirements." Another teacher adds, "Remember, there are curriculum outcomes to meet, and provincial and district assessments in June to consider." Ms. Kittle, a beginning teacher and untrained in special needs just looks downward at her folder of papers to be marked. My guess is that she just can't imagine taking on any more responsibility. I recognize and understand all that these teachers already have many professional responsibilities and expectations placed upon them. I also recognize and accept that I have a responsibility to help Sam.

I fear Sam will become progressively more isolated. Jerrod and Jose may eventually decide Sam is a burden to the quick-paced games and wisecracking that are part of their social experience. Sam's huge hugs may become an embarrassment for them. In another year, it may not be seen as cool for Jerrod and Jose to be friendly with Sam.

In the next school year, I would like Sam's teachers to take more of an active role in his academic planning. Perhaps this involvement will help them to envision ways that they could include him in more classroom activities. It is hard for me to imagine that this will ever really happen.

Will the teachers ever be willing and able to take responsibility for Sam and his learning?

PROFESSIONAL INQUIRY

Creating an Inclusive Learning Environment

- Outline the importance of developing a sense of community within a school environment for an inclusive vision of education to be effectively implemented.
- Discuss the significance of a school explicitly adopting an inclusive education philosophy as a guiding vision or the school.
- Explore the importance of the ongoing professional learning for all staff in a school that has adopted a vision of inclusion.
- Discuss the role of professional knowledge and skills in the attainment of an inclusive learning environment.

School Culture

– Describe the culture that currently exists in this school.
– Generate strategies for re-culturing this school towards a philosophy of inclusive education.
– Identify the leadership actions of the school principal that need to occur in order to enable this school to be fully committed to inclusive education.
– Discuss approaches that the resource teacher might employ to help foster a shared commitment within the school towards inclusion.
– Analyze the language the resource teacher uses in this case regarding Sam's yearly goals and educational program. (for example: "My goals for Sam this year are...") What messages does this language convey about inclusion?

CASE COMMENTARY REFLECTIONS

After reading the commentaries reflect on the following:

New Insights
Identify new insights gained from reading the commentaries.

Understandings
Discuss the impact of the commentaries on your understandings of inclusive education.

Questions
Identify questions that emerge for you from reading the commentaries.

CASE COMMENTARY 1

Sharon Rich

There are several comments that are relevant to this case but the first issue I believe is that the school staff is not working as a team. The school staff as a whole could use some professional development to help teachers understand what inclusion is and what should be happening in the classroom. The principal as school leader might consider providing opportunities for the resource teacher to work with the staff and individual teachers. Inclusion is not the responsibility of one teacher but of all working together. The creation of a learning community that has a focus on improving teaching practice and planning for inclusion would enable all teachers to develop strategies for the children in their care. From what is stated in this case it appears that the responsibility for educational planning is passed to someone outside of the classroom. The resource teacher, various assistants and volunteers have been given the major responsibility for supporting Sam.

   If collaboration and shared responsibility existed in this school then Sam would be included in more regular class activities. Part of the reason for his isolation is that the classroom teacher has little or no responsibility for him. I would involve the teacher in planning for Sam and if necessary work with her in the classroom to demonstrate ways to modify the program. Again, in my experience as a resource teacher, providing advice from outside is not as effective as working in the classroom beside the teacher to make changes. I could demonstrate how strategies such as language books on tape could assist Sam and others. In addition, demonstrating reader response activities that involve some form of artistic expression, visual or dramatic, rather than always writing responses would be beneficial for Sam and others. By working in the classroom, I could also demonstrate for the teacher that the curricular goals and outcomes were being achieved in non-traditional ways. I would encourage the use of group work in the classroom that would include Sam and would also enable the other students to see what he has to offer.

Finally, given Sam's physical challenges, it is likely that the current physical education program with a focus on sports is not working to his benefit. A better focus for someone like Sam and many other children would be a general fitness approach. Research indicates that one of the reasons many children leave physical activity behind is the focus on competitive sports rather than lifelong learning through movement activities.

CASE COMMENTARY 2

Catherine Montreuil

The classroom teacher is the key instructor for every student in the class; however they cannot be expected to do it alone. The classroom teacher needs to be responsible for the learning of all students. The Special Education teacher can assist with programming ideas, modeling different strategies or by providing a variety of materials to assist the teacher in meeting the needs of the diverse range of learners. The professional practices embodied by universal design for learning and differentiated instruction provide teachers with the skills and knowledge to affect attitudes in ways that benefit all students. Looking at the classroom as the natural and right environment for every student leads to an inclusive lens for all students. Even when it may make sense to do some skill building through direct instruction, it needs to be done with an eye to application in an authentic setting. For instance, for many students in grade 6, being in charge of making their own lunch for school is a task they are expected to do. If Sam is the only student who is planning, preparing and serving lunch with the volunteers, how does this contribute to appropriate skill development for a grade 6 student? If it is indeed appropriate, why is Sam the only student completing this task? Could it be an appropriate math and health curriculum support for more students? If it isn't appropriate for other students, then we need to find another way to meet some of the goals that Sam may be meeting through this activity that will include his learning with his peers.

Sam would benefit from more inclusive programming. Differentiating instruction strategies such as flexible groupings, differentiated materials and assessment need to be included. The educational assistant support can be reorganized to provide flexible coaching when necessary and promote appropriate learning and social skill development. Sam has clearly learned many appropriate and independent skills, evident from how he enters the school and prepares for class.

Further, the school team needs to look at what key goals are to be focused on in each term and then determine what performance by Sam will be evidence of attaining the goals. His mobility and health can be addressed through a physical education program that balances activity and teaches about nutrition. This could be supported at home by encouraging his care givers to ensure his choices for lunch contribute to healthy weight maintenance.

CASE COMMENTARY 3

Edith Clarke

The key characteristics of an inclusive school appear to be missing in this case study. Just as the unique needs of students such as Sam make every inclusive school look different, even from year to year, there are certain characteristics that all inclusive schools share:
– a sense of community complete with a philosophy and vision;
– the need for collaboration and consultation due to changing roles and responsibility;
– the use of new strategies based on research and used increasingly as new tools for successful learning;
– an awareness of the need for new forms of accountability and assessment enabling individual students to attain specific goals;
– flexible learning environments that follow individual paths of learning where the presentation of material emphasizes participation; and
– the need for flexible groupings as well as opportunities for separate instruction, as needed.

The implementation of the above characteristics can only originate through long-term planning, learned collaboration, and continuous effort. Within this framework, other factors that contribute to success must remain stable to effect and maintain this magnitude of educational transformation. These include the availability of human resources, the leadership role of the school principal, and support for school-based administration and educators through proper training. These factors can support change and make the hard work related to change, including the learning of new approaches and skills, rewarding. It is important to clearly establish that the ultimate success of providing a diverse student population with educational success and equity must depend on the deliberate efforts and support of all its participants within the system.

The principal must foster the educational achievement of all students in the school through actively involving and sharing responsibilities with the entire school staff in both the planning and carrying out of strategies that will make the school successful. Both regular and special educators must be available as teams working collaboratively to implement new strategies necessary for meeting the needs of all students within the school.

As a former teacher, I have worked with many students over the years in a variety of school settings. The issues brought to life in this case remain all too familiar: lack of school vision, absence of school leadership, and staff working in isolation. Sam's resource teacher understands his needs and how these needs should be addressed in an inclusive setting but remains isolated. While this teacher's knowledge and true goals for Sam are clearly evident they are clouded by the actual situation as it exists within the school.

A love of teaching and a strong belief that all children deserve the same opportunities in order to grow and flourish in today's society were instrumental in my learning along with the characteristics of an inclusive school as described above. In my present role as Assistant Director of Student Services, I continue to provide schools and/or individual educators with a model of inclusion that demonstrates a successful process of change. A secondary goal is to provide a means of support for individual teachers who are presently including students with diverse needs in their classrooms; and might benefit from support in the form of skills and strategies and reassurance that what they are doing is the right thing.

Every classroom, traditional or inclusive, has diverse needs and students with unique needs. These students often respond to the same learning opportunities and consideration as other students. Effective teachers are caring teachers first and instinctively know that when children belong learning is enhanced. For instance, caring teachers understand that students with disabilities must also be socially accepted. This includes efforts to make them belong in their classroom community and provide opportunities for friendships. Sam's resource teacher vividly points this out. Students such as Sam can take part in different educational activities and still be included by sitting them with their classmates and making sure that they participate in activities even though the goals might be different. It means talking and laughing with these students, teaching them and including them just like any other student.

Inclusion, however, is also preparing and supporting teachers to teach interactively thus breaking down the barriers of professional isolation. The focus should be on increasing the capabilities of the regular education mainstream to meet the needs of all students. There must be vision statements, advocates, redefined roles, and the elimination of labels. When provisions are put in place to provide the necessary support for both students and teachers it can be extremely rewarding and successful for the school community as a whole. Sam's resource teacher already understands this. She also understands that she can no longer successfully work in isolation.

CASE COMMENTARY 4

Jacqueline Karsemeyer and Jaya Karsemeyer

This is a letter written to Sam's mother from the perspective of Sam's fictional aunt. The aunt is the sister of Sam's mother and she is a teacher.

Hi sis,
It's hard to accept that Samuel is almost 13! Where did the time fly? How was his friend Matthew's bar-mitzvah? It is wonderful that they have been close since they

were 2 years old. I bet your Samuel danced up a storm at the party, and charmed everyone with his beaming smile.

So you want to pick my teacher brain about Samuel's transition to junior high. Of course, by now you know more than most people about navigating the school system. Did you hear back from the teacher about wanting to attend the school support team meeting? With the changes that Samuel will experience in adolescence, it will be helpful for the school to learn some of the strategies that you pick up from your parent support association.

Sorry to hear that Samuel hates the school bus. At least he won't have to take it next year since the social worker from the bowling club is teaching that boisterous bunch to use public transportation. You might like to know that the kids on the "gifted bus" at my school also had problems because of they were being bused out of the neighborhood at 3:45. We started lunchtime clubs that are making a big difference. Not surprisingly, parents pushed for games in the gym since so many kids are overweight. Did you know that a public health nurse will come in and talk to classes about nutrition?

When is the school going to integrate Samuel for social studies and history? Wasn't that recommended at his last IPRC? Each teacher has to take part in developing the IEP to include the expanded integration; it can even start with some of his art projects being based on a social studies theme. Why don't you bring this up with the principal next week when you are in for snack prep? Ask the principal if the classroom assistant will be staying with Samuel's class next year; it sounds as though she is supporting many students.

Why don't you tell Samuel's school about the fabulous drama workshop that he does at Famous People Players? That class you observed where they did drama games to learn about personal space boundaries would be the perfect exercise for Samuel at school. And yes, I do think that you should tell that lovely resource teacher that Samuel probably cowers because her clipboard matches that of the doctors that have prodded him since birth.

It is nice to hear that Samuel is a favorite reading buddy for the little ones at the library's Saturday program. When I taught kindergarten I used to have some grade sixes in as teacher's helpers; I would have loved to have someone like Samuel to help out during reading and free play.

Well, bye for now. You have a special son sis, but then you are a special mum.

P.S. next, we can brainstorm about how to get Samuel to wear his new glasses!

CONNECTING TO PROFESSIONAL PRACTICE

Essential dimensions that contribute to the attainment of inclusive learning environments for all learners are outlined by the commentary writers. Reflect on your own experience working in schools. Explore how these dimensions were *lived* out within your own practices and in the schools in which you were a member.

3. PROFESSIONAL KNOWLEDGE AND PRACTICE

Inclusive education is enhanced when educators and other professionals possess extensive professional knowledge and skills in conjunction with a deep commitment to social justice and inclusion. Educators that critically explore knowledge, research, literature, policy and pedagogical practices through the lens of equity, access, inclusion and achievement will be better able to provide and support inclusive educational programs for all learners.

Teachers, school leaders and other professionals need to be able to collaboratively plan coherent, progressive, accessible and simulating educational programs which align with students' needs, abilities and interests. They need to be able to articulate and effectively implement universal design and access (Jordan, 2007). Their teaching needs to reflect a wide range of instructional strategies and resources. They also must be able to knowledgably evaluate and justify their pedagogical practices, judgments and decisions in terms of curriculum requirements and research. They also need to integrate the needs and abilities of students within all actions.

Overview of Cases

The cases in this section of the text illuminate the professional knowledge and practice of teachers, principals and other school level support staff. The implications of limited professional knowledge and skill upon school level planning and programming become crystallized within the written narratives. Students require more than the well intentioned efforts of educators. They have a right to inclusive pedagogical practices that facilitate open and equitable avenues to learning for all.

The four cases and the accompanying commentaries reveal the professional and ethical responsibility of all educators and school personnel to exercise informed professional judgment. This judgment must be guided by extensive knowledge and skill. The impact of the beliefs and assumptions held by school personnel regarding learning, teaching and student's with diverse learning profiles also become visible through the case scenarios. The commentaries and professional inquiry processes invite readers to identify and critically analyze the powerful influence of beliefs and assumptions upon professional practice.

G. L. Porter and D. Smith (eds.), Exploring Inclusive Educational Practices
Through Professional Inquiry, 71–103.

CASE SIX: GETTING FRUSTRATED

"You hate me! Everyone hates me," screams Toni. "I hate you."

"We don't hate you. We just need everyone to be safe. You will have to go home," I reply patiently.

"I don't need to go home. I am not at a five!" Toni screeches. "I only yelled a little bit and I haven't hit or kicked anyone." I step back as Toni removes her sneaker and heaves it toward my leg. Mrs. Amiad, the teaching assistant, joins us in the hall. She takes Toni firmly by the arm and steers her toward my office.

I enter my office trying to remain calm. Mrs. Amiad and Toni follow. I ask the school secretary to contact one of Toni's parents to come and pick up Toni as Toni and her teaching assistant sit down. Toni's mother does not work. I expect that her mother will arrive soon. She has been very prompt in picking Toni up in similar situations.

In the meantime, I try to prevent this bright young girl from hurting one of our staff members or another student. Toni squats on the floor and pulls one of my office chairs in front of her. I sit down at my desk and shuffle some papers around pretending to work. I sneak a quick glance at Mrs. Amiad once in awhile just to get sense of how Toni is doing. Toni's teaching assistant has worked with her for almost two years. Toni will sometimes respond to her and settle down. Today was not one of those days.

"I don't want to go home," Toni hollers. She jumps into the chair and begins to spin around, almost toppling over into my lap. Part of the most recent plan for Toni included establishing a rating scale for her behavioural outbursts. An outburst that rated a five on the scale meant that Toni had to go home. Toni and her parents understand this scale and accept the consequences of reaching a five on the scale. Mrs. Amiad calmly says to Toni, "You have reached a five and your choice is to go home." I have been through these episodes many times. I know that Toni will sit calmly for a few minutes and then scream, throw something and then watch for a reaction from anyone who is near. I wait for the inevitable.

Toni is a bright nine-year old girl who is very capable of leading her class in all academic areas. Already, she has distinguished herself as a fast and competent reader. Unfortunately Toni's behaviour frequently gets in the way of her learning as well as that of her classmates. Toni can very sociable when she decides to get along well with others. She has been helping some of our younger students learn how to play chess. She gently corrects or tells them to reposition the chessmen, often creating hilarious stories about the nights and damsels-in-distress. Her chess partners share jokes with her and they giggle together like trusted friends. However, in a class setting Toni's patient nature can disappear very rapidly.

"I hate to write. I can't think of anything to write about," Toni screams. She startles her classmates. She begins to hurl her notebooks and pens, almost catching Frances in the eye.

I heard Toni scream that she hated writing almost every day last year. It seemed that the trigger to Toni's outbursts was writing. This year anything and everything appears to set Toni off. I can't begin to count the number of days that Toni has had to report to my office and finish her writing assignment outside my door. "I can't go outside for recess. You hate me! It's not fair. Everyone else gets recess. I want to go outside," Toni bellows.

Toni's angry outbursts over not completing class work always turns into a fixation with what she wants (or doesn't want) to do. Suddenly a small event grows to huge proportions. Toni becomes a tornado whirling objects and crashing into anyone that happens to be in her way.

In the two years since I took the position of vice-principal at this rural school I have been involved in numerous meetings about Toni. The guidance counsellor has worked diligently to set up individual behaviour plans for Toni incorporating each suggestion as it comes in. I would not have had the patience that Mr. Ward has had to continually update the behaviour plan. New suggestions come in on what seems to be a weekly basis. Many of these suggestions come from district level experts who have met with Toni for only a few minutes or, at best, a few hours.

Even Mr. Ward's patience is coming to an end with the constant onslaught of suggestions and changes. Toni's homeroom teacher has also expressed his concern over the rapid changes to Toni's plan. We have tried everything. Nothing seems to be working.

I remember last Friday's episode at lunch hour. "I won't take my pill." Toni yells. "I don't like bologna sandwiches. I won't put my pill in it."

Exasperated Ms. White, the resource and methods teacher, gives Toni a pudding cup and hides her pill for in it. Tomorrow there will be a second pill to administer. Toni will start a new medication. It is supposed to help Toni be able to control her Attention Deficit Hyperactivity Disorder.

Toni's outbursts have consisted of screaming, yelling and running away. Once, she even left school and raced back and forth outside the front of the school. Our resource and methods teacher ran after her and persuaded her to return.

This year we have had to use a time-out room. Toni is placed in this room until she is able to calm down. Her parents have consented to Toni being placed in this small room where she can scream out her anger. Sometimes she will scream until she is exhausted and curls into a ball on the floor. While in the time-out room, Toni often tries to leave. The door of the time-out room must be securely fastened shut. Toni still tries to open the door to run away. An adult always sits outside just in case Toni is able to force her way out of the room. Toni knows that she needs to be calm in order to be released from the time-out room. She will sit quietly and ask to leave. When she is told that she still must wait and continue to be calm for two minutes, Toni will scream in reply, "I am calm." Then she bangs her head against the door.

Now I glance in Toni's direction as she sits in my office. My glance was enough to set her off. Toni pushes over the chair in front of her and yells, "I don't want to go home. You hate me. Everyone hates me." I get up and walk towards Toni. She begins to pummel me with her fists. Once again, I am forced to use non-violent crisis intervention strategies to restrain Toni.

I calmly try to reassure Toni that we do care about her, but we need everyone at school to be safe. At this point I think of the recommendations that the district behaviour specialist made after observing Toni, for two hours on two separate days. She said that Toni should not be "wrestled with" but gently returned to her work area. This behaviour specialist has yet to see Toni when she is out of control.

As Toni continues to struggle against my arms, Mrs. Amiad asks if I need assistance. Toni has already kicked her. The large red mark on her calf indicates where the bruise will be tomorrow.

This is not the first time that Mrs. Amiad has been injured. Last month she accompanied our principal when he was driving Toni home. She returned to school the next day with several bruises caused by Toni pinching her on the drive home. She also had bruises from the two punches that Toni was able to land in her ribs. She showed them to me after I asked her why she was wincing when she spoke with me.

Both Mrs. Amiad and the principal commented that when they drove Toni home that day that her father was sitting outside the door to the house. Each time Toni has been returned home, her father who is not very tall but weighs about 300 pounds, is seen sitting on the step outside the door. The pet pit bull is standing guard beside him. Toni has assured us that the dog is friendly. We are very cautious when the dog is around.

Finally, Toni's mother arrives. "Stand up" commands the tall, thin woman. Her tone is brisk and matter-of-fact. Toni's mother has been through this many times before today.

"I don't want to go home," Toni screams again.

"Stop!" her mother yells. "I don't want to hear any more."

Toni stands up, "I'm sad," she says as she wipes her hand across her dirt encrusted face and neck. "I don't want people to hate me."

I stand, too, and I speak directly to Toni's mother. "Toni has hit staff members again today."

Toni's mother shakes her head and looks away. I notice that she has the same disheveled appearance as Toni.

"Toni has an appointment with another child psychiatrist" she tells us. "I have called her pediatrician and he will see her next week. I am doing everything I can to get help for her."

I look first at Toni and then at her mother. I feel sorry for them both. Toni has such potential, but her behaviour has a devastating effect on not only her learning, but also on the learning of her classmates. Many of her classmates have become frightened of Toni and what she might do. I am constantly aware that Toni's increasingly violent behaviour is also putting our staff at risk of injury.

In some ways I feel guilty about making my next statement. "I will be contacting the school district office about having Toni stay at home until we can get some input from her psychiatrist and pediatrician."

Toni's mother stares straight ahead. "I understand," she replies. She takes Toni's hand and walks out of my office.

I return to my chair behind my desk. Mrs. Amiad puts her hand on my shoulder. I drop my head into my hands. I feel so discouraged.

PROFESSIONAL INQUIRY

Student Needs

– Explore the school's understanding of Toni's needs.

Beliefs and Assumptions

– Identify the beliefs and assumptions that appear to be guiding the actions and decisions of the Vice Principal.
– Discuss the messages that are conveyed by the use of language such as "wrestle with", "released from the time out room" and "force her way out".
– Analyze the implicit messages that are communicated about Toni's family by the descriptors used to describe the father, mother and Toni.

Ethics

– Discuss the ethics associated with the actions of resources and methods teacher.
– Critique the ethical implications associated with the practices employed by the school in dealing with Toni's behaviour (wrestling with Toni, securely fastening shut the time out room, banging her head against the door, etc.).
– Analyze the ethical dimensions associated with the Vice Principal's intention to have Toni remain at home until information is obtained from the psychiatrist and pediatrician.

Inclusive Education

– Explore the school's vision and understanding of inclusive education.
– Identify teaching practices and strategies that could be employed to support Toni's inclusion into this school context.
– Analyze how Toni is positioned as a student and person. Discuss the implications for this positioning for inclusive education.
– Develop a plan for creating a deeper understanding and commitment to inclusive education for this school.
– Respond to this case from the perspective of Toni and her parents.

Teacher Education

– Explore ways in which teacher education can help to extend the professional knowledge, beliefs, skills and practices of the educators in this case.

CASE COMMENTARY REFLECTIONS

After reading the commentaries reflect on the following:

New Insights
Identify new insights gained from reading the commentaries.

Understandings
Discuss the impact of the commentaries on your understandings of inclusive education.

Questions
Identify questions that emerge for you from reading the commentaries.

CASE COMMENTARY 1

Chris Treadwell

The present situation suggests that a major confrontation is looming between the school and Toni. In such a power struggle the child will be the loser and the school will have lost an opportunity to have helped a student.

The school plan is not effective in including Toni and needs to have its expectations changed. The focus should be on Toni's strength's and avoid trying to force her to do activities that at present appear to trigger her outbursts, which cannot be tolerated in the learning setting.

Rather than changing the plan by a barrage of isolated suggestions from individuals, a team meeting should be held with all who are trying to help Toni. The result will be a coordinated and collaborative plan better suited to meet the child's needs and the school's expectations. A follow-up meeting date should be set so that any major adjustments to the plan will be a collaborative effort. The team should include Toni's present and past teachers, school specialists, external specialists, administrators and Toni's parents.

A case manager should be assigned. This person should be in the school and have authority to make slight adjustments to the plan. Observations and other data should be regularly collected to proactively determine how Toni is responding to the plan before a meltdown occurs. In addition to the consequences in the plan, effective reward options should be generated, in consultation with Toni, to recognize her success and to show her that people care about her well-being.

A sort of reverse inclusion could be established. Rather than have Toni continue to be suspended, her class time could be reduced and more emphasis put in one-on-one settings, or in roles that clearly give her a sense of satisfaction, such as in helping other children to read. In this way Toni will benefit socially, and academically, as she is acting as a tutor and is not missing time from school.

Unless the school can show Toni that it cares and gives her a chance to feel successful, she is at risk of long-term suspension, and others are at risk of getting hurt. Her individual educational plan should center around her needs and be flexible, rather than trying to force her into regular school hours or environments. The plan needs to support the school environment for Toni until she can better cope with her challenges in life.

CASE COMMENTARY 2

Sarah Elizabeth Barrett

Everyone in this case seems to be in crisis mode, which is quite understandable given the circumstances. Many experts are offering solutions. Several professionals are implementing strategies. However, clearly, this approach is not working. The decision to send Toni home makes sense at this point but if the situation is to be improved, I believe the perspective must shift from viewing Toni as a case or problem to be solved to recognizing her as a person.

I am not suggesting the principal in this case has forgotten that she is dealing with a troubled little girl who needs her help. Rather, I believe she, and many of the rest of the adults trying to help Toni, have slipped into viewing her as a bundle of symptoms and traits. Yet Toni is a person with connections to teachers, other students, friends, family and community. The most important resources for re-imagining Toni in more holistic terms are her parents (who have depth of know-ledge with respect to her personal life) and Ms. Armand (who probably knows her academic life best).

The administrator needs to have a conversation with each of these key adults, reserve judgment and listen to what they believe needs to be done. Education assistants are rarely consulted for their expertise about particular students. Constant consultation with experts may have discouraged Toni's mother from believing she has any expertise to contribute. Yet I believe her perspective on Toni as a child would be invaluable. In order to facilitate the discussion, the administrator needs to acknowledge and work around the power differentials that exist within the school system that work against Toni's mother and Ms. Armand viewing themselves as legitimate experts.

Finally, Toni's home life does not seem to be ideal but the information available is superficial. Though an administrator could not be expected to investigate the home life of every student, it makes sense for her to do so here, through conversations with Toni's mother.

What I propose as a possible solution in this case is neither quick nor guaranteed to succeed, but the situation seems to demand a change in strategy.

CASE COMMENTARY 3

Julie A. Stone

This case raises many issues in my mind. I wondered about the level of involvement Toni had in the development of the behaviour plan. How much actual choice was embedded in this plan for Toni? A number of additional approaches and strategies may significantly assist the school in more effectively responding to Toni's needs. These include:

- Involve Toni in all future planning. Making her aware of steps or rules may not be as effective as asking for her input into consequences. Have the district office expert, the classroom teacher, the parent(s), the Guidance teacher and the Vice Principal present at the meeting with Toni. Then, agree that the plan they develop will be in place without changes until the follow-up meeting which should be set before the meeting is adjourned.
- Have someone, possibly the Guidance Counselor do some research on Oppo-sitional and Defiant Disorder (ODD), as Toni may have been misdiagnosed or have both Attention Deficit Hyperactive Disorder (ADHD) and ODD.

She certainly appears to have the characteristics. She is in total control of the situation at school at this time.

- After the school gives Toni the out of school period referred to in the document provided, and agrees to reinstate her, refrain from sending Toni home from school if possible. It appears that there may be some difficulty in the family and besides, it allows Toni to avoid getting herself back into control. Also, begin Anger Management lessons right away. Toni is getting older and bigger and needs to learn some good cool down strategies.
- Talk to Toni about her interests and help her make a list of them – possible topics for future writing tasks. Also, provide her with some graphic organizers that might assist her with the writing process. If Toni likes working with the computer, there is a program called "Inspiration" which helps students organize their writing. I would also suggest that Toni be assessed for a writing disability. Maybe she really struggles to write, even though she is bright. She might also benefit from a program called Dragon Naturally Speaking, which turns speech into writing.
- Give Toni some tasks to carry out in the classroom – tasks which are necessary to the teacher or the students. She appears to like helping others out of the classroom and might enjoy being able to do so inside. Also, she might be viewed by her peers as being a good help rather than a bad girl.
- Have Toni keep a chart of her episodes. Allow her to visually see how often they occur and let her work to reduce them. The reduction would be positive reinforcement in itself, but the teacher may want to give her praise for her hard work, or help her to understand how much better her progress at school has become.

CONNECTING TO PROFESSIONAL PRACTICE

The commentary writers raise questions regarding the efficacy of the school's actions and planning processes. They also offer numerous practical strategies for more fully including Toni within the school. Based upon your own experience and professional knowledge as an educator, generate responses to the recommended strategies suggested by the commentary writers. Consider how some of these recommendations may be integrated into the professional practices of the educators at Toni's school.

CASE SEVEN: HOPEFUL EYES

Hopeful eyes stare at me from across the table. Mrs. Harris says with all the optimism a mother can muster. "So what do we do now that we know what she has?"

I smile gently and reply with a simple statement. "We will do everything we can."

Mrs. Harris seems satisfied with that. We proceed with a conversation about where and how to begin to best serve her daughter. Raheel is a delightful child in grade four. She has just been diagnosed with Autism Spectrum Disorder. There is a wealth of resources about autism available now and I feel hopeful about the possibility of developing a program to meet this little girl's needs. However, as the resource and methods teacher for this very special student, I also feel overwhelmed. Learning more about autism was something I knew I needed to engage in immediately.

I read whatever I can get my hands on. I call other resource and methods teachers with experience working with children with autism. I search the web. I look forward to collaborating with experts who can bring their knowledge and experience to this case. I am not concerned about the hours of careful planning involved in designing an appropriate program for Raheel and her classroom teacher. I can do all those things. I do them because that is the commitment I make to any of the children who are part of my caseload.

What strikes me with trepidation is the thought of trying to create authentic improvement in this little girl's social skills and the thought of setting realistic academic goals for her when so many years of school now seem to have been misspent. I feel so sad when I think about this undersized, pale little girl seated at the classroom edge and isolated in so many ways from her classmates.

This wonderful little girl has been so misunderstood for so long. I grieve for what I interpret to be a terrible disservice to a child in need. I am constantly thinking about the fact that Raheel's teachers have been describing her non-responsive and disruptive behaviour for almost four years.

Raheel's case history stretches well beyond her personal struggles to achieve any degree of school success. During Raheel's four years of schooling, her parents have presented their own challenges. Mr. and Mrs. Feldman are quiet individuals who seem to be resentful of any school communication efforts. I have called the home many times, left messages and received no response. Most often, I rely on written notes. Finally, today, I've had a real conversation with Mrs. Feldman. Much of the time was spent trying to assuage her fears about the results of Raheel's physiological tests.

Why didn't Mrs. Feldman realize sooner that Raheel needed this testing? Raheel has always been recognized at school as a child who seemed to have special needs. From the early days of kindergarten, Raheel's parents were made aware of the fact that her abilities and behaviours were clearly different than those of her peers. Raheel displayed rocking motions during strange times. She had odd speech patterns and inconsistent eye contact. She focused on minute details of environmental stimuli and demonstrated inappropriate reactions to what most would consider typical social situations. Raheel also displayed some endearing qualities. She was very affectionate with her teacher and had a gentle disposition. She had a ready smile and a bear-like hug for those people she let into her world.

By the second reporting period of kindergarten, Raheel's teacher had collected sufficient evidence to illustrate that Raheel was not your typical student. Raheel's parents responded to the concerns expressed by her teacher and the resource and methods teacher, most indignantly. Their response was "There is nothing wrong with Raheel. You people just don't understand her." For almost four more years they had retained this position.

Raheel completed kindergarten. Much to the chagrin of the family, her June report card indicated enormous gaps in both her academic and social progress. The family felt that the new school year starting in September would bring change. They brushed aside the challenges their child was already experiencing and the concerns that the school had raised. "After all," they asked, "How could the school know their child after only one year?"

Raheel returned to school for grade one and began the process of adjusting to the expectations of a new teacher and the dynamics of a new group of peers. As always, Raheel was kind, gentle and loving. However, Raheel was once again demonstrating many of the same unusual and inappropriate behaviors. Peer relationships were becoming a major area of concern. Raheel's classmates were often annoyed by her strange and random comments, outbursts of ill-timed affection, and fixations on topics of no particular interest to them.

Despite the teacher's attempts to foster positive and meaningful peer relationships, the situations seemed contrived and far from authentic. Academically, Raheel was also experiencing difficulty. Math and reading remained problematic areas regardless of the teacher's varied approaches to instruction.

Raheel's parents were invited to come to a number of meetings that year where they had the opportunity to meet with the school-based team. The team was comprised of a speech and language therapist, an occupational therapist, two resource and methods teachers, a guidance counselor, the school principal and Raheel's class-room teachers. A veritable army of people was prepared to meet the challenges involved with serving this child.

Unfortunately, each meeting ended the same way. Raheel's parents would state their clear denial about Raheel's struggles and imply that the problem was with the school. They felt that it was the school's job to figure out how to teach their daughter.

It was a vicious cycle and caught many people up in endless rotations. Teachers, resource and methods teachers and student services consultants were involved in numerous attempts to construct a meaningful service plan for Raheel. The situation would remain a stalemate until the parents would admit that Raheel's difficulties were worsening over time. We tried over and over to convince Raheel's parents that the school and the home needed to work together and to seek appropriate intervention.

Finally, during the latter part of Raheel's grade three year, when academic results were still not improving and peer difficulties evolved into what could be classified as bullying episodes, Raheel's parents finally conceded that perhaps there might be an issue. They even admitted that more might be involved than the school's inability to provide an appropriate program for Raheel.

This breakthrough happened after their family physician suggested that they seek a formal psycho-educational evaluation and assessment to rule out Attention Deficit Hyperactivity Disorder. After rigorous testing and evaluation, the consensus was that Raheel had Autism Spectrum Disorder.

The implications of this diagnosis were significant. Children with autism require intense individual educational plans in order to meet their social and academic needs. Collaborative planning is required in order to create a meaningful plan for the individual child. The school must work in partnership with the home to ensure a consistent approach to meeting Raheel's needs.

The implications for me, as Raheel's resource and methods teacher, were enormous. This little girl, who is now in grade four, requires a great deal of intervention and specific teaching. I still feel that this support would have been easier and more natural had the diagnosis been arrived at earlier.

In the past few months Raheel's classmates have become a network of support rather than her adversaries. Her current teacher, Mrs. Lessing, has worked tirelessly to learn about Autism Spectrum Disorder and how to teach to those needs. There is more communication with Raheel's parents.

I still find that it is difficult not to look back and wonder how this child might have developed if both the school and her family held a common vision of Raheel's school experience right from the beginning of kindergarten. I am continually reminded of the hopeful eyes of Raheel's mother and realize that I must be hopeful that together we will be able to help this student achieve success.

PROFESSIONAL INQUIRY

Beliefs and Assumptions

- Critique the assumptions and images associated with the following language used within this case: "typical learner", "army of people", "stalemate" and "vicious cycle".
- Discuss the implications of the language used to describe the learner and the parents in this case.

Identification and Support

- Explore the implications of the beliefs and assumptions associated with formal identification or diagnosis of learner's needs in this case.
- Identify other ways in which the school might have supported the success of the learner in this case.

Educational Planning

- Critique the educational programming provided to the learner in this case.

- Explore the ethical and professional responsibility of educators to provide appropriate educational programming to learners in the absence of formal identification of the needs of the learner.
- Discuss the commitment to ongoing professional learning of the educators in this case.
- Analyze the resource and methods teacher's knowledge of the learner in this case.

Relationships with Parents

- Explore approaches that schools can employ to develop trusting, accepting and non-judgmental relationships with parents of learners with diverse needs.
- Identify ways in which school personnel and parents can work collaboratively together to develop a shared understanding of the needs of learners.

CASE COMMENTARY REFLECTIONS

After reading the commentaries reflect on the following:

New Insights
Identify new insights gained from reading the commentaries.

Understandings
Discuss the impact of the commentaries on your understandings of inclusive education.

Questions
Identify questions that emerge for you from reading the commentaries.

CASE COMMENTARY 1

Pamela C. McGugan

Three key areas for discussion present in this scenario; the ability of school personnel to establish a welcoming school for Raheel's parents; the responsiveness of the school to Raheel's strengths and weaknesses and their ability to program for her and create an individual learning profile; a shared vision of how staff work together to meet the needs of diverse learners.

From the school's point, they feel that they have done everything to reach the parents. They have gathered proof that Raheel is not your average learner and tried to inform the parents. They have assembled an army of experts ready to report on Raheel's needs.

Confrontation, denial and avoidance have dominated the relationship between the school and Raheel's parents to date. Despite numerous meetings, it appears the conflict has persisted. The resource teacher feels Raheel's mother is at last ready to work with the school now that Jamie has been diagnosed with ASD. However, Raheel's mother may simply be acquiescing to what she perceives as the school winning. If Raheel's mother suffers a sense of grievance or feels pressured by the school, her animosity towards the school may resurface. Involving her in the decision making for Raheel's program goals will ensure she maintains her sense of control.

Consulting Raheel's parents about how they feel about these meetings would give the principal a place to begin in forging a relationship. I remember seeing the terror on parents' faces as they entered a formal identification, placement and review committee meeting and were immediately outnumbered by the school board personnel. Acknowledging that such a large meeting must be overwhelming conveys to the parents that you have some understanding of how they are feeling. It is also important to state early in the meeting that everyone is there to support the student. Every effort must be made to establish trust with the parents.

Establishing a welcoming school environment is key in building trusting and respectful relations with the parents. The principal may consider limiting the participants at the meeting to key players. Suggest to the parents that they may want to bring an advocate such as a relative, a family friend or perhaps a case manager if they are working with an agency.

The professional learning community structure is also a good beginning for working with parents and creating a welcoming school. This staff would benefit by engaging in a professional learning community structure where they could engage in developing a shared vision, and in particular, how they will support all students including those with special needs. A learning community that includes parents, students, and other community partners as well as staff can involve all partners collaboratively in understanding how to bring about school improvement and create learning opportunities for all students. The resource teacher expresses that she is overwhelmed. Working together and sharing responsibility will lessen this isolation and the group as a whole will feel empowered as they work on solutions together. As the understanding and knowledge of staff increases, so will their ability to work with parents in solving conflicts and finding solutions. The principal's challenge will be to create a collaborative school culture that reaches out to all students and parents.

Having a formal diagnosis is rarely a panacea for student success. Formal identification of a student ensures that they will have access to specific supports and resources and their progress followed carefully. However, a student's needs should be met regardless of formal identification. Teachers need to be prepared to continue to program effectively and use an individual learning profile as an assessment tool to determine the student's instructional level in key areas. Creating a learning profile helps to distill the data and design instruction for the student based on their strengths and needs. The resource teacher indicates that she is prepared to do this. Teachers accumulate and employ a wide repertoire of skills honed from working with students with various special education needs. A skilled leader will recognize the importance of building capacity in staff.

CASE COMMENTARY 2

Dr. Jude MacArthur

The tragedy of this case is, of course, the long delay in coming to grips with Raheel's learning challenges. Raheel has been 'misunderstood' for three years at school, she is portrayed as the object of a 'terrible disservice' as her teachers have tried to understand her 'non-responsive and disruptive behavior'. Nonetheless, clear assets in this case are the inclusive values held by Raheel's teachers. They are committed to teaching all children, and they want to learn more. They are concerned for lost opportunities, and for Raheel's experiences of exclusion that have come from a lack of understanding about her disability. The complex multiple roles of teachers are illustrated as the methods and resource teacher talks about her efforts to communicate with Raheel's family, support her teachers, and coordinate a range of professionals. They persist in challenging circumstances, raising questions about Raheel's learning and behavior, and about the implications for their own work.

The frustration of Raheel's teachers is both palpable and understandable. While teachers and other professionals at school are pasting together a picture of Jamie as having difficulties at school, ultimately the source of the problem is revealed as the failure by Raheel's parents to 'admit that Raheel's difficulties were worsening over time'. A stalemate position is identified, but one which is ultimately overcome through the intervention of the family physician who suggests a psycho-educational assessment. Raheel is found to have Autism Spectrum Disorder.

This case raises important questions about the role of schools in working closely with families and other professionals to understand students' learning challenges. Firstly, while the frustrations of Raheel's teachers need to be appreciated, the reluctance of her family to label her as 'special' or 'disabled' or 'autistic' also needs to be understood. Families live in disabling societies that are ready to separate out people with disabilities in negative ways. Schools may therefore need to focus on the early building of trusting and supportive relationships with parents as the foundation for exploring children's learning experiences.

Secondly, Raheel should not come to school as a 'surprise package'. Her transition to school can involve the early development of productive relationships between key school staff and Raheel's parents and early childhood teachers before she starts school. These relationships, along with assessments and information about her prior learning, would help to ensure that that Raheel's teachers are informed and prepared from day one.

CASE COMMENTARY 3

Melanie Panitch

The mother's role in this scenario is fascinating and complicated. She is the one who asks the burning question: "what do we do now that we know what she has?" In that question she challenges the commonly held though incorrect notion that the diagnosis will itself open all the doors. Many mothers of disabled children agree that getting a diagnosis is reassuring, but only as a place from which to build. The experienced resource and methods teacher wisely attempts to build a trusting relationship by a reassuring commitment to try her best and indeed she starts her research, willingly. But at the same time she feels overwhelmed and can't resist issuing a dose of mother-blaming for the years wasted. Reportedly, the school marshaled its core of experts to aid the student but without parental involvement or willingness to assume an active role, any hopes of a mutually beneficial partnership evaporated. In the pejorative expression often used to describe parental refusal to accept their child's disability, the parents are said to be "in denial" and are portrayed as reneging on their responsibility. We are told the parents have resisted contact with the school yet we know little of their cultural background or economic class situation which might help explain why this may be so. Perhaps they just assumed educational professionals are the experts. Perhaps they were suspicious of, or preferred not to acknowledge the assigned Attention Deficit Hyperactive Disorder (ADHD) label, a category into which countless children have been herded over the last decade and treated for unreasonable behavior. But it is clear that they recognized and respected medical authority and the valuable role a family physician can play in soliciting resources, in this case a psycho-educational evaluation for their patients. The school or the doctor might have made more headway had they tried to connect the Hains with other families or parent led disability organizations and or individual mothers raising disabled children. A final caution stimulated by this case is the following: In taking as our overarching goal the idea that no child should get left behind, we should not find ourselves stifling the possibility that any child should be prevented from getting ahead. The questions that emerge for me from reading this case include:

– How can we ensure that "diversity includes" when increasingly we use diversity to further separate from one another?
– Why do we assume we know one another much better the moment we hear short-hand identifying labels?
– What is the significance of the doctor playing such a pivotal role in this case study?
– How can supportive relationships between parents and educators be fostered and nourished?
– How can an understanding of women's traditional gendered socialization help us to explain why some mothers become vigorous advocates in their child's education while other mothers only participate passively or reluctantly?

CASE COMMENTARY 4

Krista Carr

There are three key items present in this scenario: the challenge in developing and nurturing strong parent/school relationships and how important this is to the success of the child, the view that there must be a diagnosis before intervention can be provided and the way other students can be a source of support to an exceptional learner when they understand the circumstances that surround their behaviour.

The relationship between the school and parents can be challenging at times. In this scenario it appears that the school made numerous attempts to connect with the parents and had no success. I wonder about the approach that was used with the parents. Often the presence of many professionals can be overwhelming for parents. I have been at many meetings with families where the number of professionals around the table has been overwhelming to the point that parents felt pushed into being defensive. They feel their expertise as it pertains to their child is overshadowed by the professional expertise in the room. This is often not the intent of the professionals but is often the result for the parents.

I wonder if there could have been other ways to establish a trusting relationship with these parents that may have produced better results earlier. These relationships are key in any situation but where the child is an exceptional learner, this relationship and collaboration become of paramount importance.

Diagnosis of disability, while helpful when used for the purposes of determining the most effective interventions to help a child succeed in school, can be highly overrated. This school certainly wanted to determine the cause of the student's struggles both socially and academically so they could help her succeed. I do question the amount of importance we place on the diagnosis in situations like this.

In my experience, there is no magic in diagnosis. It can be helpful in determining effective interventions but even though students may share the same diagnosis they are different human beings and they present differently as a result. Often the same interventions won't work equally effectively for different students with the same label. I wonder if interventions were attempted with Jamie and to what extent, without an official diagnosis and what the result would have been if they were.

In this case Raheel's peers were identified as a source of stress in this case and it seemed to get worse as she progressed through the grades. After Raheel's diagnosis of autism we see that Raheel's peers have become a network of support to her. We often underestimate the power of peers to include an exceptional student. The key is that they be provided with information that helps them to understand the circumstances that surround the behaviour and challenges of the student. I have seen this done very effectively by both educators and parents who take the opportunity to educate the peers that surround the student.

Going forward it seems that everyone is committed to Jamie's success at school. With parents, peers and professionals working together the sky is indeed the limit for Raheel's academic and social progress.

CASE COMMENTARY 5

Sheila Bennett

I like the idea that the teachers have the idea that they have to learn a lot. That is great. I am concerned that this case is from the point of view of special teachers. I would prefer to see the perspective come from regular classroom teachers. We do not want to promote the idea that once we get a diagnosis or a visible impairment that the 'special teacher' is the one involved.

I would also love to see a shift in the focus away from the student "adjusting to the new expectations and new teacher" towards the environment and teacher being aware and making adjustments for her!

The key issues that emerge for me in this case are building meaningful relationships with parents/caregivers, over reliance on standardized testing and diagnosis and the importance of continuous learning and self education on the part of all educators.

As I read this case, a number of questions that are relevant for this case come to mind. These include the following:

− While we often feel as educators, that we need a diagnosis prior to real intervention, why is this approach ineffective and how can we work together to provide meaningful and effective instruction and support earlier? (She has been described as non-responsive and disruptive for four years!)
− Parents can often feel isolated and disenfranchised from a schooling system for a myriad of reasons. What approaches can be used to build a relationship of trust and mutual respect with parents/caregivers?
− It would seem clear from the beginning of Raheel's school career that there were difficulties adjusting to new environments and developing meaningful relationship with peers. Want types of strategies could have been used in these early years, even without parental involvement, that might have helped Raheel function more successfully?

CONNECTING TO PROFESSIONAL PRACTICE

The case commentary writers raise issues related to relationships with parents, labeling of students, gender socialization, diversity, programming, the role of medical professionals and the impact of the assumptions held by educators. Reflect on your experience with these issues. What insights have you gained about these issues from your own professional practice?

CASE EIGHT: I DID MY BEST

Whether any of the children that I work with will ever appreciate my efforts really doesn't matter. I am happy in my role as a classroom teacher as long as I can contribute to their growth and to their successes. Being part of a student's development is truly its own reward. In my first year of teaching, I worked with a student whose challenges were so many and so complex that I began to wonder if sometimes, as a teacher there may not be many rewards.

Madison entered my grade three classroom in September. I was new to the school and did not know Madison. A brief review of her cumulative record before the beginning of school was the first indication that I had of her disability.

The fact that she had a disability was not a major concern to me. I had completed my Master of Education degree with a focus on Exceptional Learning and felt that I had the skills and know-how to effectively teach children with special needs. I had no idea at the beginning of September the challenges that Madison would bring.

I met Madison on the first day of school. Her petite frame, flowing long brown hair and big brown eyes struck me immediately. She wore an adorable new outfit that day. She appeared to be a happy girl, who seemed very curious. She seemed entranced by the patterns of light that fell on the floor. She wandered about the classroom. She looked upwards towards the ceiling tiles, and downwards towards the tiny cracks in the linoleum. She stuck her tiny fingers into small holes in the wall and floor.

It was odd that she would do these things. All of the other children were greeting one another and exchanging stories about their summer holidays. Madison took no part in these activities. She seemed inwardly focused and kept to herself.

I walked over to Madison and said with a bright smile. "Hello. What is your name?" She looked at me with this blank stare. She did not answer. I attributed this to the fact that she might just be a shy child. Her blank stare rarely vanished during the weeks ahead.

Madison had been diagnosed with Central Auditory Processing Disorder and individualized educational plans had been developed for her in previous years. After the first six weeks of school, I began to feel that there was something more interfering with her learning and her social skills. I was certain there was something else but I did not know what.

I began to see signs of an anxious child with strange obsessions and fixations. On a Tuesday in late October, Madison raced back into the school during recess. She came running towards me, tears streaming down her face and barely able to speak. I kept asking, "Madison, what is wrong?" She did not answer. All she did was sob.

"Madison, what is the problem?" I tried to turn her towards me to hold her and comfort her shaking body. I tried for several minutes to find out what the problem is. Finally, I discovered that Madison was so upset because she managed to get several tiny specks of flower pollen on her finger while she was out on the playground. She screamed, "I'm afraid. I am afraid that I have allergies. My throat will close up. I won't be able to breathe. I will die." She sobbed uncontrollably. She gulped air and choked on it.

I did my best to calm her down by holding her in my arms and speaking calmly. "Maddy, you are fine. You are such a brave girl. You are just fine." I try to reassure her that she will be all right. Nothing I do seemed to help. Madison thrashed around and screamed non-stop. She continued to sob panic stricken. There was no reassuring her. There was no way to comfort her. This was the first incident like this. Several more followed. They all revolved around Maddy's fear of death and illness.

Madison believed that when the teacher assistant touched her gently on the back with a capped pen in her hand that it would cause blood poisoning. She believed that a child accidentally bumping into her during gym class would result in a punctured lung. She believed that one day she had swallowed a bumblebee. That day she ran around in circles terrified. She shrieked over and over, "I am going to die. It will sting me on the inside of my stomach. I will die."

Later that same week, Madison adamantly refused to sit next to a child with a physical disability. She feared she would acquire the disability. Her list of irrational fears continued to grow.

Her anxiety became so severe that she could not learn. There were days where she experienced great difficulty functioning in the regular classroom environment. Madison's social skills and peer relationships had become almost non-existent. She lacked understanding and skill when it came to acknowledging and responding appropriately to social cues. She lacked tact and misinterpreted comments, facial expressions and gestures. Just yesterday, Madison grabbed Marina's hair and shrieked at her when Marina happened to come too close to Madison's desk.

Maddy was becoming more aggressive. She hit, kicked, pinched, name-called and even spit when she could not deal with her frustrations. I recall the day when I was in the middle of a lesson and Maddy jumped out of her seat, ran across the classroom, and pinched Nicholas. He had been hard at work. "Maddy", I reproached her in a stern voice, "What ever possessed you to leap out of your seat and to pinch Nicholas?" That blank stare reappeared. I could see her rage. She screeched, "He looked at me. I was afraid that he was going to laugh at me."

Nicholas looked at me in confusion and responded shyly, "Mrs. Murphy, I was not laughing at Madison. I just looked up to see what time it was." He had been looking at the clock that hung on the wall above her desk.

Madison saw the world differently. She wanted things her way. Her lack of social skills were infringing on the few friendships that she had. Madison regularly retreated to place that she called "Madison World". She seemed fixated on the belief that she was a vampire. Her real name was Zelda. When I call her by her real name, Madison, she refused to acknowledge me. She would fly into a rage if she was not called Zelda.

Finally, a meeting was set up with our methods and resource teacher, the school principal and two school district special services consultants. I passed around the documentation I had brought that outlined the nature and the date and duration of Madison's behavioural outbursts during the past three months. The meeting participants were shocked.

"Where do we start with this student?" asked my principal. We sat around the table and talked. No one offered a suggestion that I hadn't already tried. Our methods and resource teacher decided that it was necessary to make contact with our district psychologist and one of our district guidance counsellors.

They both come to the school within days and met with Madison. They both agreed that there were behavioural issues well beyond those described in the assessment that had been completed the previous year. They immediately enrolled Madison in a social learning program.

They also suggested to Madison's mother that she contact a paediatrician immediately. The school gained consent to be in direct contact with the doctor.

Eight months later Madison was diagnosed with Anxiety Disorder and Obsessive Compulsive Disorder. Her updated assessment also reaffirmed the continued presence of Central Auditory Processing Disorder. The doctor prescribes medication to help her effectively deal with her anxiety and obsessive behaviour. Madison's family indicated they cannot pay for Madison's medication. The school offered to help fund the medication. The parents refused the school's offer.

"I don't believe in medicating my child," Madison's mother responded sternly to me over the phone. I found myself begging her to consider giving her daughter medication. "There is nothing wrong with my child. Absolutely nothing," she said and then hung up the phone. My heart sank.

It had been a long and arduous process to try to even get the necessary people into place to help Madison. My frustrations continue to grow because of our lack of progress. At the end of the school year I was left with many questions. How much longer it is going to take for this child to receive the help she really needs? Did I fail this child? I tried everything that I could think of. I explored all possible avenues. I feel that there are few rewards.

I have come to accept the fact that I could not meet all of Madison's needs. She needed more that I could offer. I did my best but that was not enough!!

PROFESSIONAL INQUIRY

Commitment to Student Learning

- Discuss the teacher's commitment to Madison.
- Critique this school system's commitment to students with diverse learning needs.
- Explore the connection between developing trusting and collaborative relationships with parents and the school's commitment to student learning.

Professional Knowledge

- Identify the forms of professional knowledge that the classroom teacher appears to possess in this case.
- Recommend additional professional knowledge that may help to enhance the practices of the classroom teacher.

Challenges to Inclusive Education

– Identify the challenges and barriers to inclusive education in this case.
– Explore strategies for promoting a commitment towards shared responsibility and the integration of practices for supporting inclusive education in this case.

School Processes and Practices

– Critique the school processes, protocols and practices in this case that impact upon Madison's success.
– Identify changes that could be made to the school's processes, protocols, practices and commitments that would more effectively promote student success and learning.

Professional Responsibility

– Identify and analyze the professional responsibility of the classroom teacher, principal and the other professional in this case.
– List suggestions for enhancing the professional and ethical responsibilities of all the professionals in this case.
– Discuss the professional responsibility of educators for authentically collaborating with and involving families in the educational process of students.

Teacher Education

– Identify the implications for teacher education that emerge from this case.

CASE COMMENTARY REFLECTIONS

After reading the commentaries reflect on the following:

New Insights
Identify new insights gained from reading the commentaries.

Understandings
Discuss the impact of the commentaries on your understandings of inclusive education.

Questions
Identify questions that emerge for you from reading the commentaries.

CASE COMMENTARY 1

Odet Moliner García

The first issue concerning the transition of disabled pupils is related to the use of protocols or, in this case, the lack of a protocol containing the up-to-date, available information about Maddy. This protocol should have a double purpose: firstly providing information about this student, but not just about the diagnosis of her disability but also about other matters related to her previous schooling (provided by teachers or the family as well as specialists); difficulties that may have emerged over time, and the decisions taken regarding the response to Madison's particular needs, both in the more academic sphere (knowledge and competences) and in social and emotional areas. Meanwhile, it is also necessary to establish in the protocols the people who are most closely related to the case, forming a support network, as well as the process for collecting new relevant information and the system and frequency of monitoring and review. This would prevent an individual, intuitive approach like that taken by the classroom teacher, improvising responses to Maddy's panic attacks, irrational fears and aggressive behavior.

A support team working cooperatively is fundamental. This would encourage reflection about the changes occurring in Maddy's behavior, seeing, for example, whether they generally affect all contexts and people who have relations with her. The joint work of the specialists and the teacher would allow a more exhaustive analysis of the case and the implementation of consensus decision-making in order to develop responses along the same lines. These processes would allow agreements to be reached and made explicit. They would also facilitate the development of plans for the implementation of these agreements. Properly systemized cooperative work, perhaps led or coordinated by a specialist teacher, would help to free the teacher from responsibility taken individually. Instead, this responsibility would be shared by the team. This would prevent the feeling of loneliness and frustration experienced in the face of the uncertainties aroused by a complex case like that of Maddy.

Finally, the participation of the family is fundamental. It has been kept out of decision-making, which could have been one of the reasons for the mother's rejection of the solution adopted. Being able to share and compare information about Maddy from the beginning would have provided a great opportunity for achieving closer ties between school and family, with both sides feeling that they participated in and were responsible for the solutions adopted. Possibly a shared, gradually assumed view of the situation would have prevented the mother's denial and initial resistance when confronted with a diagnosis of obsessive compulsive disorder. The collegial work of specialists, teachers and families makes it possible to streamline decision-making and problem-solving so that responses to needs of disabled students are coordinated and effective.

CASE COMMENTARY 2

Barbara Wenders

I appreciate the self-reflection and patience embodied by the teacher. This teacher did her best. In Germany, you would hardly find any elementary school for Madison. My experience is related to our school, Grundschule Berg Fidel in Münster. We are beginning our way towards inclusive education.

In Madison's challenging case we probably would try to find a multi-professional answer. To reduce pressure and to be successful, we work in fixed teams: classroom-teacher, teacher for special education, principal, assistants or students. We would ask, what happened in Kindergarten and grade 1 and 2?

Without the collaboration of the parents success cannot be achieved. We must know about Maddy's behaviour at home? Why does the mother say that there is nothing wrong with my child? Without the trust of the parents and their collaboration there cannot be a sustained success. In Germany, we have some good experience using home visits.

Another key element in this case is the paediatrician. In some severe cases, medication makes sense and is necessary. For a period of time some students may need medication. In Madison's case we need a lot more information. We need the help of the parents and other professionals.

In Germany, we often waste time in wondering and focusing too much on the behaviour alone. For Maddy, it is normal to act as she acts and there are reasons! The development of a collaborative plan is essential for her success. In our school, we had a girl who screamed loudly every day for nearly one year. She experienced difficulty cooperating with others. We organized one to one support. One of our objectives was to help increase her confidence and make her feel secure. The purpose of having an adult alongside her was to convey the following message: "*I'm here at your side, nothing bad can happen to you*". The presence of this adult also communicated a sense of security to the other students who were often fearful of the screaming. After some months, we reduced this intensive level of support. The parents acquired behaviour therapy from a community agency and there were extensive conversations between the mother and the school. These supports commenced in grade one. She is now in grade four and her behaviour is no longer an issue and she is experiencing significant success at school.

Some students may benefit from additional adult support, therapy and sometimes medication. The key to being successful is involving the family, understanding the student and being as flexible and innovative as possible.

CASE COMMENTARY 3

Stephanie Zucko

Madison's case is a challenge, but not atypical of what teachers are faced with in the inclusive classroom. Students arrive with a range of information which is often documented in the student file. A key decision for many educators is whether they should read the student file prior to meeting the students. In this case, the teacher laments about not having information on this student, however, at times, information written in files serves little purpose but to taint your views of a student prior to meeting him or her. For instance, I had a student in grade 7, Jeff, whose file told a story of excessively violent boy—the words *aggressive, violent, and physical* were repeated to such a degree that I actually felt nervous about having this boy in my class and walked on eggshells around him for the first month. Then, I started to realize that Jeff was okay in his new class, he was adjusting just fine and I certainly had no reason to fear him. This caused me to ask myself the following questions: *What were the circumstances that triggered behaviour the previous year,*

93

in his other school? In what way was the description of his behaviour helpful for me to receive as his next teacher, there was no indication of strategies tried? Files and what is documented must be carefully thought out, as they can mislead or bias the next educator who will be working with the particular student. Detailing a particular outburst serves what purpose? What if we detailed the strategies? The events when the student performed well, or behaved—what caused the good days?

The behaviour Madison displays appear to become more disruptive to her and to others as the school year progresses. It is not clear in this case what strategies the teacher used to address some of the issues that arose. *How did she try to work with Madison regarding her fears? How did she work with classmates to help them know how to interact with Madison?* The teacher mentioned that when the school team is called in for a meeting that the suggestions offered had already been tried. I wondered about what strategies to use.

The interaction between home and school captures the frustrations felt by many teachers. Expressing concern and trying to get the parents and their paediatrician involved were good strategies employed by the school. However, there is a flavor to this case study of blaming the family for Madison's behaviour and then a quick closure to wanting her medicated as a solution. None of this sits well with me. I think the home and school relationship needs to be detailed a little more so that the reader has a sense of what transpired, with a caution to avoid blame. Parents see many teachers in the course of their child's life, often for one year blocks where it is difficult to build a trusting relationship before it is over again and they are starting with another teacher. Each new teacher may offer the parents a diversity of suggestions. Parents are partners and need to be asked, gently guided and supported—sometimes they are at a greater loss than the school.

The teacher ends the case study with a statement of "few rewards" in having taught this student. The rewards are there. The experience gained and self-growth as a teacher are important rewards to be gained from this case. To indicate twice, in such a short case, that there are few rewards to working with students with special needs is a significant concern.

I think this teacher met some of Madison's needs in that she did not give up on her. What will the teacher do to help the next teacher who will have Madison in her classroom? How can this teacher come to understand the many wonderful rewards associated with working with learners with diverse and unique needs?

CASE COMMENTARY 4

Tiffany Gallagher

This case presents a complicated situation in which the teacher truly "did her best" to support a student with several special needs. This teacher kept excellent anecdotal notes and sought assistance from support persons. Readers of this case might want to discuss how they might have handled this student in their classrooms and if they would have done anything differently (e.g., Would you as a classroom teacher, wait 3 months before calling a meeting with the resource teacher, principal and consultants?). This case illustrates an important point for teachers: do not assume that a single diagnosis appropriately defines the difficulties that a student has. As well, an Individual Education Plan (IEP) should be a working document that is in a state of constant revision based on the dynamic needs of a student.

This case brings forward some considerations of the other significant individuals in a student's life. For example, the relationships and interactions with other class-mates should be explored and explicitly addressed by the teacher. What kinds of student-appropriate resources can be used to facilitate this? The child's parents were seemingly not convinced that their daughter was not functioning successfully in the classroom setting. Readers of this case should consider alternatives for working with the parent(s) of students with special needs. How do we value and respect the role and participation of parent(s) of students with special needs?

CONNECTING TO PROFESSIONAL PRACTICE

The commentary writers raise concerns regarding the school's commitment towards and ability to effectively develop trusting relationships with Madison's parents. The lack of collaboration with and involvement of the parents, over the course of Madison's school experience, is a significant issue in this case. The apparent absence of transitional planning, lack of effective communication processes to facilitate information exchange regarding student development and limited collaborative team work are identified by the commentary writers as unacceptable educational practices.

Reflect on your own experience with transition plans, communication protocols and collaborative problem solving school teams in supporting student learning. Identify key insights you have acquired about inclusive education from these formal educational processes.

CASE NINE: SIX GIRLS AND A BULLY

"Okay girls. Tell me what's going on."

Joany looks at me. "Lolie has a lying book you know and I'm in it over fifty times! She calls me a blabbermouth. I'm not am I?"

She looks cautiously around the group of girls sitting in my office.

Another girl quickly replies, "No, you're not a blabbermouth. Lolie calls me stupid all the time."

Joany looked at me with uncertainty. "She always wants one of us to carry her book bag and hang it up for her."

I asked, "Do you carry Lolie's book bag Joany?"

"Yes. Because if I don't then Lolie won't be my friend. And she might stamp on my toe or kick me."

"Do you really want to have a friend like that?" I ask.

Joany hangs her head and quietly says, "No."

The rest of the girls in my office also tell their stories about Lolie and how she has been treating them. The stories are similar. Lolie is consistently manipulating their lives and they are very uncomfortable with it. One girl actually weeps when she reveals that she stole several dollars from a classmate's wallet at Lolie's direction. Another girl's face darkens as she whispers how she has been mimicking the child who is hard of hearing so that Lolie will give her a thumb's up sign. This has been going on all year. Each story in itself might be considered one flight into childhood cruelty. When you put together all of these incidents, however, it adds up to a pattern of bullying.

My conversation with the girls takes place at 8:30 in the morning. It took place because a mother came to visit me in the late afternoon of the previous day. She was totally frustrated and very upset. Lolie had been harassing her daughter, Darlene. Darlene's mother explained that her daughter had come home the night before crying again. Darlene was terrified that if her mother went to the school and told about what had happened then Lolie would get in trouble. She was even more afraid of what Lolie would do to her.

Darlene's mother glared at me. "What do you intend to do about the problem?"

I assured her that I would look into the matter the following morning. I added that it was my responsibility as principal to ensure that our students could come to school and feel safe.

I must confess I didn't think that a child in grade four from a small school in a rural area would have this kind of negative power over so many girls. As I began to investigate further, teachers reluctantly filled in more details about Lolie Westin's cruel and manipulative behaviour. They used words like "bully", "manipulator", "cunning", and "hurtful". These teachers provided so much information that I began to wonder why I had had to wait for a student's mother to tell me about the problem. I should have known about this problem long ago.

Finally, I was able to piece together an understanding of what was going on. Six girls in our school were involved. Each of the six girls had been cruelly manipulated and bullied by Lolie since September.

It is disheartening to realize that, as a principal, you just don't always know everything that is going on in your school. I have always tried to have open communication with teachers, parents and students. My office door is almost always open. I am visible on the playgrounds. I stop and chat and encourage dialogue. Teachers know I am willing to listen and that I have often stayed late just to be there for them.

I want to believe that teachers in my school would notice activities that look like bullying and be able to deal with them appropriately. I want to feel that I have adequate information to act and to deal with bullying. I want my school to be a safe place.

I do remember hearing murmurs of concern about Lolie in the past. She is a girl with significant speech challenges and who has difficulty keeping up academically because of these language issues. She is a pretty girl with green eyes and brown hair. But she is often scowling with her mouth turned downward. Lolie also has a delay in receptive language. In class, her teachers tell me she puts her head down on her desk to avoid being asked a question directly.

I pulled out Lolie's file so that I could reacquaint myself with her history. She is the youngest of a wonderful family of four children. The three older siblings in the family are all star students who have succeeded very well in our elementary school. Lolie's mother, Mrs. Westin, has always been supportive of the school. She is involved with the School Council and has accompanied students on many field trips. She has also provided positive feedback about all activities in which her children have participated. She has hand written many thank you notes for things done at the school.

This morning, when I ushered Joany and her friends into my office, the girls didn't want me to talk to Lolie. They wanted to handle the problem themselves. So I decided to accept their resolve and we devised a plan of action. In this way, they would be prepared to deal with Lolie when she told them what to do or which classmates they could have as friends.

Eventually, the girls began to offer suggestions. I could tell that they were relieved to talk. We discussed that it was okay for Lolie to be mad and not speak to them when they didn't follow her instructions. They reaffirmed that they had each other as friends and that they could stand by and support each other without being bullies to Lolie or to anyone else. I noticed Sarah's sigh of relief and a faint smile on Judy's face. A weight had been lifted from their shoulders. I thought of the six girls who entered my office at 8.30 looking defeated and in despair. Now they were leaving with newfound self-esteem and resolve.

After my discussion with the girls I called Darlene's mother and shared our plan. I felt that it was important for all the girls to build up their knowledge and self-confidence when dealing with bullies. It wouldn't be long before they faced even more demanding situations as young adolescents.

I had read articles about how difficult female bullies could be and how some young girls could be very vindictive. I really expected that this kind of behaviour would be more typical in a middle school or high school. I did not expect it in my little elementary school set in a community where people are really kind and hospitable to one another. I hoped that these girls might learn some coping skills from this experience with Lolie.

The six girls came to see me later in the day. "Lolie won't talk to us at recess. She is giving us dirty looks and pointing her fingers at us. Her fingers look like claws."

Joany related that in French class Lolie had told her that she could only talk to Marie three times and after that, Joany must turn her back to Marie and walk away. When Joany refused, Lolie kicked her. Joany pulled up her skirt to reveal a yellowing bruise.

I recommended to Lolie's teacher that Lolie be kept in at recess the next day. Miss Chu, a new teacher, said that she was grateful for the advice I gave her about how to handle this situation. I also gave her copies of a few of the articles that I had on the topic of bullying.

I thought about my next steps. First, I would meet with Lolie and get her side of the story. Then I would talk to her mother about my concerns regarding her daughter. I am worried about Lolie's ability to succeed in building peer relationships. I am worried about what might be causing Lolie's behaviour. I am worried about the impact that Lolie's behaviour has on her self-esteem? I felt guilty, as an experienced administrator, that I had not picked up on the seriousness and the consequences of Lolie's behaviour.

How can the school help Lolie? How can I help the parents of the children being bullied to understand the underlying problems surrounding Lolie without sacrificing student confidentiality? How can I offer support to the six girls who have been victims of bullying? It is the end of May and these students will all be together again in the fall. Should I plan activities now for the fall that will foster relationship-building skills and highlight the serious problems bullying can create? Where do I begin?

PROFESSIONAL INQUIRY

Professional Knowledge and Practice

- Analyze the professional knowledge and practices of the school principal and teachers in this case.
- Identify areas of growth and development for each of the educators.
- Discuss this school's understanding of inclusive education.
- Explore the ways in which the actions of educators can inadvertently exclude or marginalize students.

Leadership

- Critique the practices and decisions of the school principal.
- Identify actions that could contribute to the marginalization of Lolie in this case.
- Discuss the professional responsibilities of the educators in relation to the provision of an educational program that addresses all of Lolie's needs.
- Outline feedback you might provide to the principal of this school if you were the principal's mentor or professional coach.

CASE COMMENTARY REFLECTIONS

After reading the commentaries reflect on the following:

New Insights
Identify new insights gained from reading the commentaries.

Understandings
Discuss the impact of the commentaries on your understandings of inclusive education.

Questions
Identify questions that emerge for you from reading the commentaries.

CASE COMMENTARY 1

Pamela C. McGugan

The principal is responsive to the concerns of the parent, reassures her that they will ensure the school is safe and then acts swiftly in interviewing the students involved. However, once the problem is uncovered, the principal expresses surprise at what would be considered a fairly common occurrence in most school. Bullying takes place in most school environments to some degree as well as being an ever growing concern in workplace environments. The principal's underlying assumptions that it is surprising that this could happen in "a small school in a rural area" are troubling.

The principal quickly and accurately determines several areas of concern: teachers are aware of this bullying situation and yet have not brought it forward for discussion; a parent is now concerned and is demanding action; a group of students have indicated that they are being bullied and in some cases physically hurt; Lolie has been identified as a student requiring support and interventions.

Several questions are raised here. Are there clear expectations for student behaviour and procedures for staff to follow when students are at risk? Has the principal been able to convey that staff is collectively responsible for the safety of each and every student? Providing an inclusive and equitable school environment where all students feel valued, safe and welcomed includes Lolie. The principal has the responsibility of working with staff to articulate that vision and plan collaboratively to improve school climate.

Anti bullying programs and character development programs are most effective when they are integrated and embedded into the culture of the school and staff act proactively in establishing initiatives that create inclusive schools where all students are welcomed. The staff appear to be aware that Lolie is not achieving much success either academically or socially with her peers. Yet there is no indication that steps have been taken to address this situation or to involve Lolie's parents. A team effort is required to support Lolie and her parents, to identify key issues contributing to her behaviour and devise a plan of action.

The principal's remark, "Do you really want to have a friend like that?" plants the seeds for the students to isolate Lolie with the approval of the adults. Care needs to be taken to separate the student from the student's behaviour. The old adage "I like you but I do not like your behaviour at this moment" coins this sentiment. Care must be exercised when isolating sanctions are imposed on the student that she is not labeled the 'bad girl' and further marginalized. The behaviours described indicate that Lolie is moving through a cycle: low self esteem→ bullying behaviours→ isolation → further feelings of low self esteem. A successful program puts positive interventions in place that break the cycle and build 'healing' into the solution for the student. (i.e. opportunities for success and building self esteem)

The principal recognizes the need for staff training in how to deal with bullying. The larger issue though is staff responsibility when bullying occurs and expectations for the collective response to bullying. Interestingly, the staff appear to have abdicated their responsibility to Lolie. An important aspect to the success of turning this situation around will be the principal's ability to encourage staff to reflect on their own responses to this student's behaviour. The principal is responsible for engaging the entire school community and only when everyone accepts responsibility will they effect positive change in building a safe and respectful school climate where all students are valued. A nurturing and caring staff and school community are the cornerstones for school improvement.

CASE COMMENTARY 2

Sheila McWatters and Shirley Kendrick

"*...each of us is a shepherd in some way.*" (Jean Vanier, 1998)

What does inclusion look like for Lolie? How is her learning plan seen, understood, shaped and reviewed with the sphere of adults involved, student/peers and self? What is the role of each in supporting her learning and development: sense of self, social emotional learning, audience? How have all members of the community engaged in a strength-based response?

Inclusive practice for all means that "*fairness is not sameness*" (Education for All, Ontario Ministry of Education, 2005) In the context of this case, Lolie requires fair consideration, as evidenced in this principal's proactive attempts to reacquaint herself with Lolie's file and reflect on Lolie as a learner moving beyond just the behaviours she is presenting. In this reflection, this principal is able to gain a deeper understanding of the child behind the behaviour.

This also applies to the six young girls. Where have restorative practices and the reflection questions been considered in the relationships?

In a progressive context, we find that all parties need to be able to witness and name the behaviour, respond by discussing their feelings about the incident, resolve the incident, renew the relationships and for all to re-enter into community nourished and forgiven. Forgiveness is crucial for all.

Vanier reminds us that "…to forgive is to break down the walls of hostility that separate us and to bring each other out of the anguish of loneliness, fear, and chaos into communion and oneness" (Vanier, 1998, p. 162).

The case, viewed in a Catholic context, invokes reflection on Reconciliation. Reconciliation is a Catholic sacrament where interpersonal forgiveness is an anticipated outcome. In essence, reconciliation allows those within the Church to offer up their shortfalls for forgiveness in order to allow a deeper relationship with Christ in others. How would the sacrament of reconciliation and/or other faith -based expressions of shared forgiveness support the students in this case?

The reader can sympathize with the principal's feeling of shock and disappointment that she has "missed the signs" of Lolie's needs. How can the system support her practice in recognizing those signs through an understanding of, for example, the Ontario Ministry of Education's *Learning for All (K-12) document*? (Ontario Ministry of Education, 2009a). How does the evidence of academic and social/ emotional growth and development gleaned by the classroom teacher, resource teacher, support staff and other caring adults in the building and/or community, get shared in an authentic way to ensure that the community as a whole is responding within a progressive approach and with effort towards reconciliation?

The principal is open to self-reflection and, rooted in relationship with all the students and extended adult support team involved,was able to work towards healthy, supportive relationships for all, including Lolie. In a Catholic context, this case brings forward the idea of reconciliation and forgiveness and of the need for us to live in relationship: at once shepherd and shepherded. In this way, *Six Girls and A Bully* is a hope-filled case.

Also, the case allows for reflection on the notion of "silence" relative to openness. The dichotomy that exists in this case includes: the silence of each student, the silence of Lolie, the silence of other students, the silence of Lolie's parent and/or other parents, teachers and so on, relative to the principal's open door, the open teacher to teacher communication, the open student to student communication and parent involvement.

There is a shared responsibility and a shared reconciliation in this case. These are illuminated in the different perspectives of the principal. The perspectives of "not in my school", "rural area" and "being surprised" exist at the same time that the principal believes that the school has a commitment to relationships and interaction, creating the conditions for inclusion, acceptance to move beyond alienation and/or difference. The social fabric of the community knits the relationships respecting the well-being of all.

CASE COMMENTARY 3

Cindy Finn

At its core, bullying is relational in nature, meaning it involves two or more people in an unequal relationship that involves threat or intimidation. As such, solutions have to be rooted in addressing the relationship issues at play. For the victims and bystanders, it means speaking out to adults who are in a position to intervene.

For the aggressor, it often means having to learn conflict resolution and problem solving strategies. For the adults involved, it means alerting them to the signs and finding ways of responding that bring all involved together to work towards a solution.

Research shows that boys and girls express aggression in different ways. When girls engage in intimidation or bullying, they frequently use relational aggression, meaning that they use social dynamics as a weapon by ostracizing, isolating, or spreading rumours about others. Relational aggression can be a difficult form of bullying to spot and schools may be at a loss as to how to intervene effectively. Boys tend to be more physical in their approach to bullying. As a result, reactions, consequences and interventions can differ.

In this case, Lolie and her victims need to find a way to discuss feelings with an adult who can guide the conversation toward helping all realize that manipulation, threats, and isolation are hurtful. Lolie may need individual guidance to fully grasp the perspective of others and realize how harmful her actions are. Lolie's parents and the parents of the other girls involved also need to understand the role that Lolie's own behavioral and academic difficulties may be playing in this situation. The principal involved the girls in finding possible solutions. Perhaps the same approach could be considered with Lolie and her mother.

CASE COMMENTARY 4

Ulla Alexandersson

This is a sad story and I am really concerned about how this could have gone so far without any input from the teachers. I also wonder about Lolie's situation in the classroom and in what way she gets support not to feel "excluded" in the interplay in classroom.

The teachers have identified her speech problem and academic challenges so it would seem that she must have a hard time interacting with peers on her own. Her way of coming in contact with her peers will then be by manipulating and "bullying" them.

Therefore, I suggest that the teachers must focus on both Lolie's situation and her needs and how they can strengthen the relationship between all the pupils. It would be a good idea to work with the interaction patterns in the classroom. First of all observe the present patterns of interaction to understand what's stressing Lolie and then from this basis try to stimulate cooperation and interaction in different ways between all the pupils. The interaction between the individual and the learning, understanding the value of participation, and the importance of communication patterns must be a central focus.

How we are to understand Lolie's actions therefore depends on both the social practices of the classroom and Lolie's abilities and needs. She obviously needs help to build positive peer relationships and her peers need coaching on how to understand and support Lolie.

A peer mediation program could perhaps be a good strategy. In Sweden, these programs are becoming more and more common. This kind of pro-active approach stimulates an anti-bullying atmosphere where all pupils can feel they can be respected, can participate and be included.

That's what we want from our schools – for all our children.

CONNECTING TO PROFESSIONAL PRACTICE

The commentary writers discuss concepts that support inclusive practices. Relationships based on equity, safety and shared responsibility are highlighted by the writers. They also discuss the importance of restorative practices, forgiveness, self-reflection and character education. Consider your experiences with these concepts and reflect on the extent to which they are present or absent in your professional practice and professional context.

The professional knowledge and practices of the educators in this case came under scrutiny within some of the written case commentaries. How would you have handled the initial discussion with the girls in this case? What actions would you take to help colleagues understand the importance of full inclusion in the school community for a student with Lolie's profile and needs?

4. SCHOOL LEVEL PLANNING AND PRACTICES

Inclusion is enhanced and enabled when school level planning and practices are highly aligned with the philosophical underpinnings that characterize an inclusive worldview. Commitment and good will towards an inclusive educational philosophy are often not enough to enable all students to fully access educational opportunities. Action and alignment between vision and practice are required and necessary dimensions of inclusion.

Inclusive education becomes enacted or lived out in the planning, procedures, policies and practices that exist at the school level. The more aligned and inviting the school level components are with a philosophical vision of and commitment towards inclusion, the more likely full inclusion will occur. The level of alignment must be informally and formally reviewed and assessed by school personnel on a continual basis. This ongoing process of inquiry is necessary to ensure that the highest levels of alignment are achieved and sustained.

Schools and school systems need to institutionalize this regular inquiry process so that it becomes an internalized structure within the school community. This stance needs to permeate the consciousness and pedagogical practices of all educators and school personnel. It must become an integral and defining component of the school culture in order for successful inclusion and sustainability to occur.

Overview of Cases

The cases in this section of the book highlight the impact school level planning and practices can have on the attainment of an inclusive educational environment. The assumptions and beliefs held by educators significantly influence and shape the planning, policies and processes employed by school personnel.

The narratives in this section expose the power of partnership, ethical responsibility and relevant planning and practices to advance the agenda of inclusive education. The essential role of open communication, collaborative planning, shared decision making, curriculum relevancy, relationship building, professional responsibility, advocacy and principal leadership are illuminated as essential dimensions intrinsic to inclusive education. Students and parents lie at the centre of these processes. Only when they are viewed and placed at the centre of education can the hope of a truly inclusive education be realized.

The written cases that follow invite schools and systems to reflect upon and critique the impact of these planning processes and practices upon the tenets inherent within inclusive education. Some of the cases in this section reveal the negative and disabling impact of rigid school structures, inequitable relationships and exclusionary processes that do not support or enable shared decision making, advocacy and

G. L. Porter and D. Smith (eds.), Exploring Inclusive Educational Practices
Through Professional Inquiry, 105–139.
© *2011 Sense Publishers. All rights reserved.*

transparent communication. Schools and systems that fully understand and use the tenets of inclusive education, as a framework to guide practices and policies, will be better positioned to actualize the social gift and human right of inclusive education.

CASE TEN: LANGUAGE OR BEHAVIOUR?

"I don't know why you have gone to such length to develop a language program for my daughter. She communicates just fine with us at home," snaps Wendy's mother. Mrs. White glares at me.

I am greatly surprised by her statements. "I thought that you were concerned with Wendy's aggressive behaviour and frustration. I thought that you wanted us to work on helping her with her behaviour." Mrs. Whites cuts me off. "I am," she interrupts. "But I don't see what that has to do with her language. Maybe I should follow her around with a video camera for a couple of days. Then you would see just how much language Wendy has." She huffs and sits back in her chair still glaring at me.

I was surprised when Mrs. Shell, Wendy's classroom teacher, signals her agreement with Mrs. White by nodding her head. This only adds fuel to Wendy's mother's fire. I am becoming more uncomfortable and feel abandoned by my colleague.

"So", she stares me squarely in the eyes, "if the classroom teacher doesn't see a need, why are we here?" Mrs. White shrugs her shoulders. "I thought I made it clear that I want Wendy to follow the same routine of her peers and not be made to feel different."

I want to stress that this issue is not about Wendy being different. However, I decide that Mrs. White is in no mood to discuss the issues around Wendy's disruptive behaviour in a rational way. I cannot comprehend how language can be separated from behaviour. Wendy's frustration is a result of an inability to communicate. Mrs. White should be able to recognize that.

Wendy is a grade five student who completed rote tasks in the classroom quite well. Our school had provided her with a consistent and stable classroom environment. She could answer multiplication questions in class and read and answer comprehension questions. Her behaviour early in the year had been acceptable. Her communication skills, however, were limited. For example, if another student or teacher greeted Wendy in the hall she could only parrot what was said to her. Like her parents, the school staff had seen Wendy fly into a rage when set patterns were altered. She did not possess the language skills to communicate her frustration in a more acceptable fashion.

Our school has a population of 350 students from kindergarten to grade five. Many of our students have high needs. The number of teaching assistants outweighs the number of teachers. Wendy's teacher this year is well organized and structured. She does have some difficulty modifying the curriculum and being flexible in her expectations for students who have been identified as requiring differentiated instruction.

Wendy is exempt from French and it is during this one period a day that Wendy and a teaching assistant work on social skills and language skills. As her resource teacher, I am responsible for designing and delivering these programs.

I am an experienced resource teacher. But I feel very confused. Did I misunderstand Wendy's parents at the beginning of the year meeting when they voiced their concerns about Wendy's unacceptable behaviour? In the last few weeks, Wendy had twice overturned bookcases in her classroom. She repeatedly slammed doors in the faces of her classmates and teachers. Wendy has also ripped up her teacher's collection of student reward stickers. She is becoming more and more non-compliant and disruptive.

I remembered Mrs. White's words at the beginning of the year. "Wendy's behaviour, when we have to change routines even for something like attending a doctor's appointment is so frustrating that my husband and I are at our wit's end." What had changed? Why couldn't Mrs. White acknowledge Wendy's behavioural issues?

I look around the table at the other support staff members who worked with Wendy. The speech language pathologist, Meghan, had remained silent throughout this meeting so far. I am feeling increasingly alone. I look to Meghan for support. She does not make eye contact with me. Instead, her eyes drift to the floor.

I think again about the meeting that we had with the school-based team and the parents earlier this year. We all agreed that we must focus on Wendy's lack of communication. The parents had shared their concerns regarding the simple changes that drove Wendy into tantrums. Even arranging Wendy's stuffed animals in her bedroom was an event that quickly escalated into a major incident. Mr. And Mrs. White had felt that her daughter was getting too big to force her to comply with their requests. They said, "We are looking for direction from the professional staff at Founders' School to help us address these situations." Mrs. White's fingers had gripped the edge of her chair and she tried hard not to cry as she asked for our help. The school staff had left that earlier meeting feeling valued and trusted as members of a collaborative circle that included Wendy's parents.

After that fall meeting, I asked for our speech and language pathologist to assess Wendy's language skills and to come back to the team with her recommendations. The school team developed and implemented Wendy's language program based on these recommendations. Wendy seemed to enjoy those new strategies and was making progress in transferring her new language to social situations. Meghan had beamed when she told me that Wendy was actually making friends because she no longer threw her fists at her classmates. Wendy was beginning to understand how to integrate herself in a group setting.

I look directly at Wendy's mother sitting across the table. I try to reassure her. I try not to plead. "Mrs. White, we have Wendy's best interests at heart. I thought that we had all agreed at our meeting at the beginning of the year that we would work on building Wendy's language skills."

Mrs. White restates her position. "I don't see what language skills have to do with her behaviour."

I once again look to my colleagues. I am again met with silence and no eye contact. I begin again. I paraphrase, "Mrs. White, I hear you saying that you don't see any connection between Wendy's language skills and her behaviour". Mrs. White nods in agreement. I now realize that we, as a school team, need to take a step back and begin a conversation about this connection with Mrs. White. We need to develop a shared understanding among all of us.

PROFESSIONAL INQUIRY

Communication

- Critique the communication exchanges and the processes related to the team meeting.
- Identify recommendations you would suggest, as Principal of the school, to enhance communication with parents and among the members of the school team.

School Level Planning

- Identify strategies to enhance the school level planning associated with Wendy.
- Explore reasons for the lack of consensus and shared understanding at this team meeting.
- Generate methods to enhance the school level planning related to students at this school.
- Identify next steps for the school staff facilitating this meeting.

Instructional Practice

- Identify strategies that can be employed by the classroom teacher to honor Mrs. White's request for her daughter to be provided with opportunities to "follow the routine of her class and not be made to feel different".
- Discuss how specific evidence related to Wendy's language skills and behaviour can be effectively documented and shared with Mrs. White.
- Discuss how the collected evidence regarding Wendy's development can be effectively analyzed.

Parent Involvement

- Critique the school's attempts to involve Mrs. White in the decisions, planning and ongoing education of her child.
- Explore the possible reasons for Mrs. White's comments and feelings.
- Brainstorm methods for inviting more involvement of Mrs. White in the educational vision and planning for her child.

CASE COMMENTARY REFLECTIONS

After reading the commentaries reflect on the following:

New Insights
Identify new insights gained from reading the commentaries.

Understandings
Discuss the impact of the commentaries on your understandings of inclusive education.

Questions
Identify questions that emerge from reading the commentaries.

CASE COMMENTARY 1

Dr. Kathryn Noel

In discussions with parents, it is important that problems or issues be discussed in ways that enable parents to understand the situation and the suggestions being offered. The use of clear, everyday language and concepts with which the parents are familiar is critical. Parents should be part of the discussion of the issues as well as of the plan of action, and regularly scheduled follow-up discussions of evidence that point to progress or lack of it are important. Both learning and changing behaviour need to be viewed as long-term projects. Small changes might be difficult to notice so it is important to record base-line data and to document evidence regularly. On-going communication is critical to forging a learning team to support Wendy.

CASE COMMENTARY 2

Tammy Dunbar

It is evident that this school is making efforts to create an inclusive environment for students with special needs. The Resource and Methods Teacher has taken the lead in establishing a school team to discuss Wendy's programming needs. The team included parents and support personnel who could assess and make recommendations relevant to Wendy's needs.

The team met and there was consensus around the focus of Wendy's program would be. The Speech Language Pathologist completed a screening and generated recommendations for strategies that could be put in place. School personnel and the Speech and Language Pathologist were using the strategies and progress was being seen.

Where did things start going off track? On closer review, it appears that opportunities for ongoing communication between the parents, the classroom teacher and the Speech Language Pathologist may have broken down. The Resource and Methods teacher set up a review meeting not realizing that the team was no longer on the same page.

Experience tells us that classroom teachers work diligently to include students with special needs into their classrooms when they feel supported. We also know that teachers must have a sense that their classrooms are a safe and productive learning environment. Programs breakdown when behaviors escalate.

Regularly scheduled observations and meetings with the Resource and Methods teacher, the classroom teacher and the Speech Language Pathologist would have kept the lines of communication open. Mrs. Shell would have had support in planning for differentiated instruction and the team would have quickly been able to adapt the strategies being used to prevent an escalation in Wendy's behaviors.

Communication with parents is also a key factor in the success of any child's school program. Mrs. Shell is organized and efficient. It is likely that she was keeping Wendy's mom informed about Wendy's behavior in the classroom. What that communication looked liked and sounded like may have contributed to the miscommunication expressed by some of the team members during their team meeting. It is possible that while expressing concern about escalating behaviors, the team members did not take the opportunity to talk about proactive strategy changes. Regular contact between each of the stakeholders (parents, school personnel, and outside agencies) must be collaboratively facilitated by the school personnel.

CASE COMMENTARY 3

John Lundy

This case study presents a clear example of missed communication opportunities among the professional staff, and missed diagnostic opportunities between staff and parents. Mrs. White, Wendy's mother, is obviously very frustrated with both her daughter's behaviour and the school's apparent inability to help solve this. The protagonist, Wendy's resource teacher, has many years of experience and has assessed the situation as solely a "language problem." That is, she sees Wendy's limited communication skills as the sole causal variable for the inappropriate behaviour and she too is frustrated and upset that other professionals around the table seem to be supporting neither her assessment of the problem nor the intervention strategies thus far.

Mrs. White does not appear to understand the resource teacher's use of the concept of "language" as meaning Wendy's inability to express effectively her feelings in words as opposed to unregulated and intemperate behaviours. In effect, this theory-in-action (Schon, 2002) centres on the social and communication skills problem-solution approach. This ineffective parent-staff communication adds to the parental frustration since the parent knows "how much language Wendy has." We can all guess the type of crass language emanating from Wendy's mouth. Given the equivocal use of the term "language" it is no wonder the parent is exasperated.

The resource teacher needs to work more diligently with all of the relevant school staff to determine the exact causes of Wendy's inappropriate behaviours. Taking a problem solving approach may be a better start to deeper resolutions. Staff and parents may want to investigate whether or not Wendy has undiagnosed special needs (including physical problems: hearing loss, allergic reactions to environmental or dietary elements, etc.). Wendy's deficient communication skills may indeed be the intervening variable that is masking other, more significant issues. The parents would need to take the lead on ruling out potential physical problems while the school staff could set in place any further relevant testing to rule out specific special needs. Other school staff would need to take the responsibility to give relevant feedback when warranted so that a simple causal variable does not become that simple solution to what may be a much more complex problem.

While it is normal for professionals to feel isolated in meetings when they are certain that they right about a diagnosis in the face of both silent and vocal opposition, it is essential to step back from the situation and reassess – to reflect on the potential multiple causes for student behaviour and the overriding responsibility of professionals to work meaningfully with parents/guardians.

CASE COMMENTARY 4

Isabel Killoran

Communication, communication, communication! Underlying many of the issues in this case study is communication. Wendy is using behaviour to communicate her frustration in a way that is interfering with social and academic development. The parents and teachers are not effectively communicating their hopes and concerns for Wendy and the general education teacher, special education teacher and other resource staff have yet to find a way to meet Wendy's objectives in a proactive rather than reactive manner.

Let's first look at behaviour as communication. What purpose does behaviour serve? When Wendy is upset she communicates this by becoming disruptive or aggressive. Everyone knows that she is unhappy so if her ultimate objective is purely showing frustration it is actually an effective mode of communicating her feelings. If the objective is really one of inclusion then Wendy needs a method of sharing her feelings that will not be disruptive or impact her negatively. How can Wendy communicate her frustration (preferably before it becomes overwhelming) so that her needs are met? Is there a way for her to do this non-verbally? Defining what each member means by communication is an important place to start.

Bringing together all of the stakeholders (including Wendy) to talk about what is triggering the outbursts is critical. Transitions and change seem to be difficult for her. Her parents and the school team acknowledge this, yet the team is not working together to try to reduce the triggers while they are teaching Wendy to communicate more effectively. If transitions are difficult and language interferes with communication, creating visual schedules or graphic organizers may help Wendy with the anxiety she feels around change and transition. These are strategies that could benefit Wendy at school and at home. Working together to create them would foster a sense of collaboration between the two settings.

Ultimately, everyone has the goal of wanting Wendy to communicate her feelings in a way that is less disruptive; however, the reason behind this may be different for each team member. Wendy's mom wants Wendy to be included. The teachers seem to be working more towards reducing disruption rather than fostering inclusion. It is clear from the case study that some of the ways that the school is providing service/support may be working against the goal of Wendy's mom, which is to have Wendy "follow the routine of her class and not [be] made to feel different." Is there a way for the resource teacher and teaching assistant to work with Wendy on her social and language skills with her peers present? How is Wendy going to practice these skills and transfer them to other settings if she is learning them in isolation?

CONNECTING TO PROFESSIONAL PRACTICE

The commentary writers respond to the issues of communication and planning among the school staff and between the parents and school personnel. The lack of ongoing and informed communication may have contributed to the lack of shared understanding among the parents and the school team.

Discuss your experiences with school teams and the role communication has played in the success or failure of these collaborative problem solving forums.

CASE ELEVEN: PLANNING AHEAD

"How do you prepare for your first student with autism and a history of frequent biting, hitting, kicking, screaming and pinching the adults and children around her?" asked the exasperated grade five teacher.

This was the question we were faced with at our transition meeting for the new students who would be joining our school next September. In addition to being identified with autism spectrum disorder, Serena also has a central auditory processing disorder. She has difficulty communicating. Her academic ability is at the kindergarten level.

As principal and chair of the transition team meeting, I go over Serena's school history and profile with the group. My concern is evident to all those present. We all remember Stanford's arrival at our school. He was a student who physically lashed out at both his teacher and his classmates. He was a large and surprisingly muscular boy. When he became angry his punches could break a board. We had to remodel a storage area and turn it into a safe place for him to be during his violent outbursts. We even needed to have a door with a plexi-glass window installed in the area. We all were wondering if Serena would present similar challenges.

I am wondering to myself which teaching assistant, out of the nine that we have, would work best with her? I think about Josephine who is gentle and patient and who waits for to approach her. I think about Marvin and how he anticipates each child's needs. I also wonder about the teachers on our special response team? Who in that trained group needs their non-violent crisis intervention knowledge and skills updated?

Later that day, I stop the resource teacher, Elisha, in the hall and ask, "What services does Serena have access to already? What are her strengths and weaknesses? What will her daily schedule look like? What will be our plan if she exhibits these violent behaviours?" Elisha looks concerned. She stands erect and seems to be listening to me. One question leads to another. Soon we both are pacing.

Elisha adds her own questions. "What are her parents like? Do we have any information about them?" I seem to recall that Serena's former principal had inserted some hand-written notes on a separate page into her file. I remember seeing the word uncooperative. Should I share that information with Elisha before she has a chance to actually meet the parents?

We continue. Elisha tells me that Serena's mother, Mrs. Greenway, works in the school building. I had not been aware of that fact. Will the approach we take change because her mother is working in our building?

Suddenly both Elisha and I realize that we are both focusing on potential problems even before we begin to make plans for Serena's transition. We pause and laugh. We are both embarrassed by how readily we had fallen into the trap of thinking only about the potential problems.

We resume our discussion in a more positive way. "To whose class do you think we should assign Serena?" I enquire. Elisha and I both know that we have only two grade five teachers. One is an experienced teacher, Mrs. Jones. Her classes are orderly and her students respond well to the structure. Ms. Wallace is just starting her teaching career. Our school is her first assignment.

Wisdom and patience often come with the kind of experience that Mrs. Jones would have. On the other hand, Ms. Wallace has that enthusiasm and openness that comes with being a new teacher. We considered the pros and cons of each teacher but didn't make a decision.

"Elisha," I ask, "Can you go over Serena's file to find out if there been any charting done on her behaviour? Also check to see what types of strategies have been tried in the past?" I am feeling overwhelmed. I can tell by the troubled look on Elisha's face that she too is concerned.

I know how hard she has worked with some of our other exceptional children. There are rarely complaints about Elisha. I believe that she takes responsibility for every single one of her students with special needs. Perhaps, I should have prepared more before engaging her in this informal brainstorming session. I leave a perplexed Elisha and return to my office. I slump in my chair. I feel a headache coming on.

I pull out Serena's file again. Her previous teacher says that she has a cherub face and is not very tall for her age. Suddenly, I remember exactly who Serena's mother, Grace Greenway is. Grace has tattoos up and down both arms. She is our school custodian. I did not even know that she had a daughter.

We plan a meeting of our school-based resource team. Our guidance counselor is preparing to review all the information that we have about Serena for the team. We need to try to imagine what the school day for Serena will look like. We will need to consider all the variables that are possible influences on Serena's placement and program.

We meet the following Friday. In spite of my hard and focused work, it doesn't go as I had imagined. We began the discussion by looking at some of our best practices that have worked with other children with similar challenges. People around the meeting room table seem tense and worried. Suddenly, Elisha breaks the silence and says, "I feel that we should wait until Serena gets here and see what she is like before we do any planning." Some heads nod. Glances are exchanged.

Elisha continues, "Remember Jake. We prepared this much when he was coming to the school and it wasn't at all necessary. Jake was not anything like his previous teacher described. We had very few problems."

Again there are nods around the table.

I respond by trying to convince Elisha that our careful planning for Jake ensured that things went so well. I wonder if I had misinterpreted her troubled look when we spoke in the hall. I thought that we were both on the same page. I had trusted her expertise and expected she would see things that way I did.

I look directly at Elisha. "We had the safeguards in place for Jake. We ensured that he was getting all of his basic needs met every day. We had provided a structured program for him with a very organized teacher. He was assigned a highly skilled teaching assistant. His day was custom made for him. He had a time out plan in place. We made sure that his program was explained and acceptable to his parents. Jake's family was supportive." I pause. Elisha does not meet my gaze.

My eyes finally meet Elisha's. She looks away. She has a blank look on her face and her arms are crossed. I realize that my passionate speech has been pointless.

How can I get her to see my point of view? As a principal, I know that careful planning is the answer.

PROFESSIONAL INQUIRY

Beliefs and Assumptions

— Explore the beliefs and assumptions that appear to be guiding the thinking and actions of the school principal.
— Explore the beliefs and assumptions held by the resource teacher.
— Explore the beliefs and assumptions that may have guided the initial questions of the grade five teacher regarding preparation for Serena's arrival at the school.
— Comment on the impact that the beliefs and assumptions held by educators can have upon inclusive education practices.

Leadership Practices

— Critique the actions and decisions of the school principal.
— Generate suggestions for enhancing the professional judgment of the educators in this case.

Inclusive Practices

— Analyze the school's knowledge of Serena.
— Critique the school's commitment to involving Serena's parents.
— Analyze the school's actions towards acquiring information from Serena's previous school.
— Explore the inclusive pedagogies being considered by the school.
— Discuss approaches and strategies that the school might consider in attempting to include Serena's parents in the education of their child.

CASE COMMENTARY REFLECTIONS

After reading the commentaries reflect on the following:

New Insights
Identify new insights gained from reading the commentaries.

Understandings
Discuss the impact of the commentaries on your understandings of inclusive education.

Questions
Identify questions that emerge for you from reading the commentaries.

CASE COMMENTARY 1

Anthony H. Normore

Autism is a word most of us are familiar with. Children with autism can present educators with some difficult challenges. Autistic disorders generally have lifelong effects on how children learn to be social beings, to take care of themselves, and to participate in the community. We often place important responsibilities on schools, teachers and children's parents, as well as the other professionals who work with children with autism. Thus, educational planning must address both the needs typically associated with autistic disorders and the needs associated with accompanying disabilities. In this case, Serena has autism and also has a central auditory processing disorder which complicates her ability to communicate. Research indicates that children with autism experience challenges communicating ideas and feelings, have great trouble imagining what others think or feel, and frequently find it hard to make friends or even bond with family members (Abend, 2001; Timmons, Breitenbach, & MacIsaac, 2006).

Based on my experiences as a former school administrator, it has been my practice to regularly seek out and provide opportunities to raise awareness about diversity within the school community; and to respect similarities and differences of others. In this case, it is equally crucial that Serena's classmates understand the characteristics of autism so they may help understand special skills or interest in relation to Serena as well as the social interaction dimension of her disability. A recommendation is to assign the resource teacher - with the help of the parent - to describe events in the school that may be particularly stressful for the student and to provide peers with specific ideas about how they can best get to know the student with the disability and how they can help the student with the disability on a daily basis.

Having a child with an autistic disorder is a challenge for any family. In this case, rather than pre-judge Mrs. Greenway because of her tattoos (as indirectly suggested in the case), she should be supported in Serena's education through consistent presentation of information by the local school system, through individualized problem solving, continuous consultation and providing opportunities to learn techniques for teaching Serena new skills and minimizing behavioral problems. Mrs. Greenway should not be expected to provide the majority of educational programming for Serena. Her concerns and perspectives should actively help shape educational planning for her daughter.

At the root of questions about the most appropriate educational interventions for Serena are differences in assumptions about what is possible and what is important in Serena's education. The appropriate goals for educational services for Serena ought to be the same as those for other children: personal independence and social responsibility. To the extent that it leads to the acquisition of Serena's educational goals, she should receive specialized instruction in a setting in which ongoing interactions occur with her typically developing classmates. These goals should be an integral component of the Individual Education Plan process.

The Individual Education Plan team must adopt an attitude that is collaborative and responsible. At the moment, this does not seem to be the case for Serena's team despite the principal's efforts to create it. Before developing an Individual Education Plan, Serena's Individual Education Plan team must learn about Serena, be able to envision the future and possibilities for Serena - her dreams, fears, strengths and needs (see Timmons et al., 2006). With so many complexities, challenges, and emotionally charged decisions involved, creating an appropriate Individual Education Plan can seem like navigating through a minefield. In the best interest of Serena, the Individual Education Plan team must work with Mrs. Greenway as a unified team to design, review, and modify Serena's Individual Education Plan as necessary.

A final issue that needs to be addressed in this case involves personnel. Relevant to Serena's instruction are the teachers and other professionals and paraprofessionals who will provide the bulk of service. The formal preparation, training, and familiarity with the course of autistic disorders and the range of possible outcomes must be provided to those who are in charge in the instructional delivery. The school district must choose and implement effective approaches for personnel preparation, beyond a single training effort, to provide a continuum of services across time. Attitudes, behaviors, and dispositions of the principal are critical in improving this school, as are explicit strategies for program development and keeping skilled teachers within the school. Providing knowledge about autistic disorders to special education and regular teachers as well as education administrators are critical in proactive change – if Serena is to be successful.

CASE COMMENTARY 2

Lois Kember

This is not an unusual scenario found in many of our schools where fears, concerns, and questions, like this do come up on a regular basis. The secret to smooth transitions is having well informed leaders employing open communication and ensuring information is available and accessible to all involved. It is essential that all relevant information and strategies are shared at meetings that include everyone concerned.

It is clear to me that Serena's principal and resource teacher are doing their best with the skills that they have and mean well. Their strategies and planning seem to be a bit "scattered" and unorganized. They need a systematic way to plan for this incoming student. Serena deserves to have a smooth transition to her new school and in my opinion this would mean a meeting with the following people attending: sending and receiving principal, sending and receiving resource teacher, sending and receiving guidance counselor, sending educational assistant and most importantly, the sending classroom teacher. Meetings such as this provide valuable information such as strategies that work or don't work, ideas tried, etc. We have consistently used this type of meeting and find it is effective! A separate meeting with the parents would be necessary for this case due to the "uncooperative" note in Serena's file.

The issues that I believe need to be addressed in this case include: individuality, parent involvement, communication and choice of teacher and educational assistant.

Individuality- Not all students are the same and to link Serena's behavior to Jake's was an unfair assumption! Always remember to treat each student according to their needs.

Parents- If parents are uncooperative it is usually due to lack of poor communication on the school's part, or lack of understanding of what is happening with their child for which they need information given- not information withheld. Fear for their child and can be linked to receiving poor service in the past when their requests have gone unnoticed or unfulfilled. Labeling a parent as uncooperative from a past school is not correct. Start with a new experience and ask for parents concerns, questions, ideas, hopes... after all, parents are the experts on the child!!

Communication- It is evident to me that the principal is very concerned about having Serena in his school. After the transitioning meeting, he asks the resource teacher in the hallway what services she has and what Serena's strengths and weaknesses are. This should have been information readily available at the transition meeting, from her IEP and from the sending school history and profile. What was in the profile anyway? There appears to be work to be done on both areas!!

Another note on communication- At the end of the case description the resource teacher has a blank look on her face and her body language is negative. The principal didn't ask her for her thoughts, ideas, or input. Earlier the principal asks the resource teacher to go over the files and even admits to engaging her in an informal brainstorming session without doing any preparation himself! He leaves the resource teacher perplexed without any explanation, and returns to his office to slump at his desk. I do hope the principal's headache was a good hefty one! I would be furious if my principal had done this to me. Formal meeting need to be well planned and communication needs to be open and clear with plenty of time to share concerns, questions and strategies. Informal meetings in the hallways need to be discouraged. The student's privacy of information is threatened and teachers are caught off guard which leads to miscommunication and defensive attitudes.

Choice of teacher and educational assistant- This is always a tricky one! Deciding on the best match with the teacher who can cope with the behaviors presented in this case is challenging. I do feel that Mrs. Jones' class would be more appropriate because of the structure and order that she has. Students with autism usually respond well to structure and order, as well, the quiet and orderly classroom might help alleviate some of the sensory issues often seen with central auditory processing disorder. I think it would be wise to have a meeting with the grade five teachers, present the scenario, and ask if either of them would volunteer to have Serena in their class. Explain to Mrs. Jones that it could be a very positive growth experience for her and that you are impressed with the level of her expertise over the years. If the new teacher volunteers that would be great as they usually have considerable insight regarding inclusion. Both teachers need to know that they will have extra support during the year and that they will not be left alone to solve all the problems. It needs to be a team effort!!

I totally agree with the principal's final statement, "Careful planning is the answer. Isn't it?" The information presented in the case is not what I call careful planning, in fact it seems the very opposite to me. As a resource teacher, I would like to work with this principal as he seems to be trying his best. I would suggest to him some improvements he could make and help him to follow through with the suggestions so that he could see how an organized and effective system works.

CASE COMMENTARY 3

Joanne MacNevin

This case study outlines a common issue faced by schools when a new student is expected, especially when the new student has special behavioral or educational needs. Teachers often don't know what to expect or how to prepare. In this case, I feel the staff did a good job of asking the right questions and trying to prepare properly. They were trying to get a plan in place for the new student. However, because of the anxiety of the teachers and administration, which seemed to stem from previous experiences, the members of the staff were finding it difficult to agree on a specific plan. The question asked at the end of the case study, 'Careful planning is the answer. Isn't it?', is a good question and I believe the answer is 'yes'. However, what constitutes careful planning? Is it really possible to plan carefully without knowing the student? How do you decide on a plan?

Truthfully, I don't know what I would do if I were the principal in this situation. I do know that I, like many other teachers, have faced a similar issue. Two years ago, I was told a new student would be joining my class. His file reported he needed an educational assistant with him all day due to a variety of behavioral problems. He was also on an Individual Education Plan, was low academically, and so on and so forth. As a staff, we worried over this new arrival. I was worried because I already had a classroom full of individuals who needed a bit of extra care and attention everyday and I didn't know if I could handle another 'enthusiastic learner'. However, when the student came in on his first day, he proved to be a wonderful boy with a great sense of humour and a desire to learn. All the worrying, careful planning and the team work of the staff contributed to this student's success.

CASE COMMENTARY 4

Dan Goodyear

The school has not formulated a transition planning process that is clearly communicated to all team members. It is not clear how the receiving school is going to connect with the transferring school. As well, I do not see how the parent is going to be meaningful engaged in this process. The staff is primarily focused on Serena's needs and not on her strengths.

The school needs to develop a transition planning process that will be followed for all student transfers. Otherwise, a hit or miss approach will be taken as students transfer into the school. The development of such a process needs to happen in consultation with feeder schools, so that everybody will be clear about the expectations and their roles. Parents/guardians need to have meaningful participation in the transition process. Thus, the school needs to communicate clearly to all school community members regarding the transition planning process. It is important that the transition process focus on the student's strengths as well as needs.

The transition planning process must happen with all stakeholders, including the student, other service providers, and relevant staff members from both schools and parents.

As educators it is easy to fall into the trap of comparing issues of previous transfers and assuming that the needs will be the same. It is important as well not to prejudge parental response. The setting up of too many red flags will not facilitate positive discussion.

In my experience at the college level when the transition planning process was adhered to by all team members issues were minimized, stress was reduced, required services were in place and there was no gap in program implementation. The process worked well, when the student was involved at all stages.

In instances where the transition plan was not followed, students did not have the required resources, instructors were not informed of required interventions and there was an increase level of stress and decrease in positive outcomes.

CASE COMMENTARY 5

Emily Dwornikiewicz

This is a very common situation that I have observed as a Developmental Services Worker. I have noticed the strain school transitions can place on teachers, educational assistants, parents and the student. A well thought-out planning process is vital to ensure that students with unique needs will be successful.

A student's academic file can become his/her worst enemy. These files often point out all the concerns associated with the student. They frequently tend to highlight issues related to behavioural challenges and focus more on the negatives than the positive attributes of the student. Reading these files in isolation can lead to preconceived judgments. This can result in negative attitudes and opinions being formed about the student and the family. This can particularly occur when principals and teachers who are not consciously aware of their own biases and judgements read student files. It is important to always read these reports with an open and non-judgemental attitude. I have found that when educators meet students and families prior to reading a written report they are more likely to form more positive perspectives. My experience in school settings and working with students in both their homes and in community programs has revealed the benefits and consequences of reading student files prior to actually meeting the student. The content of a student file can impact upon the acceptance and inclusion of students and their families.

Students with Autism Spectrum Disorder generally do not feel comfortable with new people quickly. This is why the transitioning period is often very challenging for them. It is very important that their strengths and needs remain the number one concern for all involved. Aside from just meeting with the staff that will be working at Serena's new school, I feel it is vital to include other key people as well. I would suggest that the following actions be considered in attempting to provide a successful transition for Serena:

– Organize meetings with Serena's Parents. Often when students files have notes deeming the parent "uncooperative" there is a preconceived judgment upon meeting the parent which can emplace barriers when trying to work together. It would be effective to not inform the resource teacher, educational assistant and others meeting with the parents of the fact that the parents are considered "uncooperative". This will help to ensure that everyone enters the meeting with an open mind. Discuss with the parents how they handle Serena when she is exhibits challenging behaviour.

– Create an opportunity for Serena to visit the school and have her meet with both Mrs. Jones and Mrs. Wallace individually. Observe Serena's reaction and level of connection toward each teacher. This process will help Serena become more comfortable with the new school and provide insight into placement decisions.

– Meet with Serena's support workers involved in the programs she attends in the community. Often these workers observe things that the parents or teacher may not taken note of because they get to view students in very different settings. By incorporating things Serena may be comfortable with at home or in community programs into her time spent at school (for example: type of workspace she works best in, familiar scents, colours and textures) will help make the environment not seem so foreign to her and allow her to become comfortable faster.

– Invite Serena's previous teacher and educational assistant to a planning session with the new transition staff for Serena to identify effective strategies.

– Educate other students in Serena's grade about her needs and strengths so that they can be comfortable around Serena and accepting towards her as a fellow classmate.

For Serena's transition to be effective there needs to be good communication between her parents, workers and educators as well as a focus on what will work best to make Serena be successful in school. Serena is there to get an education just like every other student. It is important for the school staff and students to see and understand Serena's uniqueness. Just like everyone else in the school, she is completely unique and different. Serena will have a better chance of being included when she is viewed first and foremost as a student with strengths and not as a student that has special needs.

Careful and thoughtful planning is very important for the success of all students. Entering the planning process with a positive attitude towards each other, the family and Serena will help support success. By planning for all aspects of Serena's school day and each possible outcome it will not only guarantee a smooth transition but also put the educational staff and Serena's parents at ease knowing they have plans on how to handle different situations. Collaborative planning will also communicate to the teacher chosen to be Serena's teacher that she is part of a team that will support her. Teachers that are not given these messages of shared support may feel stuck and uneasy about planning on their own. Teachers that feel included and supported in the educational process are more empowered to be able to include and support learners.

CONNECTING TO PROFESSIONAL PRACTICE

The commentary writers comment on the assumptions of the educators in this case, the lack of communication with parents, transition issues and the importance of informed planning.

Reflect on an experience from your own practice when the beliefs and assumptions of educators impacted significantly on professional practices and decisions. Explore how this situation may have been different if these beliefs and assumptions had been critically reflected upon and analyzed.

CASE TWELVE: PLANNING FOR INCLUSION

"Oh, Mr. Nielsen, don't be unrealistic! I am a teaching assistant, and I know what it's like for teachers to have kids with special needs in the classroom. My husband and I don't expect Carole to be in the classroom a lot."

I had never met such supportive and caring parents. They were pleasant, cooperative, and were willing to work with the school. I was a bit worried about Carole's arrival because I did not know if we would be able to meet all of her needs.

I am the principal of a kindergarten to grade eight school. The school population is 600 students. The student services learning specialist contacted me during the summer. He explained that a new student with special needs would be starting in our school in September. He said, "We need a transition meeting for this student with his parents." I agreed to meet the parents at the school.

Carole has severe epilepsy and has been diagnosed with autism spectrum disorder. She takes multiple medications. During the meeting the parents explained that Carole would require a private washroom area in order to use the facilities. The learning specialist indicated that the necessary structural changes were going to be made to our building.

Carole arrived in September. She is currently in grade six. She is a tall girl with the angelic aura about her. She leans towards you as you talk to her. Carole often seems fascinated by what you say and do.

Two teaching assistants work with Carole on a regular basis. She eats her snack and lunch in the cafeteria, walks outside and in the hallways, visits the office area. I keep wondering if Carole needs to be more in classrooms.

One Thursday morning, I am walking down the hallway and see her. I instantly smile, and move towards her. I am eating a bowl of fruit, and she moves towards the bowl. I offer her a piece of fruit, and she accepts. She moves towards the bowl again. What a wonderful moment! She is not only responsive but also trying to get her message across. I can almost hear her saying, "I want another piece of fruit."

I keep thinking of what her mother said about it being unrealistic to think about having her in the classroom. Am I being unrealistic? If her parents are happy with her program, the resource teacher is happy about it, the school staff is content with what is happening and Carole herself seems pleased with her daily routine then why do I have this nagging feeling that she is missing out on something really great? Why do I think that she could be achieving more?

Carole will make noises and grunts as she is walking in the school or moving about with the teaching assistant. Her teaching assistant holds her by the arm at all times. I continue to wonder if I need to encourage the teachers who are already overwhelmed with high expectations from everyone to accommodate her noises and her dependency in an already disruptive classroom.

I believe that Carole is a great addition to our school. She has taught us so much. Are the other students missing out on seeing Carole work on her computer in the classroom? Could they benefit from seeing what her day looks like and what she works on? Are they missing out from interacting with this student and working alongside her?

As she gets older, I keep wondering what her life will look like? She has come a long way since she has been with us. She has learned to point out and identify her needs with visual images. She manages to communicate without words by using physical actions and facial expressions to show her feelings. She also has mastered a program designed to point at pictures as a communication aid.

I feel privileged to work with a group of teachers who enjoy working with students with special needs. How do I help support these teachers in holistically meeting her needs as well as all the other students?

We have another student with high needs coming next year. I already have the same questions about him. Will he follow the same program? Will the teachers connect with this student? Will most of the responsibility for his day-to-day care rest with the resource teacher and his teaching assistant? What will be the expectations of his parents?

"Good Morning Mrs. Salta!" I said. Mrs. Salta is our resource teacher. "I was wondering how Carole is doing with her program."

"Well, she is doing just great. After all those changes in medication, she seems to be more settled, and doing better," she responds.

"That's great." I said. Please keep me posted on how she is doing, I added. "I certainly will", she replied.

The resource teacher has become very close to Carole. She has developed her program with the help of her parents and the teaching assistants. The teachers have not been part of her collaborative process. She takes great pride in structuring Carole's day. She believes that Carole's needs are not curriculum based and that it is her job to develop Carole's program.

I am so glad Carole is doing well. It is really great that we can offer programs for all students. I begin to realize that I need to really look at her special education plan a bit more in detail. I will make a point of doing that. I want to make sure we are meeting all of her needs. I wonder how we decided what were her needs were? Was it a collaborative approach? Did all stakeholders have a part in developing her program? I think that the classroom teachers may be a bit disconnected from the plan.

I will have to ask the teachers if they feel part of the planning process for Carole. How do I make it possible to help them have time to do that? I realize that the issue isn't just around the time involved. It is all about fully including Carole. Will all the teachers want to do that?

PROFESSIONAL INQUIRY

Inclusive Pedagogies

- Identify a set of holistic goals for Carole.
- Discuss how curriculum, teaching styles, instructional strategies and the learning environment can be adapted to allow Carole to be more fully included in this school.
- Explore approaches for fostering Carole's social and academic inclusion within the school.

- Analyze how the current program being offered to Carol is supporting her independence.
- Discuss professional learning experiences that may assist the staff in this school to become more aware and knowledgeable about inclusive education.

Commitment to Inclusion

- Identify the overlying philosophy of this school regarding students with special needs.
- Discuss this school's understanding of inclusion.
- Define inclusion from your own perspective.
- Describe what an inclusive environment might be like for Carole.

Leadership

- Discuss the principal's responsibility for advocating for Carole to ensure her program is designed to enable her to achieve at the highest level possible.
- Explore the ways in which the principal can establish a clear vision of inclusion within this school community.
- Generate strategies for creating a community that is committed to developing and maintaining inclusive education.
- Identify next steps that the principal could take towards establishing a more inclusive learning environment for Carole.
- Discuss how the principal can include the parents in shaping a vision of inclusive education for Carole.

CASE COMMENTARY REFLECTIONS

After reading the commentaries reflect on the following:

New Insights
Identify new insights gained from reading the commentaries.

Understandings
Discuss the impact of the commentaries on your understandings of inclusive education.

Questions
Identify questions that emerge for you from reading the commentaries.

CASE COMMENTARY 1

Pamela C. McGugan

There is a vast skill set required to understand the complexities of providing for students who have complex medical issues as well as challenging academic and social needs. School boards that embed their philosophy for students with special needs across all aspects of curriculum and school services, provide the groundwork for conveying their philosophy and support mechanisms to their principals. Integral for success is the need for principals to have a clear vision of what is needed for students with special needs to be successful.

The principal is on the right track in questioning Carole's program and whether all stakeholders were involved in the process. Determining a clear definition of inclusion and ensuring that staff understands what an inclusive classroom looks like will also be important. The students themselves also need to be part of this equation.

I worked with staff to create an inclusive environment with the goal of providing greater opportunities for all students to understand and accept diversity. Interestingly, when assessing our progress, it soon emerged that staff felt they were providing inclusionary experiences simply by taking the students into the community or to the classrooms. However, in most cases, the students had primarily interacted with their own assigned staff.

Through a visioning exercise, staff revisited the definitions and goals of inclusion versus integration. They looked at what inclusion would look like and not look like and what one should see when visiting an inclusive classroom. They concluded that every step needed to be carefully thought out in order to provide students with the skills to interact with others and build their independence. Careful orchestration of those interactions resulted in increased opportunities for all the students as well as an increased comfort level and understanding for the needs of all students.

However, the individual path created for each student can be highly complex. The task of the teacher in preparing and supporting all students is cognitively and academically challenging and requires intense concentration. The task for the student with special needs should be a parallel task that is meaningful and relevant for the student while moving the student forward in terms of skill acquisition or task completion.

Another point that surfaces in this case is that the staff needs information. I was often struck with the sheer panic that came over my colleagues when faced with receiving a student with severe medical or behavioural issues. Information sharing can go a long way in dispelling some of these fears and myths. Providing support personnel to be there for the initial transition period can also help alleviate fears and anxiety. Having a parent assist for the first few days can provide a very positive start for all.

It is advisable to provide in-service education for all staff. Support staff also requires specific training so that strategies are constantly updated, refreshed and practiced. The principal has observed staff holding on to Carol - a questionable practice unless for safety. Staff may require additional training to ensure they fully understand how to best support the student.

Inclusion takes work. It encourages people to understand each other and gain an appreciation of one another. It celebrates differences and welcomes everyone's contributions. Staff should be aware of their collective responsibility to enlighten students' understanding of inclusion.

Inclusion involves adjusting curriculum, teaching styles, and the physical environment to allow all students to participate. Each member of the teaching team, although with varying levels of skill and experience, presents a valuable tool in setting up non-traditional programs. But each member of the team must also be supported in acquiring the needed knowledge base to be able to program for students with different abilities.

A probable goal for Carole is to increase her socialization with her age appropriate peers. Staff that is working with Carole may be furthering her isolation by providing for her in a parallel situation where she interacts primarily with them. Carole may not be able to sit in the classroom while the students are working on math seatwork, but she can participate in a host of other classes where she can interact with her peers with assistance from staff. The goal for Carole must be to have her an active participant, not just an observer on the sidelines. Creating a community that values everyone as a contributing member will benefit all students. Carole's individual needs will dictate various learning situations and program modifications. A balanced approach in creating a menu of experiences and situations will help develop Carole's areas of strength and her sense of self and move her towards independence.

Success can be measured by the other students' understanding of Carole's abilities and their respect for those differences, their empathy, their acceptance and their desire to communicate. Friendship can be the greatest teacher of all.

CASE COMMENTARY 2

Darren McKee

All too often in today's education system we work from a deficit model rather than an appreciative model. This creates a focus on what students can't do instead of what they can and focusing on what they bring.

In my experience, children are sacred gifts, and children with special needs are the most sacred as they provide us with significant opportunities for growth and development around how we as societies and communities support diversity and inclusion and believe that everyone can contribute.

We must engage a broad group of experts in the design of a plan that is strength based and recognizes parents as experts. Relationship is the foundation for successful planning and must be in place for a process to be successful.

I have difficulty understanding the aversion of some people (teachers, administrators, or parents) to moving away from a dependency model with paraprofessionals to one of having experts and specialists collaborate and provide programming - do we not all want our children to have dreams, goals including learning objectives? Instead, we often place them in the care of the least trained individuals and feel they are best served in this model.

Accountability is the key to supports around a learning program. If we, as consumers, utilize a service, we have expectations. We clearly articulate those expectations and if the service is not satisfactory we take recourse. In the education system, we as consumers should feel that we have the opportunity to collaborate on expectations and be informed of how we will know what has been accomplished towards those expectations.

There are many caring professionals who work in the education system, much like the principal in this "case" who has the best intentions but simply may not have the experience necessary to take a leadership role in inclusive education. We as parents, caregivers, and or professionals must recognize that this is a journey of shared understanding led by establishing relationships with key people focused on the best interests of children.

CASE COMMENTARY 3

Lois Kember

On my first reading of this case scenario, I did not find certain elements plausible. However the more readings I complete of this case the more I elements I notice! The collaborative full team approach of the administrator, the classroom teacher, the resource teacher, the parents, and perhaps the student are missing. This case has some elements in place, but lacks in others. Very caring parents and an empathic administrator don't necessarily make the plan for inclusion work. Careful, creative, innovative, and specific planning, using the talents and skills of all team members, as well as open communication are required. Strong leadership with a vision of having each student working to his potential is of benefit to the Student Services team. In this case the principal assumes the position of leader, but at the end of the case he's left thinking, "... the teachers may be a bit disconnected," and ponders some very important questions regarding inclusion, to which I don't believe he knew the answers.

Transition meeting- A meeting took place during the summer with the principal and the parents. What about the other support staff? At our school this type of meeting would have been conducted in May or early June. The following people would attend this meeting: parents, sending school Student Services Team members, and various representatives from the community such as Disability Support Services staff, speech language consultant and autism consultant. Our School Services Team members would also attend and they would include a guidance teacher, administrator, and at least two resource teachers. Each person would share relevant information in a round-table style and each would be able to express concerns that that have. Short term goals would be set and recorded in an Individual Education Plan. An action plan would put into place and a date noted for when the necessary team members would meet again.

Parents- Although Carole's mom is an Educational Assistant she might not know what is best for her daughter. The parents are very kind, co-operative, and caring, however, I wonder if they are hindering or sheltering her too much. Just how much can Carole do? Parents sometimes don't have high enough expectations for their children with special needs and tend to overprotect them, not intending any harm, but this does limit the extent of their development. I think the principal suspects this from several of his comments.

Goals for Carole - Carole walks the hallway and eats in the cafeteria. What about being included in the regular classroom? She can participate in many of the classroom activities, especially the social ones, even if her parents don't expect her to! As well, she might benefit from music and physical education. Carole has a right to her education as much as the other students in her grade. I think she could be achieving more! She could have a special time in the day to share her work with a buddy, and the other students could show her their work as well. Many social skills can be learned within the regular class.

Accountability- The resource teacher's glib response of, "she's doing just great... she seems to be doing better" is far too vague. What is better? How do you know she is doing great? How are you measuring what is better? The classroom teacher is not part of the collaborative team process in structuring her day! "Pride, or no pride" taken in making the schedule, Carole needs to have more curriculum based goals in her schedule and needs a team approach to help decide what these goals might be and how they can be attained! Behavior support strategies and social stories could be added to her program to increase her skills.

"Another student coming next year... will he follow the same program?" Carole has mastered making her wants known through PECS (Picture Exchange Communication System), however, the student next year will have different needs. No two students are the same. Each student needs creative and innovative ways to have their needs met. The 'mould' doesn't fit everyone! Three or more team members are always better than one! That is why we work together to assess the needs, strengths, and then make an individual plan that "fits the student."

In conclusion, it is important to be proactive, positive, and prepared! This principal seems to take the 'padded leather chair approach.' A teachers-helping-teachers meeting would help to solve some of the problems encountered in adding some curriculum based goals to Carol's Individual Education Plan. Professional learning sessions focused on adapting and modifying programs for students would be helpful. Also, another professional learning session on multi-level teaching would help any teacher in their classroom.

At our school, our School Based Student Services Team, consisting of an administrator, guidance counselor and all resource teachers meets weekly. Here we address student referrals, teacher concerns and any new documentation that has arrived on any student which is shared on a need-to-know basis. An action plan is quickly made identifying who is responsible for specific tasks and a review plan is established.

An Individual Education Plan meeting is held for each student that requires one. This meeting is attended by at least two resource teachers, an administrator, the classroom teacher, and the educational assistant. These meetings are conducted at least twice a year. The goal of this meeting is to discuss and change the student's strengths and challenges, decide which goals have been attained and set new goals, adjust any area of the plan which is not working, and to update any part of the history that has changed. This meeting takes approximately one hour. I think this collaborative approach supports classroom teachers and conveys that they have valuable input.

The educators in this case want the best for Carole. This desire and intention requires much more than adjusting medication and eating fruit from the principal's cup!!

CASE COMMENTARY 4

Carson Allard and James Moloney

Missing Out

Inclusive education is central to the achievement of high-quality education for all learners and the development of more inclusive societies. Inclusion is still thought of in some countries as an approach to serving children with disabilities within general educational settings. Internationally, however it is increasingly seen more broadly as a reform that supports and welcomes diversity amongst all learners. (UNESCO as cited in Ontario Ministry of Education, 2009b)

"Why do I have a nagging feeling that she's missing out?" The principal's intuitive reaction that Carole was missing out in the educational experiences provided for her at the school is central to this case. Additional thoughts that others may also be missing out from learning and interacting with Carole cause further discomfort and worry for the principal. This theme of missing out reverberates throughout this case. The feeling that someone or something may be missing is perhaps the fundamental concern that underlies the complexity of what is meant by inclusivity and how it is nurtured throughout the culture of a school. This case provides additional insight into that complexity.

There appears to be a good foundation in this school towards an inclusive culture. The principal is deeply reflective and shares the nature of his professional inquiry through his case writing. In the principal's view, he leads a dedicated and hard working staff who expresses satisfaction in working with students with diverse needs. The resource teacher shows great care and commitment in supporting Carole. She has developed Carole's program in consultation with the parents and the teaching assistants. Parents and staff seem pleased that Carole's educational program appears to be going smoothly. Yet, the principal continues to sense that something is missing.

The principal wonders whether it was a collaborative approach that was missing in planning for Carole's participation in the school community. Can inclusive schools really exist without collaboration? Can a school community truly understand and respond to the needs of all participants without a vibrant and continuous conversation that includes all its members and especially those who are most vulnerable?

The principal wonders whether other students are also missing out on the gift that is Carole. Here he struggles with the notion of what it means to truly belong. Carole must be perceived as more than an appendage to an existing community. In the full sense of belonging, she must participate in the co-creation of what the community is to become, what it can be. To belong fully to an educational community means that the potential for transformative experiences exists for all participants as they learn from and with one another? It is ultimately embracing and celebrating diversity that can lead to the transformation of community.

In wondering whether Carole could be achieving more, the principal reflects on the educational practices and school community processes that surround her. This principal is quite rightfully concerned about not "pushing the teachers who are already overwhelmed with high expectations". This would do little to address Carole's belonging or achievement. The 'push' for change best comes from within when a sense of moral imperative drives our actions.

The challenge then becomes one of developing a communal sense of moral imperative. There is potential to fundamentally alter the culture of inclusivity in this school if the principal is able to share his reflections on Carole's inclusion with the staff. This may help the staff to frame the principals' reflections and concerns into a shared professional inquiry that empowers them to explore the gap between Carole's lived school experience and the beliefs, assumptions and values espoused in the professional practices of the educators.

The final outcome of this shared professional inquiry cannot be determined but certainly this would be an important step in moving toward a more inclusive community, one in which no one is missing.

CONNECTING TO PROFESSIONAL PRACTICE

The role and responsibilities of the principal in shaping an inclusive school environment was raised by the commentary writers. Reflect on your own experiences of inclusive education. Identify effective approaches from your own professional practice that have contributed to helping staff gain a deeper understanding of the meaning of inclusive education.

CASE THIRTEEN: STRIKING A BALANCE

"You people do not understand. She needs to be in the classroom with the other kids, doing the same things, covering the same topics and being like any other grade five student." demanded Mrs. Potts.

After a year of massaging a relationship with Mrs. Potts and working through her fears and concerns for her ten-year-old daughter who had been identified with autism - something had changed. Sure. We have had challenges with programming and learning. We explored different practices to use with Jillian to help identify the most effective approaches. However, the demand for answers and action from this mother was packed with a new intensity. It was going to be a long year of grade five. As a new principal, I knew that I had a lot of issues to address..

Mr. Rolf, our learning specialist, is skilled with working with parents. Once again, he refers Mrs. Potts to the learning plan that we had set up for Jillian's year. She would focus on a morning of in-class reading and mathematics and participate in an afternoon program consisting of physical education, life skills and expressive language development. Through this program Jillian was able to work on specific skills with a full-time educational assistant. The program appeared to be progressing well and was highly successful.

A frustrated Miss Greenlee, an experienced resource teacher, shares with Mrs. Potts the language program developed by the district's Resource Teacher for Autism, the Speech and Language Pathologist and herself. This comprehensive plan was being implemented and assessed by this highly specialized and knowledgeable team. Considerable gains had already been noted as a result of this innovative and individualized program.

"I know that we said that we would try to include her more in the regular classroom this year but she is doing so well in the program that has been specially adapted for her this year," says Mrs. Potts. Miss Greenlee smiles with pride as she lists Jillian's accomplishments. "Jillian is participating in projects. She is reading well above her grade level and her math is really coming along." All of this was true.

When I walked the halls and glanced into her class, I saw Jillian in reading circles, and engaged in purposeful chatter with her peers. Sometimes she moved her chair back and forth against the floor but, for the most part, she looked interested and engaged in the lively discussions. Her achievement in math was slowly improving. Jillian was even volunteering to answer in class.

Today Jillian's mother had arrived at our meeting and indicated that she had rethought the school's desire to provide instruction for Jillian both in and out of the classroom. I was shocked. I recalled meeting last term when Mrs. Potts had strongly asserted that she wanted to see significant improvements in Jillian's language abilities regardless of the educational environment in which she was placed.

Puzzled, I found myself asking why Mrs. Potts had changed her mind about Jillian's placement and program. Why would she want her to be placed full time in a regular classroom? And then I heard the reason.

Mrs. Potts said, "Mr. Smith, Jillian's teacher, told me that he was amazed by the abilities Jillian had demonstrated. He could not see why she needed specialized skill development in language. She could read better than most of the children in his class. He had a capable educational assistant to help him to modify Jillian's work and that she could do most of what the others were doing in class."

Apparently Mr. Smith had gone on to add that Jillian was consistently interacting in appropriate social ways. Her prior extended bouts of silence were now just notations on old reports. Mrs. Potts quoted Mr. Smith again. "Jillian is making tremendous gains in the language area."

Mrs. Potts tearfully looked at the team of teachers sitting around the table, "I just don't understand the differences in what you are telling me? This is the first time that Jillian has been treated like a normal child. Do you know how good this makes me feel as a parent? I want to trust you. I am confused. Is it better to provide her with the specialized help outside of the classroom or is it better to keep her in the regular classroom? Which one will best meet my child's needs?"

PROFESSIONAL INQUIRY

School Level Planning

- Critique the process involved in planning a program for Jillian.
- Identify suggestions for helping the school personnel acquire a deeper understanding of and respect for the perspectives of the parent (Mrs. Potts).
- Discuss the importance of the role of communication in planning processes that result in the provision of the most enabling learning environments for students.

School Culture

- Identify aspects related to the culture of this school that are revealed within this case.
- Describe this school's understanding of inclusion.
- Generate recommendations for fostering parent trust in the school.

Leadership

- Explore the new understandings and insights the new principal gained about the school through this meeting.
- Generate a list of next steps for the principal in this case.

CASE COMMENTARY REFLECTIONS

After reading the commentaries reflect on the following:

New Insights
Identify new insights gained from reading the commentaries.

Understandings
Discuss the impact of the commentaries on your understandings of inclusive education.

Questions
Identify questions that emerge for you from reading the commentaries.

CASE COMMENTARY 1

Carla Digiorgio

This case provides much food for thought as it reflects a very common situation in the education of students with learning challenges. In this case, the child was making progress in her language and reading due to a focused program developed for her by her resource teachers. They were pulling her out of class to develop these skills. The child was also spending time in the regular classroom with her peers and interacting with them in meaningful ways while learning in language arts and other subject areas.

Some advocate full inclusion for all students with special needs as a right. However, as in this case, it seems that the student benefits from both regular classroom and specialized one-on-one learning. In one-on-one teaching and learning, specific skills are taught to the student based on her needs. The lack of distraction allows for a special bond to develop between teacher and learner. Challenges such as autism rely on this one-on-one work to develop particular skills. Sometimes the quiet focused time is quite necessary as a balance to the noisier times spent in the classroom, which can overwhelm the student over time.

The parent in this case is trying her best to provide what she feels her child needs and can benefit from. She is listening to the teachers and principal and trying to imagine the best world for her child. Of course, the supposed ideal for any child would be to be in the regular class full time with their peers as a 'normal' child. However, the advantage of one-on-one attention has provided the child in this case with focused, directed teaching which has resulted in the gains they have witnessed. In a regular classroom, it may have been very difficult for the regular classroom teacher to develop and provide this support on his own. I understand the teacher's enthusiasm for the child's progress, and applaud his positive attitude in wanting her in his class.

Perhaps the school team needs to include the classroom teacher and the parent in its planning for the child so that both are aware of what the child is doing in resource and how this is complemented by regular classroom experience. Both should have input into the planning for the child and should meet regularly to discuss progress and adjust programming as necessary. They should also be planning for the child's transition to middle or junior high school, and preparing the student for the challenges this next level will bring, through increased responsibility for her own learning and self-care.

CASE COMMENTARY 2

Ann Marie MacDonald

This case is about Jillian, a ten year old with autism who is entering Grade 5. Her mom has become confused and unsure about the amount of time her daughter will be in the classroom after talking with the classroom teacher. The resource teacher, speech language pathologist and the learning specialist have set up an individualized program and are very pleased with Jillian's progress in language development.

The current plan for Jillian is to be in the classroom in the morning for reading and math and outside the classroom in the afternoon for expressive language development and life skills. The learning plan for Jillian seems to have been made without any input from the classroom teacher or other members of a school based Student Services Team. The classroom teacher has spoken to the parent and expressed how well Jillian is doing and that she should be in the classroom.

The teacher has a full time educational assistant to help deliver a modified program to Jillian and now the mom is questioning her daughter's programming and where it would best be delivered. Although the teacher recognizes Jillian's potential and her need to be in the classroom, the approach taken by the teacher has put the team and parent on different pages as far as the priorities in Jillian's program. The teacher almost seems to be undermining the work that has already been done with the student and parent.

Although the teacher wants the best for Jillian the approach taken was not as collaborative as it could have been. The principal, who is new to the school, has to take a leadership role and ensure there is a more collaborative approach to planning. The principal needs to initiate a meeting with all stakeholders to discuss Jillian's program to try to get everyone on the same page.

There needs to be more involvement in planning for Jillian at the school level, especially with the classroom teacher and members of the school based team. I agree that Jillian should be fully included in the classroom for academics and to foster relationships with her peers, but the teacher's approach was wrong by discussing it with the parent first without the knowledge of the rest of the team.

The teacher should have brought his concerns to the Principal and the school team to discuss the plan and possible changes at this level before bringing it to the parent. The language development plan could be implemented in the classroom setting. Life skills could be taught within the context of the classroom. These adaptations would enable Jillian to be included full time in the classroom.

Jillian has a lot of strengths, has a teacher who has her best interests at heart, and has additional support within the classroom to deliver a modified program where she can participate in learning and socializing with her peers in the classroom setting.

I think the teacher is right in being an advocate for Jillian and wanting her to be fully included in the classroom. His approach has caused confusion for the parent and he has not worked collaboratively with the rest of the team to ensure Jillian has the best possible program to meet her needs. There may be times when a student needs to be outside the classroom but there has to be a good reason for it. In Jillian's case I think she should be in the classroom full time because she needs to be learning with her peers as well as have the opportunity to continue to build relationships with her peers.

CASE COMMENTARY 3

Brent Langdon

A new principal, committed professionals a strong parent advocate and a deserving student, will collectively lay a fertile ground for growth in this case. It appears as though there are number of competent players involved in this student's life with no shortage of ideas or expertise. Despite the knowledge and good intentions, there does not seem to be any consistency in their message. There are conflicting ideas about programming and in turn, services for the young girl in question. It is even difficult to ascertain the service delivery model of the school and/or board. There is an Education Plan in place, but no evidence that it was developed collaboratively, used to support transition planning or even shared with the student, parent or classroom teacher. There has been progression with this plan and also considerable gains with separate programs prescribed by other professionals. The classroom teacher is also reporting a good amount of success happening in the class. It is interesting that the story begins with confusion and a demand for answers.

There are a number of program options being communicated, taking place in varied settings, and facilitated by different individuals; each seemingly committed to "their" model. In order for a plan to move forward, or any balance to be struck, school personnel will need to begin functioning as a team. In order for differences of opinion to become opportunities for creative solutions, there will need to be a commitment to open dialogue. A systematic approach is needed to ensure this dialogue results in coherence and meaningful change. The principal must make sure that the plan(s) is reviewed and that the team has purpose (Jillian) and direction. Every piece of this team seems strong, but there is a need for a unified plan.

First, a discussion, between the parent Mrs. Potts and the new principal, needs to occur. Such an exchange should result in insight about school and family history as well as clarity around the current concerns. The new administrator may apologize on behalf of the school for the mixed messaging and ensure that future correspondence between home and school takes on a new level of professionalism. This will put both Mrs. Potts' and the new principal in a better position as they journey through a team problem solving process.

Second, dialogue needs to take place amongst the school team and could begin with recognition of the good things that are currently in place for Jillian. This meeting will be the forum for defining the issues at hand while advocating for the views of individual team members. Advocacy will need to be balanced with a commitment to inquiry where team members feel free to air concerns, ask questions and challenge assumptions. All efforts should be aimed toward finding common ground and arriving at a shared plan. It will be vital to have a clear understanding of the school/system service delivery model to ensure that the plan "fits" within this context. Communication, for a period of time, may need to come from fewer sources to ensure consistency and clarity.

At the third stage of the process, team members need to be delivering clear ideas and a proposed program plan with Mrs. Potts (and possibly Jillian) at the table. This will allow for the parent to reflect on the work that has been done, ask questions and offer feedback. Upon conclusion of this sharing, all team members should be moving forward with common purpose, satisfied that each has been heard. The plan will require on-going reflection and input from all parties. Much like the IEP itself, the plan will evolve with the student. It would be helpful at this time to set incremental follow-up meetings to gauge progress and develop next steps.

A personal, school and board vision of education will have a great impact on how this program actually "looks" in practice. I will highlight some ideas around a potential outcome, which is based on my own experience and coupled with the parents expressed concern for having her daughter learning with her peers. These parameters will lead us toward the development of an Inclusive model for learning. Such a model will reflect the following beliefs:
– All students Belong
– All students can learn
– All students must learn to live in Community
– Inclusion is the pre-requisite for Healthy Living

If we are guided by these beliefs, the school team will need to engage in courageous conversations by addressing the following questions:
– What is the optimal classroom set-up to promote learning for all?
– How will we Differentiate Instruction to meet the diverse needs in this classroom?
– How do we optimize the support from our educational assistant? How do we utilize peer mediated supports?
– What recommendations for specialized programming can be embedded into the classroom program? How? (the time for creativity)
– Are there needs that must be met outside the classroom (medical, sensory)? If so, how can we make this seamless?
– How do we function as a collaborative team to ensure that we are all working toward measurable goals and guided by common purpose?

Within this context for learning, I anticipate a blend and balance of ideas resulting in effective partnerships and programming. Such a balance will optimize and streamline supports, encourage collaboration between school and home and lay the foundation for Jillian's future success.

CASE COMMENTARY 4

Jerry Wheeler and Darquise Leroux

Mr. Smith, Jillian's teacher, does not seem to be fully aware of her learning needs. His conversation with Jillian's mother contradicts the program and course of action identified by the team of specialists which up until then had yielded excellent results. This conversation has created confusion in the mother's mind as to whether Jillian should be in a regular classroom or receive individual programming.

This kind of situation highlights the importance of collaboration and team work. Somehow, Mr. Smith has either been left out of the loop or is in disagreement with others about Jillian's learning needs. The Ontario Ministry of Education document "*Standards for School Boards' Special Education Plans*" highlights the importance of collaboration by stating that the teachers are to work "with special education staff and … with other school board staff" (Ontario Ministry of Education, 2000, p. 24) to meet the needs of students.

Misunderstanding and lack of information may hamper relationships between teachers and parents (Keyes, 2000). In this case, it is clear that Mr. Smith and the members of the specialist team are not on the same page with respect to Jillian's learning needs.

This scenario heightens the importance of ongoing communication and a team-work approach to appropriately respond to Jillian's educational needs. True commitment to student learning is reflected in responsible relationships with students and parents and expressed through positive influence, professional judgment and empathy in practice.

The case underlines the need to promote and participate in the creation of a collaborative and supportive learning community where individual roles and responsibilities are recognized in order to facilitate student success.

CONNECTING TO PROFESSIONAL PRACTICE

Inclusive education requires collaborative planning and the authentic participation of all involved in supporting the learning and development of students. In this case, the commentaries reveal concern with the apparent limited involvement of two key members of the collaborative school team: the parent and the classroom teacher. Reflect upon your own experiences in education as a teacher, student or parent. Have there been occasions when you were excluded from forums or from opportunities in which your knowledge, experience, insights and perspectives may have been helpful? How have you responded to these occasions of exclusion? What have you learned from these experiences? What would you do to ensure these forms of exclusion do not occur in education?

5. CHALLENGES AND BARRIERS TO INCLUSION

Extensive visible and invisible challenges and barriers exist that influence or prevent full and authentic inclusion from occurring within educational systems and society. It is imperative that educators become increasingly aware of these barriers and work to remove and prevent obstacles that prevent full inclusion of all learners.

Inclusive education is complex, intricate and multifaceted shared work. It requires highly talented and versatile individuals that are deeply committed and resourceful. Their work often involves creating environments and systems that are adaptable, flexible and accessible for all students. These individuals are also often required to demonstrate and act upon their extreme dedication to inclusion with unwavering courage and conviction.

Identifying and responding to the many challenges and barriers to full inclusion requires educators to be deeply skilled, knowledgeable, and influential. The successful removal and prevention of obstacles to inclusion requires collaboration, mutual understanding and respect. Ultimately, the goal is to foster a shared inclusive consciousness and commitment within all schools and school systems. This shared consciousness and commitment needs to be nurtured and acknowledged among all students, educators, school personnel and community members.

Overview of Cases

The cases in this section reveal a myriad of challenges and barriers that can exist within educational systems that result in the exclusion of students. These barriers or challenges can manifest within the individual attitudes or beliefs of school personnel; school and system policies; pedagogical practices; assessment approaches; school environments; school organization; school culture and within the language used by school personnel. Ongoing education is essential to the identification and elimination of these unnecessary challenges and barriers to inclusion.

G. L. Porter and D. Smith (eds.), Exploring Inclusive Educational Practices
Through Professional Inquiry, 141–172.

CASE FOURTEEN: BRIDGING THE GAP

"What have you heard? Do you have any news yet? Do you know the name of Joyce's new teaching assistant? We can't wait to hear. Who have you talked to? What can I do to help?" Mrs. Campbell, Joyce's mom, fires the questions at me. I am Joyce's grade eight teacher. I have been trying to build in support for Joyce's transition from middle school to high school. Joyce has been identified with autism spectrum disorder and her parents and I are greatly concerned about her move to high school in September. Our middle school is much smaller than the high school and has only 400 students.

At the beginning of grade eight, Mrs. Campbell expressed concern about Joyce's future in high school. "This school has done so much for her. Joyce has had the same teacher assistant for two years. Can the teaching assistant transfer to the high school with Joyce?"

Joyce is an average-sized girl with brown pigtails that seem forever in her mouth. Her teaching assistant's name is Marjit. The two are an inseparable pair. Mrs. Campbell already has been told that Marjit will not be moving to high school with her daughter. "I know, I know" she says, "We have been so lucky. I don't want Joyce to know that Marjit will not be going with her. I'm scared that it will really upset her."

I, too, am aware of the wonderful support that Marjit has provided for Joyce. She has taken extra courses to help her better support Joyce, smoothed out so many difficulties and helped all the staff and students embrace Joyce as a significant member of our learning community.

At one time, Joyce would scream non-stop without cause. Staff and students would actually cover their ears as they passed Joyce in the halls. I cringed at the thought of her classmates trying to learn in that environment.

Now Joyce is ready for high school - or so we hoped. She attends all classes except her second language class. That time is used to continue developing social skills, learning basic cooking skills and practicing the use of money. Joyce can be seen bubbling with joy as she shares her most recent dishes with her teachers and classmates. Joyce loves to share the food that she makes and enjoys being around others. Will this precious time continue during the high school years? What type of citizen will Joyce become? What role will the next years at high school play in her life? I want to imagine Joyce in the midst of laughing peers, sharing secrets, her body relaxed and her eyes shining.

I know that Joyce does form strong attachments when she feels safe. Her attachment to Marjit proves that she can make significant strides under the right circumstances.

At the end of last year, I knew I would be teaching grade eight and that Joyce would be in my class. Prior to the end of June, I introduced myself to Joyce. I sought her out, took both of her hands in mine, looked directly into her blue eyes and calmly and quietly spoke to her. As she tried to move away, I stood my ground and gently reissued the invitation to talk with me. After the initial meeting, I made a commitment to touch base with Joyce on a regular basis to prepare her for entry into my class the following year. Based on our experience here at the elementary school, we knew that Joyce needed to start building a relationship with the high school staff and to familiarize herself with the much larger school.

Our resource teacher organized a small outing to Bluestone High School for Joyce before the entire grade eight student body went for orientation. The visit was a success, thanks to the sensitivity of our resource teacher and the staff at Bluestone High School. Later, an experience during the orientation visit for the grade eight students reaffirmed our belief that Joyce would be welcomed and supported in her new school environment. During this orientation visit, Joyce was very proud to let her peers know that she had been to visit Bluestone a few days earlier. "The gym is down that hall over there!" she exclaimed. She pointed her arm toward the double doors with excitement. We all shared in her moment of triumph.

While at Bluestone, I approached the principal and asked if we could plan an individualized transition day for Joyce in the fall. She replied, "Yes. We already have programs in place. I promise I will be back in touch with you."

I contacted the district school board office in order to facilitate this special day. I was told that this procedure was not within the board's transition planning procedures. I shared this information with Mrs. Campbell. She was disappointed but thankful for our attempt.

The next obstacle was the one Mrs. Campbell had asked about today that being the assignment process for a teaching assistant for Joyce. I immediately contacted the Students Services supervisor. She responded, "Joyce may not know who is working with her until the first day of school." She questioned me about Joyce's needs. "Joyce requires a teaching assistant with whom she can form a strong attachment," I replied. "That strategy has been shown to work exceedingly well for her. Mr. and Mrs. Campbell understand their daughter very well. They realize, as we do, that Joyce requires time and coaching to help build the necessary relationships for her academic and social growth."

We made changes at our middle school to try to help Joyce make her transition to Bluestone in the fall. The teaching assistant has requested that our teachers now wait for Joyce to ask questions when she needs help. For Joyce, this will be a huge change. She is used to being asked if she needs help. We know that Joyce has difficulty with this concept. Sometimes she reverts to previous behaviours of fidgeting and making loud, screaming, unintelligible sounds.

I am fearful that these behaviours will affect the sense of community that has developed since her early screaming days. Her classmates, who have become accepting, may not tolerate her regressive behaviours.

Joyce has had a buddy system that has served her well. Jasmine is her reading buddy. She makes extra notes for Joyce and even underlines, in purple, the most important concepts. Jasmine is proud of the role she takes as Joyce's reading buddy. It was Jasmine's idea to use Joyce's favourite colour of purple to highlight key ideas. Thomas also cues Joyce when it is her turn to go to the blackboard. He stands by her desk, offers his hand and accompanies her to the front of the class. He stands beside her as she writes on the board. The other students fully accept her and display genuine understanding, compassion and sensitivity towards her. They have grown to accept and support her.

Despite the success of this program Joyce's parents and our teachers realize that there will be four schools feeding into Bluestone High School and that the buddy system may not be implemented. Joyce's closest buddy, Sarah, is also graduating to the high school. Mrs. Campbell was thrilled when we told her that we have requested that Joyce and Sarah be in the same classes. We know, however, that there are no guarantees that our request will be addressed.

Mrs. Campbell understands that requesting and receiving are two different concepts. This realization adds to her growing list of fears. We have talked to Joyce multiple times about the challenges and excitement of high school. Outwardly, she appears content in knowing that she can come back to visit. Her twitching body and unconscious grunts though tell us that she is uncomfortable with the unknown aspects of her high school future. Joyce is obviously troubled by this next step.

I, too, am deeply troubled.

PROFESSIONAL INQUIRY

Leadership and Professional Knowledge

- Identify the forms of leadership demonstrated by the educators in this case.
- Analyze the leadership demonstrated by the grade eight teacher in relation to Joyce's education.
- Analyze the professional knowledge and commitment of the educators.

Transition Planning

- Identify the issues and challenges associated with supporting the transition of Joyce from elementary to secondary school.
- Develop an effective transition plan to support Joyce's move to secondary school.
- Discuss processes for involving Joyce and her parents in the development and implementation of a transition plan for secondary school.

Inclusive Practices

- Critique the system level practices associated with transitioning students from one school to another.
- Explore the impact of these practices upon the inclusion of students with special needs.
- Discuss the inclusive practices that have enabled Joyce to achieve considerable success in the current elementary school.
- Comment on the significance of the professional knowledge and commitment displayed by the teaching assistant (Marjit) for Joyce's inclusion.

Challenges to Inclusion

- Identify the barriers, obstacles and/or challenges presented in this case that impact upon the full inclusion of Joyce.
- Critique the planning processes employed by the school district related to transition planning and the assignment of teaching assistants.
- Develop an action plan to respond to the barriers, obstacles and challenges that are apparent in this case.
- Analyze the culture of the school district and discuss how rigid and policy driven practices can negatively affect student success.

Advocacy

- Explore the forms of advocacy employed by the educators in this case.
- Identify strategies to support the self-advocacy of Joyce.
- Discuss approaches to assist Joyce's parents to become more effective advocates for their child.

Ethical Practice

- Identify the ethical dimensions associated with this case.

CASE COMMENTARY REFLECTIONS

After reading the commentaries reflect on the following:

New Insights
Identify new insights gained from reading the commentaries.

Understandings
Discuss the impact of the commentaries on your understandings of inclusive education.

Questions
Identify questions that emerge for you from reading the commentaries

CASE COMMENTARY 1

Jean J. Ryoo and Peter McLaren

The transition from middle to high school can be a stressful experience in multiple ways—physical, mental, emotional, and spiritual—as young adolescents find their bodies transforming, academic competition increasing, sexuality blossoming, and friends changing. For students with autism, this transition can be especially clouded with frustration and even fear. While the case author's deep compassion for this student with autism (Joyce). Her transition into high school should be applauded, such attention to students' needs should also be the norm expected of all educators and administrators. The case author's ideas and actions of introducing Joyce to her new high school before her middle school classmates, aligning Joyce's schedule with her close peer-buddies, organizing an individualized transition day for Joyce before high school begins, etc, should be the minimum that we provide to students with autism or other special needs.

Based on the case study, it appears that Bluestone High School wants to support Joyce by welcoming her early school visit. It is disappointing that the district school board is unwilling to facilitate Joyce's autumn individualized transition day. Yet, since the Bluestone principal supports the transition day idea, efforts must be made to implement this program for both Joyce and all other students with special needs as well. While it is too much to ask of the case author to organize such an event, a lot of strength and support can clearly be found in the *parents* of these students. Joyce's parents should be embraced by the Bluestone High School to help organize an event jointly with educators from the four different middle schools feeding into the new high school to ensure that all students with special needs experience positive transitions.

Indeed, students like Joyce and these students' families may find empowerment during the middle to high school transition by creating their own community support networks. If parents of children with autism and special needs were given the opportunity to openly communicate with one another, they could learn from each others' experiences and create the united front necessary to ensure that schools and district school boards facilitate the programs and supports their children need to excel. On the larger, community-wide scale, parent-educator organizations could make sure that children with special needs meet the new high school teaching assistants well in advance of the first day of school and are placed in classes with supportive friends. This way the knowledge that teachers, like the case author or Marjit, and parents have about children can be better communicated from middle to high school.

For Joyce's case, one might see a multitude of other possibilities to support her transition into high school. It may be possible for Marjit to provide professional learning to Joyce's new teaching assistant in the high school. Or, Joyce's parents might consider hiring Marjit as an after school tutor until Joyce feels comfortable with the new assistant. School-wide professional learning could be organized for Bluestone faculty in which the educators from the middle school who are familiar with students with special needs could prepare the high school for their new students' needs. Finally, one should consider how Joyce's passions and strengths could be incorporated as supports during her transition into high school and into her adult life. How, for example, can culinary arts be something she continues to learn about in the high school since it is something she loves to do and share?

CASE COMMENTARY 2

Jacquie Specht

Joyce's case is unfortunately not that uncommon. Elementary school is a place where students spend time with one teacher for most of the day. This setting lends itself well to creating positive relationships. We know that relationships are the key in creating supportive environments for all students. When students feel supported, they do better socially, emotionally and academically. Secondary school, on the other hand, typically involves students traveling from class to class at least 4 times a day with different students and different staff. By the very nature of the environment, it is much more difficult to form relationships with fellow students and staff. The elementary school staff, in conjunction with the family, seems to understand what Joyce needs for a successful transition, but the bureaucracy of the system does not seem to be aiding the implementation of these strategies.

Although there are more students with exceptionalities at secondary school, it is imperative that a one size fits all understanding of transition not be the view. When there are students that have issues with change, more attention needs to be paid to this issue. Working to help Joyce feel comfortable with her new school will be best for everyone involved. It is not clear why the teaching assistant for Joyce cannot be determined before the first day of classes. It is not dependent upon numbers because s/he will be working directly with Joyce. Students from the same elementary school are often placed in the same classrooms in their first year of secondary.

Ensuring that those who have developed a relationship with Joyce in elementary school (e.g., Jasmine, Thomas, and Sarah) will aid in the continuation and development of natural friendships in her secondary school classes is important. Helping Joyce to become a self advocate will be very important. We know that self advocacy is largely related to life success. It seems that there is a move in this direction in that she needs to ask for help. Given that she is having difficulty with this process, her parents would be advised to continue the support of this development over the summer. Finally, because she seemed to be excited about her new school and is now having some issues, I would question how much teachers and parents are discussing the barriers that they have encountered in front of her. Students who are anxious about change need to be given the message that it will work and it will be fun. We need to be careful not to discuss the negative issues with students as it may increase anxiety.

CASE COMMENTARY 3

Zuhy Sayeed

The practice of inclusive education must be borne out of the conviction and the cultural belief that inclusion is absolutely the right moral, ethical and best practice for students with disabilities. If the cultural belief and the values play a critical role in our practice of Inclusive Education; we will automatically do our very best to bridge every gap, to ensure that each concept, each class and each transition will be smooth and successful.

Teachers play a huge part, as Joyce's teacher does to ensure that all these elements are in place. Their support is greatly valued, their ability to create collaboration and teamwork is necessary. However, the absence of a team around this teacher is obvious. The absence of a supportive team around Mrs. Campbell is clear. The teacher has obviously been a sole source of support to the parent. Mrs. Campbell has not been able or encouraged to make some of the inroads required for Joyce to transition smoothly and effectively to the High School.

Parents are integral and valued members of a school community. They are the tax payers, whose contributions to schools and their community is taken for granted. In addition, parents spend considerable time and resources organizing the extra-curricular activities that are pivotal to every school in every community, town or city.

Yet, in the case of the parents of students with disabilities, we are often viewed as outside of the stakeholder group within education. We are part of the recommend-ations of people to be 'included' in teams and discussions about our own children, but very seldom as an integral part of the whole team or as part of the deliverers of education for our own sons and daughters.

If we examine the history of any progress that has been made to enhance the lives of people with disabilities- no matter what their ages- we see clearly that this progress has only been made due to the hard work, advocacy and insistence of parents and allies of individuals with disabilities. Yet, we continue to be extremely undervalued and subliminally set aside. Even within the hierarchy of the disability movement, families have been viewed as not being part of the process and the progress that has been developed to include our own sons and daughters within community. It is no wonder that in school based settings, power has been shifted to decision makers and we, as families, just have to be 'included'- that's all.

For those who are reading this book; the key point is the belief that schools must embrace and value our sons and daughters. If our children are valued as integral to the school; there will be no barrier to their inclusion and schools and educators will do everything in their power to make it work. Transitions will be smother and flexible, parents and students will be part of a caring and consistent team. In this context, school policies will state that every educator and administrative member will do 'whatever it takes for as long as it takes' to really include and welcome our children.

CONNECTING TO PROFESSIONAL PRACTICE

The commentary writers identify issues associated with advocacy, professional responsibility and parental leadership. What value do you place on these concepts within your own professional practice? How are these concepts reflected or lived out within your professional practice?

CASE FIFTEEN: DIRT BIKES AND COMPUTERS

"Martin. He's not here. He never comes. When he does show up, his behaviour disrupts the other students and he doesn't do a thing in class."

I had heard this complaint from every grade eight teacher each time I asked to see Martin. I sighed. Martin was another name on a list of eighty students from the caseload list that the previous resource teacher had left on my desk.

The first task I took when I had arrived at my new school was to familiarize myself with my middle school students. I wanted to know about their individual profiles, their exceptionalities, their accommodations, their modified outcomes and their previous assessments and interventions.

I was in a new school district and also new to the grade level. That meant that I had to ensure that I was up-to-date on school procedures, district policies and the new curriculum. I needed to know the dates for parent interview nights, the names and contact information for the agencies that worked with the school, and the resources I could quickly access in the community.

It was all a bit over-whelming and I felt more than a little apprehensive. However, I was excited and eager to get started at this large kindergarten to grade eight inner-city school. I knew I was in for a challenge with more than half of the 300 middle-school students reading below grade level.

My strength came from remembering students that I had worked with in my previous school. I remembered Jonathan who had struggled with letters. I recalled the look on his face when he finally made meaning of his first simple word. I think it may have been the word ball. That ball had started him rolling into reading larger words and eventually full sentences.

Sometimes it is just so hard to know where to start. I decided to start with my first student at my new school, Martin.

Apparently, Martin attended school occasionally and when he did he would invariably get himself into trouble throughout the day. Teachers would report outbursts and foul language. Then he disappeared for weeks on end. We called his home. No one answered. We were beginning to plan for more aggressive measures.

I overheard the frustrated comments in the staff room. Paul said, "He disrupts my classes and his behaviour encourages the others to act out." Tasha added, "In my class, his has even threatened other students." I had also looked through his cumulative file and noted that numerous suspension letters had been sent home. How should I react to this information and the comments made by the grade eight teachers? I didn't know if I should feel shocked or defeated by the challenges that lay ahead.

Weeks flew by. I settled into a routine. I found plenty of students with a diversity of needs to keep me occupied.

One afternoon in the middle of October, the vice-principal poked her head around my office door. She had that pained look of exasperation. "Got a minute?" she asked. "It's about Martin. He got into trouble again, first thing this morning. He wasn't even in the building five minutes and he ended up at the office." She paused and looked directly at me. I could tell she was holding back tears.

I recalled all the things that I had heard so far about Martin. I felt guilty about the fact that I had not yet met him.

The vice-principal continued. "I sat him down in my office to give him the usual lecture and plead with him to behave in class. This time it was different." Again, she paused, obviously very upset about what had happened. I listened as she repeated Martin's words and I imagined how his young voice would have sounded.

"Miss Harper, I don't know how to read. I can't do math, either." I realized then that Martin was a big boy with a big secret,

The story didn't end with Martin's confession. "Then", said my vice-principal, "he sat in my office and started to cry." I wanted to cry too.

Here was a child crying out for help. "I'll see him as soon as I can," I said. I thought about this scenario that had been shared with me in confidence by the vice-principal. I wondered how I would engage Martin when I caught up with him.

A few days later, I did meet Martin. He eagerly accompanied me to the resource room. I noted his swagger when he walked down the halls. Martin's smile and relaxed mannerism suggested that he was more than willing to cooperate. Over the next hour I tested him in reading and mathematics. His skills were weaker than I had ever imagined.

I also got to know Martin a bit during this first session. Realizing how he really felt about himself made his bravado little easier to swallow. I understood why his teachers found it difficult to have him in the classroom. He seemed to have a charisma - a charming quality that made you trust him.

Martin was easy to engage. He was happy to talk about himself and readily rambled on. "I have so many hobbies. Like I go dirt biking." Then he stopped and offered a wicked smile. "I also hack into other peoples chat lines. It keeps me busy on the days I don't go to school. I also do some computer programming for Microsoft," he bragged. How was that possible? Was this more bravado? I wondered if they knew at Microsoft that he couldn't read.

Martin did admit that he would like to learn to read the signs along the dirt bike trails. He suspected they were danger signs but added, "Right now I'll just continue to zoom by them and hope for the best." He shrugged his shoulders and smiled at me again.

At our next weekly student services meeting, Martin was at the top of the agenda. With several of his former resource teachers at the table, it became evident that attendance had been a chronic problem since kindergarten. Years of sporadic interventions had proven fruitless. They had all tried. Most felt that weak parenting skills or parents that were just not around to watch him or even discuss his problems were major issues. Martin's mother had not entered the school in years and had told a previous resource teacher, "I didn't do good in school when I was a student." Martin's father did not seem to be in the picture at all. The school had already held back Martin in both grade two and grade seven. With his achievement scores in reading and math there seemed to be little for him in the grade eight classroom.

The student services team began to look at the school through Martin's eyes. He knew he was different from the other students and he was embarrassed. At the same time, he wanted desperately to be successful enough to graduate from middle school and get into high school. From his perspective, school was not doing anything for him. He still couldn't read.

The big question was how to get him hooked on school again so that we could keep him here long enough to teach him functional reading and math skills. We seemed to have nothing to offer this boy who did not fit into the regular school system. If we could get him to grade nine, the district offered a placement for him in an alternative school setting. What were we to do for him until then?

We devised a plan that would set up a type of apprenticeship program for Martin in his current school. He would become the assistant in the elementary gym at the other end of the school. He would assist the classroom teachers during gym class and organize the equipment trolley at the beginning and end of each day. All the teachers involved in the program would initial his daily schedule. This would allow the school to keep track of his attendance and make him accountable for his time at school. Twice a day, Martin would go to the resource room to work on functional reading and math skills. It looked like a great plan on paper. Would it work? Martin had not been subject to many rules or routines in his life. Could we sustain his interest in the apprenticeship program and the resource sessions? Would this plan work for the remainder of the school year?

The next day I attended the grade eight teacher's team meeting and enthusiastically outlined the plan we had devised for Martin. Their response was disheartening. "Good luck," they said. "It will never work." They were wrong. It did work for a week. Martin then went back to his dirt bike and his computer.

PROFESSIONAL INQUIRY

Leadership Practices

- Discuss the impact of the vice principal's actions upon the support provided to Martin.
- Identify additional actions that the vice principal could have engaged in to ensure Martin received immediate and effective learning support.

Teaching Practices

- Critique the practices employed by the school resource teacher.
- Analyze the professional knowledge of the resource teacher.
- Discuss the possible impact of Martin not receiving support from the school resource teacher immediately at the beginning of the school year

Instructional Strategies

- Review and critique the learning opportunities provided to Martin.
- Discuss how the assumptions and beliefs of each of the educators in this case influenced their decisions and actions.
- Review the level of responsibility for Martin's success that each educator demonstrated.

School Culture

- Critique the culture of this school.
- Contemplate the impact of this school's culture upon learners with diverse needs.
- Discuss the impact of the attitudes and beliefs of the grade eight teacher regarding Martin.
- Develop a plan to respond to the attitudes and beliefs of the teachers regarding Martin.
- Identify strategies for fostering a shared school commitment to inclusive education where all learners are welcomed, included and meaningfully participate in learning opportunities that help to develop their potential.

Professional Judgment

- Analyze the decision of the resource teacher to wait a few days before connecting with Martin after receiving important information from the Vice Principal.
- Discuss alternative actions the Vice Principal may have taken to ensure Martin received appropriate and timely support from the resource teacher.

Assumptions and Beliefs

- Analyze the messages that are conveyed about the resource teacher in this school.
- Identify the assumptions and beliefs about teaching and learning that are associated with the perspectives and practices of the grade eight teachers and the resource teacher.
- Discuss the assumptions that the Vice Principal may have held regarding the role of the resource teacher.
- Explore how curriculum and education are understood by the educators in this case.

Ethical Practice

- Discuss approaches for fostering a sense of shared moral responsibility for the success and well-being of all learners within this school.
- Identify strategies for fostering a moral stance among educators that is fundamental to ensuring all students are valued, honored and respected in a school community.
- Discuss the ethical responsibility schools, school systems and teachers have when teachers assume the educational role as a new resource teacher.

CASE COMMENTARY REFLECTIONS

After reading the commentaries reflect on the following:

New Insights
Identify new insights gained from reading the commentaries.

Understandings
Discuss the impact of the commentaries on your understandings of inclusive education.

Questions
Identify questions that emerge for you from reading the commentaries.

CASE COMMENTARY 1

Dr. Lauren Hoffman

It is unfortunately not uncommon for students to slip through educational systems without having their academic, behavioral, social, or linguistic needs understood. In this case, the educators did not understand or recognize these interconnections. They did not understand the needs associated with Martin's behaviour. The educators had a superficial understanding of behavior and apparently used suspensions and punishment throughout Martin's years in school. Unfortunately, Martin was seen as an "object", not a human being with different experiences and needs that need to be uncovered. Rather than demonstrating care and compassion, the educators' responses were blame, punishment, control, and exclusion. This obviously is not a productive approach to supporting students with academic and behavioral needs.

Moral Responsibility: All faculty need to assume responsibility for all students. Responsibility involves the ability to respond to the challenges and demands that arise from being socially conscious (Purpel & McLaurin, 2004). Creating a sense of responsibility as a moral impulse among educators is fundamental to assuring all students are valued in their school community. A major issue is how to promote a sense of responsibility among educators to care about each and every student. The apparent lack of responsibility and pessimism are indicative of larger educational, societal, and political issues. It is recognized that educators are often overwhelmed in this era of accountability with high stakes testing, narrowing of the curriculum, and funding issues. Perhaps this contributes to their lack of self-efficacy in making a difference because of being so overloaded in so many ways. Although this is understandable, there is an urgent call for the provision of systems of support as well as larger systemic transformation.

Three major issues emerge in this case. They are the ethic of care and compassion, professional competence and curriculum.

Ethic of Care and Compassion: Education has overemphasized the technical and mechanical aspects of teaching and learning and consequently the human impulse to be caring, compassionate, and concerned about the welfare of others has been compromised.

Professional Competence: It is critical that educators learn the relationship between academic, behavioral, social, and linguistic development. This will assist in understanding the individual learner and his/her personalized needs while building the ability to act on the student's behalf.

Curriculum: Curriculum should be conceptualized in a broad manner recognizing the "funds of knowledge" that can be gained from the classical, critical, and community bases (Gonzalez, Moll, & Amanti, 2005).

This case raises questions about how to avoid students slipping through the system without receiving the proper support. In addition to creating a sense of responsibility among educators, following are additional suggestions:
- Include a holistic understanding of the interconnections of child development in teacher preparation;
- Broaden the understanding of curriculum to include "funds of knowledge" as described by Gonzalez et al. (2005);
- Assist educators in recognizing and questioning inequities and injustices in the educational system;
- Establish professional communities of educators whose responsibility is to personally know each and every child, question unjust practices, and create systems of support;
- Involve the community and parents as active contributing members of the school community and embrace community leadership in school/community partnerships;
- Provide leadership for educators to know how to work with students with various needs, hold expectations for them to be responsible for every student, create systems of support for every student, and provide space for ongoing dialogue about these difficult issues.

CASE COMMENTARY 2

JoAnne Putnam

Martin is a student who is seriously at risk for school failure and drop out. His erratic attendance and behavior in school contribute to poor academic achievement. He appears to be unmotivated by the school curriculum, although he clearly wants to succeed in middle school so he can attend high school. It is evident that he is dissatisfied with his lack of success in reading and math and seems to be covering up his inadequacies with misbehavior in school.

Martin does not possess many of the advantages that contribute to school success. His mother has not been involved with Martin's school for years and there is no father in the picture. The new resource teacher is committed to supporting Martin and has worked with teachers to develop an apprenticeship program in the gym class, coupled with two days in the resource room for math and functional reading. While teachers predicted the plan would fail, it worked, but only for a week. Nonetheless, it was a worthwhile experiment. The next step is to plan another more enduring apprenticeship that is built with Martin's interests and strengths in mind, such as an apprenticeship in the computer lab.

Martin's resource teacher should continue to find ways of encouraging Martin to participate in school. How can Martin's strengths be used to foster his involvement in school? Are there websites and magazines and other media that can stimulate his interest in reading? Both reading and mathematics could be built into his curriculum with more creativity. Participation in meaningful tasks that are relevant to Martin's future is likely to be the most successful. For example, capitalizing on his interest in computer programming is likely to increase motivation and self-esteem, in addition to preparing him for the future.

Martin needs to be more positively engaged with his peers, especially positive role models, through cooperative learning activities and extra-curricular activities. Are there community organizations that provide youth activities that Martin enjoys? Identifying nonparent adults to support Martin should also help, such as a favorite teacher, community member, or staff member. These are a few examples of many external and internal resources that can be utilized. A student support team, or a *problem solving team* (Porter, 2008) can be formed to generate many creative ideas and possibilities for supporting Martin's education.

CONNECTING TO PROFESSIONAL PRACTICE

The commentary writers raise issues related to the moral responsibility of educators, curriculum relevancy, relationship building, teacher commitment and community involvement. Explore how these issues relate to your own experience and commitment to inclusive education.

CASE SIXTEEN: WHO IS BLIND?

Imagine being blind.

Now, imagine being the parents of a blind child. This may be harder still since you as a seeing person can see what your child is missing. You can see the blue sky, the warm sun, waves at the beach, beautiful plants and flowers, frosty, snow covered mornings, birds singing in the trees, horses in the pasture. The list is endless.

Sure, Jamie can hear and feel these things and he even talks as if he can see them. He often says, "Oh, it is sunny out today." I quietly turn him towards me and ask, "How do you know?" He smiles, his lips turning up slightly at the edges, pleased to explain, "I can feel the warmth on my cheek." He points to the exact centre of a soft cheek.

It may be even more difficult as a parent to watch a child struggle with day-to-day tasks such as grooming, cutting their own meat, manipulating utensils, and shaving. The list continues to expand and becomes increasingly difficult every year as Jamie grows into a young man. I notice the change in his face as the shape elongates and his body begins to stretch out. I am also aware of the restlessness that accompanies those sudden growth spurts.

A tremendous amount of patience is required to teach a blind child life skills. We take those tasks for granted. Sometimes it is easier and less frustrating to just do things for Jamie.

It is easy to forget how detrimental this so-called help is on his independence and how incompetent it may make him. I wonder, will he always need someone to comb his hair or tie his shoes?

Now, as Jamie is a young man with only two years of high school left, I worry. How will he ever make it in the real world? How will Jamie be able to support himself, cook for himself, shop for himself and be his own person? Strangely, thinking about Jamie's independence doesn't seem to be a priority for Jamie's family. That is what worries me the most as his resource teacher.

I think that his parents are holding on too tightly. How much can we as teachers and support staff intervene? I ask Francine, the teaching assistant, to sit down with me and discuss how she thinks Jamie will eventually cope. I ask, "Why are Mom and Dad confining Jamie and keeping him so isolated? Who needs whom? Do the parents need to be needed by Jamie? How can we convince them to let him grow and spread his wings?"

I have told his parents that Jamie can successfully navigate the school halls with his cane. He somehow even recognizes several of his classmates before they speak. Jamie appears to have progressed a tremendous amount at our school. His school records illustrate just how far that he has come since entering kindergarten. He has overcome his fear of fire drills and loud noises. I read about how the sound of the fire alarm bells frightened him so much that he rolled into a ball, screamed and flung his arms in search of help.

Jamie has even spent a couple weeks each year at a special school for the blind. He always returns with renewed confidence and proudly demonstrates his new

What can J do when J got ?
What is the role of
class/subject teacher?

CASE SIXTEEN: WHO IS BLIND?

learning to his classmates. By the end of grade seven, Jamie could travel to the school for the blind five hours away on a special bus with other visually impaired students. Attending this school was a huge step for Jamie and for his family.

For several years, I have helped and tried to teach Jamie to be as independent as possible. Sometimes I joke that I am working myself out of a job. I have learned so many things by having the opportunity to work with Jamie. I even had the occasion to travel with him on one of his weeklong placements at the school for the blind and visually impaired. It was here that I learned better ways to teach Jamie to be more self-sufficient. These experiences enabled me to become increasingly hopeful that someday he could obtain a job and live on his own. It is my hope that I can help him achieve this.

When I reflect on working academically with Jamie I see that it is easy compared to overcoming obstacles of independence. We can easily order textbooks in Braille or provide him with special reading devices. I have learned some Braille so that I can help Jamie. He has an abundance of technological equipment available at his fingertips. I have found that itinerant teachers are an invaluable resource available to students who are blind. They offer expertise in areas of technology, computer programs, Braille equipment, Braille books, learning white cane techniques, learning familiar routes, teaching life skills and providing endless opportunities for growth and experience.

but if they don't read Braille

Jamie has a wonderful memory. He can read anything and answer any factual question based on the text. However, he is not as good at reading between the lines though. His thinking does tend towards the literal. Math is another story. We keep it to basic everyday life skills math. We give him real life problem-solving so he can make applications to his own life.

Jamie loves to write stories. He always worries that his stories or homework won't be good enough for the teacher. I fear he is somewhat of a perfectionist although he can really put together a good story.

I spend a lot of my time with Jamie writing stories. We act as editors for each other. We share the same books and talk about the characters. These conversations make me think of Robert Coles and what he has written about the power of stories to transform lives. The books I choose for Jamie have messages of hope. After reading some of the stories he compares himself with the protagonists and feels empowered. We have laughed at Tom Sawyer and his antics because recently Jamie and a friend attempted painting a fence.

Sometimes I can sense that Jamie has a bit of developmental delay and that he has not had many life experiences. Most of his stories are about his family and music. Only the odd one revolves around antics with friends. Maybe that is why he loves to read. Through his reading he can travel or be with friends.

Jamie is a wonderful musician. He can play a variety of instruments by ear. Everyone in our town knows who Jamie is and has heard him play. Jamie's dad shadows his every move. His father is always there with Jamie at all his "gigs". Jamie's dream is to be a famous musician. Perhaps that will happen.

Of course most of us do what we love and are good at, but I don't want Jamie to close any doors to other careers. Through career assessments we have found that

Jamie could be capable of doing several other kinds of jobs. He has very good people skills, loves to meet new people, has good phone skills and communicates well.

Developing lasting friendships with his peers is one of the hardest things for Jamie. In a school complex with nearly 800 students most are familiar with Jamie. A lot of young students call out, "hello" or just "hi" as he walks by. Jamie always acknowledges them. Jamie is asked to play at school activities such as pep rallies, school band performances and drama plays. These are wonderful opportunities for Jamie to interact with his peers. Jamie is always very polite, pleasant and willing to help out.

Despite all of this Jamie has a very hard time maintaining a friendship. A friend to Jamie is always somebody who helps him. He can't see outside of his little world and is very socially delayed. Jamie doesn't know how to reciprocate a friendship. When he moved to high school it seemed that the students had even less time and desire to be a friend to Jamie. It saddens me to see Jamie sit alone day after day in the cafeteria at lunchtime.

I think this inability to make friends his own age stems from the problem his family has generated by sheltering him too much and always doing everything for him.

Even though Jamie's parents are not assisting him to become a self-sufficient, independent young adult, they do promote his musical abilities. Jamie gets many invitations to entertain people at dinners, festivals, and charity events. Last summer, he even worked at our community music festival. The full time that he was there, however, he was under the watchful eye of his father.

This parental support may seem great to some but who is benefiting the most from all of this? Sure Jamie gets to play in public but his experiences are all mainly adult oriented. On the positive side, Jamie interacts very well with adults. He even has the opportunity to make some money. Again, who benefits from this? As a young adult Jamie should be learning life skills. He can't even manipulate a knife to make a sandwich for himself.

There are only so many hours in a school day. With only two years of school left, I wonder what will become of Jamie. I know he will always have his family to take care of him. I also know that deep down he would like to take care of himself. I believe he is very capable of achieving this goal.

I do think about the "what ifs" for Jamie. His family may not always be there and there will be a time in Jamie's life that they will not be there. With a set routine, organized home, and familiar community Jamie could surely be a capable and successful adult. How will he manage on his own as a middle-aged adult if we don't try to force the parents to understand that they are not helping their son to be his own person?

Jamie's family loves him so much but they cannot see that they are his biggest obstacles to independence. When we first mentioned the option of Jamie going to Ottawa for an exclusively blind camp we saw a glimmer of excitement but then it was quickly followed by apprehension. Jamie's family would not allow him to go such a distance away from home. They said that he could not handle the many new experiences that would come with going to camp. They didn't even give him the chance to try.

I think Jamie wants to try new things and be independent. But he knows that his family will worry about him so much and so he declines any opportunity to even discuss possibilities.

I think that maybe in a sense Jamie's parents are blind. They don't see what we as educators see. When I look at Jamie, I see a person with great potential. Will Jamie live a normal life? Will Jamie have a family of his own? Will Jamie be a productive individual who can support himself in his community?

I believe that Jamie has the ability to do anything he wants to do. Why can't his parents see this?

PROFESSIONAL INQUIRY

Assumptions and Beliefs

– Describe how the educator in this case understood inclusive education.
– Analyze the educational vision that the educator in this case had for Jamie.
– Identify the assumptions and beliefs held by the educator in this case.
– Discuss the significance of these assumptions and beliefs for Jamie's growth and development.
– Explore professional learning strategies that will help invite the educator this case to revisit the beliefs and assumptions held about Jamie, his parents and blindness.

Language

– Critique the language used by the case author to describe Jamie.
– Analyze the messages about individuals with visual challenges (impairments) that are embedded in the language used by the case author.
– Identify statements in this case that convey negative images of Jamie.
– Discuss how the language and images that are used to describe students can serve as barriers to inclusive education.

Professional Knowledge and Practice

– Critique the professional knowledge of the educator in this case.
– Analyze the practices of the educator in this case from an inclusive education perspective.
– Explore methods for enhancing the knowledge, skills, practices and dispositions of the educator in this case.

Programming

– Critique the educational program being provided to Jamie.
– Generate recommendations for enhancing the educational program designed for Jamie.

- Explore methods to promote an inclusive educational philosophy within this school that will be reflected in the educational programming provided to all students.
- Discuss strategies for directly involving Jamie in the identification and implementation of his educational goals.

Working with Parents

- Identify barriers and challenges that influence the school's ability to work effectively with Jamie's parents.
- Discuss strategies for more fully including Jamie's parents in his education.
- Critique the assumptions that are held about Jamie's parents in this case.
- Explore how the teacher's assumptions and beliefs influenced his/her perception of Jami and the support provided.

Inclusive Education

- Write a response to this case from Jamie's perspective as an adolescent wanting an inclusive education.
- Write a response to this case from the perspective of Jamie's parents.
- Develop a plan, as a new principal, for re-culturing this school towards a vision and philosophy of inclusive education.
- Explore the ways in which this case does not advance the field of inclusive education.
- Explore the ways in which this case and the associated commentaries can be used to advance the field of inclusive education.
- Describe what an inclusive learning environment might look like for Jamie.

CASE COMMENTARY REFLECTIONS

After reading the commentaries reflect on the following:

New Insights
Identify new insights gained from reading the commentaries.

Understandings
Discuss the impact of the commentaries on your understandings of inclusive education.

Questions
Identify questions that emerge from reading the commentaries.

CASE COMMENTARY 1

Sheila Bennett

Throughout the case study I had a very uncomfortable feeling with the tone. There seemed to be a tone of pity and limitation on the part of the educator. Even in the first paragraph, I suppose it was supposed to emit an emotional response but the response I feel is, "Oh my goodness, this does not bode well… (Also, you cannot see a bird singing)". What is the child missing? I don't know, but I also don't know what s/he has that I don't as a seeing person. Were it my child I would hate their experience to be characterized this way. Beyond that, in the first line to use **disability language** first is actually quite shocking to me. Reading the words, "Blind Child" is very offensive to me.

Returning again to the tone of this case, I am not sure that because a person is visually impaired that their struggles are anymore poignant than any child across a myriad of challenges. I would be encouraged to watch a child attempt and persevere at any task.

I like the point of helping too much, it is true for all parents but perhaps more so when a child struggles, whether it be through the social, physical or cognitive, socioeconomic or ethnic arena. I would prefer this point be made within that context.

I am wondering why a child of his age would still be combing his hair and tying a shoe. I am questioning why Velcro was not considered? I am also wondering why these issues related to combing hair and tying shoes were not dealt with much earlier by the school. Developmentally, if a child such as Jamie were not combing his hair or tying his shoe in primary I would be concerned then.

This case really disturbed me!!!

In paragraph six, there is actually a reference to how the student would make it in the real world. He is in the real world, the one that is real for him. If we characterize students with disability as needing to get ready for the "real world" then we support the fantasy that two worlds exist, one in which the child with disabilities must earn his/her way into. While I realize that this was not what the author meant, I believe that leaving it in the case study perpetuates a line of thinking that is detrimental to inclusive thought.

The paragraph then goes on to life skills training. Is Jamie intellectually impaired? If not, then why would we as a school system be concerned about this (My 18 year old sighted university bound son can't boil an egg!) If he is not intellectually impaired then perhaps our worry should be how he will get through university registration procedures as a person with visual impairment.

The author also starts to veer onto the edge of the blind mystique, with the statement, "he somehow even recognizes several of his classmates before they speak". There are many reasons that many of us know a walk or a smell but it is not because we are "blind". To characterize this ability in this way to make it seem like one of those superpowers that "blind children" get. Again, I am not sure, about the author's intent but not a good representation either.

I cannot even begin to comment on the next paragraph that describes the school as not just the school for the blind but the "special school for the blind". This school has a "special bus". Not only does Jamie go to this school but he demonstrates his skills to the class upon his return.

I am more optimistic when I read that the teacher actually received some training that made her a better teacher for a person with visual impairments, which is the direction that I believe we should be promoting. Specialized education and professional learning for educators that enable them to work with students with exceptionalities is essential. Imagine a world where as a teacher I went to a "special school for a week and then the student got a whole year of great instruction! (I can dream!!). But just as my optimism kicks in the paragraph ends with ...."someday he could obtain a job and live on his own." Again the tone of pity re-emerges in the tone of this case.

I like the next paragraph. The technology and translation of information into a usable format as well as accessing expert help are terrific ideas. It continues on for a few paragraphs with some good content. When the educator talks about choosing "stories of hope" again the pity shines through. The next paragraph though is when all hope fails for me as a reader... Sometime I sense that Jamie has a bit of a developmental delay. Don't we know at this stage? I am assuming that she means developmental delay in a special education context which would mean modified intellectual testing, or does the educator mean he is behind socially. If he is behind socially perhaps it is because he is spending too much time reading hopeful stories and going to the school for the blind and not out kicking around with the "normal kids"

The next couple of paragraphs are more optimistic and one can see the value of being part of the larger community within the school. That is what I would be working on as an educator. The next few paragraphs support the need for social skills building. Why isn't the story about a circle of friends or how they navigated a trip to Canada's Wonderland or how Jamie has been taught from a young age to meet and greet? While I do not disagree that the family is culpable as well I see ño evidence in the story that this school has been proactive on this front.

Later the discussion is about Jamie relating well to adults (he will be one soon) and the fact that he gets paid gigs as a musician. However, there seems to be no recognition that these are valuable experiences and the concern seems to be that he cannot use a knife? Why can't he? If he has the manual dexterity to play an instrument why can't he use a knife at this age? And again, why are the concerns centered on life skills?

Now our solution is to send him to a "blind camp". Alright, I might be convinced to admit that given the right set of circumstances an exclusively blind camp may be a good thing. Certainly, I have had experiences with students from Finland who attended a teachers college for deaf students and they were fantastic....but why is this the example of Jamie's independence adventure???

Finally, the statement in the case that says, "Will Jamie live a normal life?" once again illustrates the extensive work needed to change attitudes and beliefs held by some educators. This statement is so far removed from inclusion that it does not justify a response. HE IS LIVING A NORMAL LIFE! If we don't believe that then we shouldn't be in the inclusion world at all.

CASE COMMENTARY 2

Jackie Fewer-Bennett

The situation that this teacher finds herself in is not uncommon. Many parents of children with a disability have difficulty in letting their child "spread their wings" and while this is very understandable, they need to be aware of the power of building independence. Parents also need to understand the importance of building social capital and their vital role in helping their child maintain friendships outside the school setting. Life skills and social skills need to be embedded within the student's program. It is critical that the teacher builds positive rapport with the student and his/her family. This rapport will enable the teacher to gain credibility with the family in respect to the student's programming.

The development and implementation of the Individual Education Plan process is an avenue through which appropriate and realistic goals can be developed. The student should be a key member of the Individual Education Plan team, especially when he/she is able to articulate their wants and needs. The team will help develop goals and outcomes to address the life skills and social skills for the student. The team could also provide suggestions on how to transfer the acquired skills from the school to the community.

This case reminds me of a situation during my teaching career. It involved a young man with autism who was very high functioning. His class was going on a four day field trip quite a distance away. The parents were very apprehensive about letting him go with his class because he had never spent a night away from home. When I called and asked them to reconsider their decision in allowing their son to go on the fieldtrip, I cited reasons why I felt he was ready for this experience.

Fortunately for the student, the parents agreed and a contingency plan was put in place to support the student. During the fieldtrip, he fared extremely well. He was very engaged in the activities and actually won the respect of his classmates and teachers who discovered just how much knowledge he had on the subject being discussed. This experience changed the perception of his classmates and teachers on a positive note. It also gave the student and his parents the confidence to allow him to experience new things.

I feel that my relationship with the parents and the rapport I developed with the student set the stage for him in extending himself into new life experiences. Therefore, building a relationship with the family is vital.

CASE COMMENTARY 3

Alicia de la Peña Rode

The case author believes that Jamie has grown inside a protected family environment. This overprotective attitude is positioned as needing to be dealt with in a professional way in order to reduce barriers and fears.

At Jamie's age strategies have to be found to strengthen his independence in all environments. The school needs to strive to understand Jamie's goals and support him in achieving his all of these.

Jamie needs to participate in activities with more people. Teachers need to work with peers to support Jamie's full inclusion within the school and community. The teachers all need to investigate how their own views and beliefs are influencing Jamie's success.

Jamie's musical gifts and involvement in the community can be used to help the school expand their understanding and actions towards this young man. The school appears to be one of the barriers to Jamie's growth, independence and success.

CONNECTING TO PROFESSIONAL PRACTICE

The case commentaries identify the barriers and challenges to inclusion that exist within this case. The assumptions, knowledge and practices of the educator in this case are problematic for some of the commentary writers. Reflect on your own beliefs and assumptions related to students with diverse learning needs. Explore the impact of your own dispositions, assumptions and beliefs upon your practices, decisions and actions as an educator.

CASE SEVENTEEN: HIT HARD

In all the years that I've been working with and meeting with school principals (10 years), why did this principal's remark hit me so hard?

"Just think about this…if you keep your son here, as a parent, and I'm a parent myself, you wouldn't be doing what is best for him."

Standing in that school hallway, hearing those words, I felt a cold wave wash over me from my gut to my head. I had no control over what was coming out of my mouth: "You need to stop talking now. You are bullying this parent". I then turned to look at the mother beside me.

The principal tried to spit out some excuse, the Vice-Principal standing stiff-lipped behind her, was not coming to her aid. "Well', I interrupted, "you need to keep those thoughts in your head."

Thinking back to that moment, I was so relieved that there were no students or other staff in the hallway over-hearing this very inappropriate dialogue. This dialogue that had started out as an end-of-school meeting was actually a last-ditch effort to discuss school placement for the coming September. The placement options were either a home schooling program in Grade One, or an alternate placement in a Primary Diagnostic Program in a different school.

I felt very protective of this family. I had known and worked very closely with them since their little boy was 3 ½ years old. I'd been to the developmental assess-ment, speech therapy sessions, and made countless visits to the home and daycare centre. I had become, essentially, a member of the family.

I was curious, slightly hopeful of a good outcome when the mother and I entered the principal's office that morning. Unfortunately, dread soon set in only seconds later. The mother sat across the coffee table looking nervous, distrustful and some-what defensive. Past experiences with this principal had already coloured her opinions of this school.

The principal proceeded to desperately wave the speech-language and the senior kindergarten reports in front of her. "Look at this, read what it says!" Once again, I attempted to remind her of the parents' choices, the social learning implications, the duty to accommodate and the need for an Individual Education Plan. My attempts to educate and communicate with the principal were ignored. The principal turned to the mother and placed additional pressure on her prefacing her comments with, "Just try this program for 2 months, if you don't like it…...!!!"

She then urged us to observe the open-concept framework of the Grade One classroom first-hand. We were shuffled down the hall. Once in the classroom, the principal whisked me to the reading area. Over my shoulder, I could see that another woman had approached the mother and began speaking to her in a serious tone.

It was very difficult for me to initially comprehend what was actually unfolding. I wondered, "What was happening here?!" and paid little attention to what the principal was saying about the student not being able to do well because of x, y, z. I thought, "Was this a set-up? Were we split up intentionally?"

I walked back over to the mother and encouraged her to come back to the school office to continue our meeting. The woman who had cornered her was an educational assistant in the school. Her own son apparently had a disability and she appeared to be given the green light by the principal to tell us her educational philosophy. The educational assistant seemed angry and her eyes were wild. Her attack turned to me and my agency. She preached about how inclusion hurts kids and prevents them from getting the special help they need. Her words were like weapons designed to hit hard.

"That's one perspective", I firmly retorted. My angry response stopped her in her tracks. When this dialogue finally came to a close with the principal's concluding remarks, I understood that this was no meeting, but a carefully-planned ambush.

The actions I had witnessed were appalling to me on both a professional and personal level. Knowing that the family appreciated my presence and my input, and that they will need my support again for what was to come, made this struggle for their son's acceptance worthwhile. My role to help support and prevent families from being hit hard from the often misguided blows from the educational system is important. Why does inclusion have to be so difficult?

PROFESSIONAL INQUIRY

Ethical Practice

— Explore the ethical dimensions related to the professional judgment and actions of the school principal.
— Discuss the professionalism and ethical practices of the teaching assistant.
— Identify the ethical principles that were not honored in this case.

Challenges to Inclusion

— Identify the challenges and barriers to inclusion in this case.
— Analyze the underlying issues that may have contributed to the silencing of the parent's voice in this case.

Advocacy

— Discuss the role that advocates can play in supporting the inclusion of learners.
— Identify the professional knowledge, skills and dispositions that contribute to effective advocacy.
— Explore ways in which schools can accept, respect and work collaboratively with advocates that support families and students.

Leadership

Critique the leadership actions and decisions of the school principal.
— Generate strategies for enhancing the understanding and professional knowledge of the school principal.
— Identify approaches for changing the thinking and actions of the school principal.
— Develop a plan for facilitating a respectful, open and transparent meeting with this parent and advocate.

CASE COMMENTARY REFLECTIONS

After reading the commentaries reflect on the following:

New Insights
Identify new insights gained from reading the commentaries.

Understandings
Discuss the impact of the commentaries on your understandings of inclusive education.

Questions
Identify questions that emerge for you from reading the commentaries.

CASE COMMENTARY 1

Jean J. Ryoo

The first question that arises when reading this case is: why would a principal try to dissuade a student from enrolling in her school?

As the core ideals of capitalism—competition, individualism, and economic efficiency—grip the minds of people in a world that values money over humanity, today's schools have embraced identities as miniature businesses. Schools commit themselves to creating sterile environments and manufacturing "quality products" with as little effort as possible (i.e. push students through every grade level whether they are ready to move forward or not and, based on their gender, ethnic, and class backgrounds, prepare them to be well-paid CEO's or poorly-paid laborers). In such an era, it comes as little surprise that a school principal would actively dissuade certain students—children with disabilities or who need "special help"—from enrolling in her school. Under a capitalist model, why should a person running a business (school) want to work hard to create a product (educate a student until s/he graduates) if that same product could be manufactured with less work and money (students with disability require more attention and effort than students without disabilities)?

Indeed, this unfortunate attitude appears to be the defining characteristic of the principal described in this case. Instead of embracing a visiting mother and high-lighting the strengths of the school, the principal introduces it as the *wrong* place for children with disabilities. Instead of asking the mother what type of education and learning experience she envisions for her child, this principal "waves" speech-language and senior kindergarten teacher reports in the mother's face in order to point out how her child has "problems" and is "unfit" for the school. Rather than looking at these reports with the desire to understand the child's needs and discuss how the school can meet those needs, the principal uses them in a condescending and prejudiced way to label the potential student as "undesirable." Without even meeting the child, the principal has already calculated in her head that she doesn't want the child using her school's educational resources.

While some may debate whether mainstreaming students with disabilities into traditional classrooms is "good" for children, none should question that schools are supposed to be safe spaces for *all* children—regardless of class, gender, ethnicity, sexuality, ability, etc.—to learn, socialize, and grow into critical thinkers and citizens who are positive participants in the greater society. Everyone deserves equitable access to education.

This case clearly illustrates a school under poor leadership. Sadly, many schools are filled with people like this principal who judge children based on their physical appearance, accents, test scores, and other superficial measures. While the principal's behavior is appalling, the case writer's approach to education is one that should be both commended and upheld by all people who spend time in schools.

The case author's self-descriptions as a person who is "protective" of the student, who made home and daycare center visits, and who became a "member of the family" should be how every educator and school leader approaches students and families. Schools should be spaces that embrace communities and value the voices of parents. School leaders should listen to student and parent perspectives as well as teacher and student-advocate opinions, and be able to create a united community of diverse members.

CASE COMMENTARY 2

Gordon Kyle

We live in a society that is increasingly aware of the value of diversity in all elements of community life. As citizens, we have elected to formalize our commitment to diversity through human rights codes, human rights commissions and enabling legislative structures that promote the rights of all citizens to be fully included within our society. This recognition of the value of diversity is reflected in many places within our education system, from the ethical standards (Ontario College of Teachers, 2006) that guide the teaching profession, to the excellent report of the expert panel on literacy and numeracy *Education For All* (Ministry of Education, 2005). Despite this, there remains within our education system those who feel that the value of diversity and participation do not apply equally to certain students including those who have an intellectual disability. Some in the education system, as this case study demonstrate hold to the idea that for students who have an intellectual disability separate and "special" is better.

The type of battle faced by the mother in this case study should not be necessary in our modern age. While nobody is saying it is simple to create an education system that differentiates and responds to the unique characteristics and needs of each individual student, educators are largely committed to make this a reality for most students. One has to ask why this cannot and should not be true of those who have an intellectual disability.

While the treatment of this mother is appalling, what is even more disturbing to consider is how a parent would fair in such a circumstance if they were not as well prepared and sophisticated as this mother clearly was. As the case study outlines, this is a parent who had identified clear expectations for her child's education, understood the Individual Education Plan (IEP) mechanisms and had worked to ensure that her child's accommodation needs were spelled out. Further, this is a parent who understood the dynamics of school/parent relationships and the value of coming to a meeting with an advocate who could assist her in her interactions with the school.

Many parents do not fully understand the complexities involved in dealing with their child's school. They therefore trust educators to provide them with the information and guidance they need to make the best decisions regarding the educational options for their son or daughter. We must find a way that the overriding value that our society places on diversity is reflected and strived for by all in our education system. Rather than pressuring parents into choosing non-inclusive options, educators must work with parents to figure out how to include and teach each and every student.

CASE COMMENTARY 3

Shelley Arsenault

This case study involves several passionate perspectives regarding the potential school placement of a grade one student with varying needs. The principal feels that the student would be better off in a home schooling environment or in a Primary Diagnostic Program in a different school. Though it was obvious a meeting was to take place, the principal should have taken a greater leadership role to prepare for an effective meeting. Her approach, with a confrontation in the hallway before they entered her office, was not appropriate. It would have been more productive to have a case conference with all the partners involved and perhaps inviting someone from the local school board to be in attendance.

This principal does not display appropriate leadership qualities and this is seen in her tone of voice and body language that has set the stage for a hostile and unproductive outcome. It was also inappropriate for the principal to draw on her own personal experiences in parenting to bully the meeting participants. In this case study, the role of a classroom teacher, resource teacher, or guidance counselor is not evident, but that may be due to the fact that the principal has already decided that the child will not be coming to her school so no other staff member needed to be aware of the situation. It would be important to know how the other staff members feel towards inclusion.

Even the vice principal, who doesn't respond to the principal in the hall, may have a different view on inclusive practices. A few people with the loudest voices many not really be speaking for the whole school. Though this case study is written from one person's perspective, several statements leave the reader wondering if indeed the principal did have a hidden agenda when the parent and the parent advocate were intentionally separated during a visit to the grade one classroom. The principal and some members of her staff had obviously discussed the situation prior to the visit and had strong opinions formed before any sharing of information could take place.

This type of leadership weakens collaboration and is not an effective way to communicate. The remarks made by the educational assistant also crossed a professional line and concern should be relayed to the principal and the school board. In his/her capacity, the comments were not appropriate and added pressure to the situation.

The parent advocate also has a very important role to play in this case study. He/she is emotionally attached to the family and may need to step back to see how he/she can continue to be a leader while moving things forward. Instead of using a verbal rally with the principal he/she may have been better served in helping to educate the principal as to what, how, and why inclusive practices are essential. This learning session on inclusive education would need to take place at a different time, perhaps a professional learning forum or through an in-service session. The parent advocate could also have asked for more partners to be involved in the meeting, especially since she did have prior experiences with the principal's philosophy and must had attended other meetings leading up to this "last ditch effort". One would hope that a parent advocate who truly wanted to be effective would have a pocketful of calmly rehearsed statements used to response to various myths surrounding inclusive practices. The advocate's role should also have included teaching the parents how to speak up for their child and themselves and this did not show through.

The parent advocate could also have taken some responsibility for the lack of focus to the issue as it was clear his/her mind was stuck on the possibility of being set up. Perhaps the critical role of the advocate would be to support the child and parent in contacting the local school board and in possibly filing a formal complaint against the school with the Human Rights Commission. Clearly, no accommodation is being offered to the child in a regular class in their community school.

The parents, too, need to find a voice and may need more support than just an advocate. Perhaps a community organization, pediatrician, or family and friends could also lend support. If there is a second parent involved in the child's life they too should have attended the meeting.

The parents will need a great deal of support to look past the views of the principal and the educational assistant. They may give up their vision for their child as a result of the principal's pressure. They may begin to believe that their child is better off in another school. Their desire for their child to be "wanted" may overshadow the best educational opportunities needed for the child. They must see beyond these narrow views and hope they can be part of a change process for this school and their community.

The situation described in this case study will need a lot of collaboration to have a positive result. This one individual, the principal, may not be able to be easily changed and a more forceful pressure may need to be applied. Ultimately, if the child is not given a placement opportunity, then strong action should be taken at the school board level. This requires the Human Rights Code to be applied then that path should also be taken. This child is entitled to an inclusive education – education in a regular class, with peers, and in the home community.

CASE COMMENTARY 4

Krista Carr

There are three key areas for discussion that present themselves in this case study. Firstly, the inappropriateness of the treatment the parent in this case received from the school administrator. Secondly, the incredible strain faced by parents when they are told that what they want for their child is unrealistic and not in their best interests. Thirdly, the unwillingness of the school to individualize a learning plan and outcomes for this child results in parents having to revisit their own goals and intentions for their child.

Far too often parents feel bullied by the school system. They are told their children will not be safe in the school environment or that they will not learn what they need to learn. In this case, pressure is being put on the parent to comply with what the school administrator wants. The principal employs a strategy to convince the mother to agree with the views of the principal by talking "parent to parent". The fact is this administrator is no doubt not the parent of a learner with special needs. The principal has not stopped long enough to think about the fact that all the things she wants for her child, this parent also wants for hers.

I often ponder the incredible strain parents are put under when they are told or made to feel by the system that the expectations they have for their children's school experience are unrealistic or not in the best interests of their children. Parents are their child's first teachers. They have spent more time with their child than anyone else. They know their child best. They know their child's capabilities and their also know far too well their limitations.

No, parents aren't always right. They do the best they can by using their best judgment. In my experience parents are the "experts" on their children. When that parental expertise is matched with the educational expertise of the school staff, the result can be wonderful outcomes for the child. In this situation, a "we/they" relationship is being established and no one benefits from that, particularly not the child.

There seems to be no discussion in this case about the development of an individualized plan for the child. We hear only of an offsite program or home schooling. Far too often we try to place children in programs rather than building individualized plans to meet the needs of each child.

Setting up programs that slot children in is in many ways easier than individualizing for each child that needs it. Developing individual plans takes more time, more effort, more energy and more teamwork between parents, school staff and other professionals. Sometimes you try things and they don't work and you have to revise the plan and start again. The experience I have had over the past thirteen years of supporting parents has shown me that the results are worth every ounce of energy expended.

In general, this case demonstrates the plight of parents to have a real say in the education of their children and to not be overwhelmed by the wishes. Parents have every right to pursue the best education for their child.

CONNECTING TO PROFESSIONAL PRACTICE

The practices, skills and ethics of the school principal and educational assistant are scrutinized by the commentary writers. The purpose of education and the significance of human rights emerge in some of the commentaries. Explore your own thoughts related to ethical practice, human rights and the purposes of education.

The case commentaries also convey respect for the role of advocates that provide supports to families. Reflect on your experiences working with advocates. Identify the knowledge, understanding and insights you gained from your professional encounters with student and family advocates.

6. THE VOICE OF PARENTS

Parents are situated at the heart of inclusive education. Their love, understanding and hopes for their children must be respected and honored in the complex process of education. Parents often serve as a reflective mirror for conveying to educators the impact of educational practices and decisions upon child and families.

As essential educational partners, parents offer unique, informed and experiential wisdom that can extend and deepen the understanding and professional knowledge of educators. Parents must be included as integral components of the educational process. Their insight, knowledge and expectations regarding their children need to be genuinely invited and responded to by all educators and school personnel.

Respecting and honoring the voice and perspectives of parents is an essential component of inclusive education. The cases in this section of the text illustrate the multiplicity of experiences some parents have encountered in their attempt to help support an inclusive education for their child. These experiences illustrate the many challenges and barriers that parents encounter in their quest for educational inclusion.

The attitudes, beliefs and assumptions held by educators often play a significant role in shaping their professional actions, decisions and judgments related to student learning. Educators that possess the belief that parents are a valuable and essential resource and partner in the educational process will ensure that parents are invited and included to participate in the teaching and learning process. These educators respect and privilege the active involvement of parents. The authentic inclusion of parents becomes a key component in the pedagogical practices of these educators.

Conversely, educators that do not recognize or respect the lived experience and knowledge of parents, as valuable educational resources, may implicitly and explicitly exclude parents. This exclusion often results in limiting the educational experiences and opportunities for learners.

Overview of Cases

The eight cases in this section reflect the perspectives of parents. Most of these case have been written by parents. These narratives of experience illustrate the many faces of both inclusion and exclusion. The hopes, dreams and anguish of parents are told through these stories of schooling.

The parent authors accepted the invitation to reflect upon their experiences as parents hoping for and envisioning an inclusive education for their child. The re-collection and writing of the lived experiences of exclusion was painful for some of these parents. For others, the case writing process served as a source of transformation and healing. Remembering moments and occasions of authentic educational inclusion for their child reinforced feelings of joy and hope for some parents.

G. L. Porter and D. Smith (eds.), Exploring Inclusive Educational Practices Through Professional Inquiry, 173–247.
© 2011 Sense Publishers. All rights reserved.

These parental cases invite educators, support personnel and policy makers to reflect upon their own professional practices and beliefs. This process of critique will hopefully encourage these professionals to collectively adapt educational practices that will result in the enhancement of inclusive practices. Deeper insight, empathy and knowledge can be gained though interaction with the case narratives in this section.

CASE EIGHTEEN: PARENTAL DEMANDS

How could I get so lucky I thought as I walked home from my first day of school?

After ten years of teaching, I felt I had won the "dream class" lottery. The children in my fourth grade class were bright, eager to please and extremely keen. "What a year I am sure to have with this class from heaven," I explained to my roommate. I could see my class test scores up in lights. I was so excited that I immediately started to plan for the term. I was absolutely certain that everything would fall neatly into place.

After a wonderful first term, I felt that I had gotten to know all the students. They were all experiencing success. I would challenge this group and watch them flourish. The parents were happy with their children's progress and were ready to help out when they could.

It was a brisk spring afternoon when a parent of one of my students scheduled a meeting. I was sure it would be to discuss how well his son was doing and I was ready to tell of his accomplishments on the most recent math test. This was when my dream changed to a nightmare.

I greeted Mr. Cross and invited him to sit down at my reading table. He refused. He stated coldly, "This won't take long." I was taken aback and stared silently at him. Mr. Cross announced, "Tom is not progressing."

I couldn't believe my ears. Tom was a good student. He worked well in small groups. According to my assessments and evaluations, he had demonstrated competency at the appropriate level.

I quickly recovered and went to retrieve Tom's portfolio. I was just about to show Mr. Cross Tom's results in mathematics when he held up his hand and said, "I don't need to see that. I have seen some of the homework that my nephew is doing."

"I am not sure I follow you, Mr. Cross," I stammered. I could feel my face start to flush. My hand was trembling as I held Tom's portfolio. I realized that I was a long way from the office. I recalled the principals' recommendations that conversations between parents and teachers should be held in locations other than closed classrooms. Now, here I stood with no support present.

Mr. Cross was emphatic. "You are not doing your job. Tom needs harder work to develop his potential." He almost shouted, "Tom will not be coming back tomorrow or the next day until you decide to teach what needs to be taught."

Silently, I prayed for a member of the custodial staff to interrupt the meeting or for the office to page me over the intercom. I had to get away from this parent. Mr. Cross was looking around my room. I felt that he was peering into all the corners of the classroom for signs of my incompetence. I wasn't sure how to proceed. What should I do or say?

"Well, Mr. Cross I am sure we can resolve this issue. Your son is a good student and really enjoys our class." I knew by looking at him that my comments hadn't made any difference.

Mr. Cross is well-known professional in our small community. He works with the public and is respected in his business. I waited to see what he would say next.

"Get me all of Tom's notebooks and personal things from his desk," he demanded. "I'm withdrawing Tom from your class as of today."

I was stunned but managed to gather up Tom's possessions. I stammered, "I'm sorry that you feel this way," Mr. Cross grabbed the books from my trembling hands and stomped out the door.

I stumbled to my principal's office and slumped into her chair. "What is wrong?" she asked and immediately closed her door. I just sat there and stared at her desk. "I'm not sure what just happened." Mr. Cross said that he was just withdrawing Tom from my class. He accused me of not teaching what I should be teaching. He said that other students were excelling in more complex subjects. My eyes filled with tears. "I have never been accused of being too easy on my class." I put my head in my hands. "I don't think this is the end of it. He seemed out for blood. What do I do?"

After a few minutes of contemplation, my principal smiled as she said, "I know you are teaching what you need to teach. Your students are doing very well. As hard as it is, let Mr. Cross have a few days to think about what he wants to do. I think he will be back and when he comes back in to see you, I want to be present. We will get to the bottom of this. For now, just give him some time."

I thought that was a great suggestion. But I still was worried. How was I ever going to let this parent's intimidating tirade go? What would happen to Tom?

I began to realize that this is one of the realities of being a teacher. I wondered if this was my issue and if I had let Tom down in some way. On the other hand, perhaps Mr. Cross was simply an overzealous parent wanting the best for his son.

After a restless night I dragged myself out of bed and got ready for school. I was a bit hesitant about my lesson plan that day. Was I meeting all the requirements? Was I looking beyond the average student? Was I enriching those who needed it? My list of questions grew and became endless. I felt that I could honestly say, "Yes, I was meeting the needs of all the students." I would not let Mr. Cross dominate my thoughts that day.

My week flew by as they always do and I rarely thought about Mr. Cross. I did wonder how Tom was doing. I wondered what he was learning at home.

As I was getting my room ready for the next day, I heard someone coming down the hall. I looked up to see Mr. Cross enter my classroom. My stomach churned. I looked him in the eye and asked if I could help him.

"I want Tom's homework," he said. "His what?" I asked with disbelief. Mr. Cross wanted to have the homework and assignment sheets that I had given my other students that week.

I reacted more assertively this time. "Mr. Cross I think we should set up a meeting with the principal to discuss Tom's program."

PROFESSIONAL INQUIRY

Beliefs and Assumptions

– Explore the beliefs and assumptions that the classroom teacher appears to hold regarding her class and education.

- Discuss the possible assumptions the principal and teacher may have held regarding the parent.
- Consider the possible implications of the educational assumptions held by this teacher and principal.

Communication with Parents

- Generate strategies for communicating information regarding educational expectations and programming to parents.
- Critique the professional judgment of the principal regarding the decision not to communicate with the parent for several days.
- Explore alternative methods for responding to the issue(s) in this case.

Educational Programming

- Explore ways in which teachers can receive meaningful and ongoing feedback regarding the educational programs they establish and implement.
- Generate approaches for obtaining feedback from students regarding their educational program.

CASE COMMENTARY REFLECTIONS

After reading the commentaries reflect on the following:

New Insights
Identify new insights gained from reading the commentaries.

Understandings
Discuss the impact of the commentaries on your understandings of inclusive education.

Questions
Identify questions that emerge from reading the commentaries.

CASE COMMENTARY 1

Diane Richler

This case demonstrates the challenge to schools when dealing with students who are academically capable and who have parents with high academic expectations. It is not clear from the case study how knowledgeable the teacher was about how to ensure that her students were truly being challenged to reach their full potential and that adaptation to the curriculum was taking that into account. The teacher's initial thoughts about having a "bright" class and having high test scores raises questions regarding her philosophy of education as well as her beliefs about teaching and learning.

The case also raises questions about the interaction between school and parents. It was already the spring term when Mr. Cross expressed his anger and disappointment. What prior opportunities had there been for him to meet with the teacher to discuss his son's progress and individual goals?

The attitude of the principal is troubling. If a parent was angry enough to withdraw his child from school, shouldn't the principal have acted immediately to call the parent, express her concern over his dissatisfaction, and set up a meeting between the parent, teacher and herself? No child should be absent from school without the principal knowing why. If there is an issue then it needs to be addressed immediately.

The parent also showed poor judgment in how he approached the situation. He should have called in advance to schedule an appointment. He could have also expressed his concerns that his son was not being challenged and given the teacher a chance to modify her approach.

This case suggests that there was very poor communication between the school and parents. Did the school convey a commitment to parents that it would strive to meet the needs of all students? Did teachers receive in-service training to assist them to individualize their teaching methods in order to address each student's learning style? Did parents have regular meetings where they could learn about the school's approach and also about the progress of their own child?

Clearly the teacher wanted her students to do well, but it is unclear that she knew how to challenge her students, or how to modify her requirements according to each student's academic ability. The principal did not seem to be aware of how she could foster a better relationship with parents by demonstrating her commitment to helping teachers meet individual needs. And the parent did not know how to translate his "work with the public" into forming a collaborative relationship with the school, rather than a confrontational one. Only when teachers, administrators and parents find a way to work together can all their expectations about providing a quality education to each child be met.

CASE COMMENTARY 2

Kara Walsh

After years of teaching this educator has a "perfect class" of fourth grade students, all appearing to experience academic success. It appears that this teacher is challenging the students appropriately and is assessing and tracking their progress individually. It also appears that the majority of parents are happy and some are involved regularly in the classroom activities.

The professional judgment of the teacher to meet alone with Mr. Cross without inquiring into the purpose of the meeting is questionable. The teacher was prepared for a very positive meeting with Mr. Cross' but his demeanour at the meeting comes as a huge surprise to the teacher. Tom is experiencing success in the program and the teacher has this all documented in his personal math portfolio and with other forms of assessment. After the initial statement by Mr. Cross, the teacher should have asked Mr. Cross if they could reschedule this meeting for a time when the principal was available to discuss the matter further. At this point, neither side is prepared to hear the other. Emotions begin to cloud thinking. It appears that Mr. Cross has not been communicating his concerns with the teacher up to this point in the year. It also seems that the teacher has not had any direct contact with Mr. Cross up to this point to build a relationship with him. If there was a relationship, I think Mr. Cross would have felt comfortable to come and discuss this situation with the teacher earlier rather than let it come to the point of high frustration resulting in a rash decision to pull his child out of the classroom.

It seems there are many issues guiding Mr. Cross' decision to pull Tom from the class. Mr. Cross has a set of expectations for Tom's learning that he feels are not being met. He feels like his child is not being challenged enough. These expectations may not be age or developmentally appropriate for Tom at this point, however, he doesn't appear to have been told what is appropriate at this age. He also has a misconception of what homework should be – homework should be something that the child is familiar with and can have success with, not something that is extremely challenging and could potentially bring the child to the point of frustration. I wonder if this has been communicated with all of the parents at any point in the school year by the teacher.

The principal's response to the teacher's situation and concerns are a bit unnerving. Waiting for the parent to calm down is important however I do not think that waiting for the parent to come back to the school is the right move, especially since Tom will not be in school for however long Mr. Cross takes to calm down. My personal feeling is that a day to calm down is appropriate. It is important then to immediately contact the parent. This would show effort and concern on behalf of the teacher and the school. Setting up a time to meet and discuss the situation with the principal and possibly even another teacher at that grade level (or a resource teacher) would be a good next step. Addressing all of Mr. Cross' concerns is important. The teacher needs to have a prepared list of grade and developmentally appropriate outcomes (written in parent friendly language) and evidence of Tom's progress in relation to these outcomes. It is also important for the teacher to communicate the content of the homework assignments in terms of review material. Most importantly, it is important for Mr. Cross to feel like his concerns are being heard and for the school team to begin to meet his concerns. Follow-up communication must take place to monitor and continually reassess the situation so that it does not escalate again.

I would also want to have Tom talk with either the teacher or someone else on staff (maybe the guidance counselor) about how he feels about school, whether he feels like things are too easy or if there is something that is concerning him about the situation at school or at home. It may be appropriate to have a "Can do" folder of work that delves deeper into the grade level material (i.e. open-ended math problems on the same outcomes) that Tom can do to further challenge him, if this is decided as something that is appropriate and desired by all (including Tom).

This case is a "teacher's nightmare" in many ways. To be unprepared for a meeting with parents that does not go well can be avoided. Having been on the receiving end of this kind of meeting before (though much less dramatic) I have learned that communication of expectations and procedures upfront and providing progress reports continually throughout the year is key to positive parent-teacher relationships. Defusing the situation before it snowballs is the best way to prevent a situation like this from happening. Remaining calm and not becoming defensive is essential. Listening and problem solving with the parent will lead to a much more productive resolution.

CASE COMMENTARY 3

Angela AuCoin

As a school teacher, I came to understand the importance of involving my students' parents in their child's learning development. Although at first I was nervous and hesitant at how to keep them informed, the following practices made it easier to involve everyone and avoid unfortunate incidents.

To begin with, fostering a positive relationship with all parents as soon as possible is essential. Establish a rapport with them at the beginning of the school year is also very important. As a teacher, I would call the parents at the end of the summer vacation to introduce myself or shortly afterwards with a positive comment about their child. If behavioral or scholastic issues arose with a student later in the year it made it much easier to deal with the parents if that initial effort to connect with them had been made.

Using differentiated instruction helps teachers accommodate the different ways that students learn and enables us to become better teachers. In this case, effective planning and ongoing evaluation needs to be strengthened.

Sharing expectations with students and parents at the beginning of each unit is an effective pedagogical and communication strategy. This information enables parents to feel involved and informed about their child's learning. Parents are then empowered to support this learning at home.

Teachers will prevent misunderstandings and promote a positive learning experience for all by establishing a positive relationship with all parents by means of keeping them informed of their child's progress in relation to their educational outcomes.

CASE COMMENTARY 4

Catherine Montreuil

Today's classrooms are diverse places with a wide range of learners. Some students are strong students and are "demonstrating competency at the appropriate level" but may not be progressing at their potential. This difference in expectation seems to be at the base of the parent-teacher conflict in this scenario.

Commitment to helping every student reach his or her potential is fundamentally different from helping every student reach a level of competency. Assessment in the classroom needs to determine where students are achieving with respect to the curriculum or an Individual Education Plan. Teacher feedback needs to be timely, constructive and should help the student identify his or her next learning goal. Record keeping and providing ongoing feedback to the home are critical to ensure that communication is open, effective and supportive of student learning.

In this case, while the teacher is assured that she is doing all she can, we don't get a good sense of the data she has to establish her assertion that she has evidence that she is challenging Tom to work to his potential. The principal missed a valuable opportunity to review work samples, curriculum expectations, teacher feedback and record keeping. Had the principal done this with the teacher, they would have an evidence-based conclusion on which to plan. They would also have a collection of information and data to share with Tom's family. They would also be able to have a plan in place to share if their data reveals that Tom should be challenged more.

Finally, while conflict is often uncomfortable, it can also be an opportunity to review, reflect and make changes to professional practice.

CASE COMMENTARY 5

Denise Silverstone

Over the last decade more opportunities have emerged for parents to be involved in their children's education. In my own research on this topic, I have found numerous studies that demonstrate that learning improves when parents are involved in their child's education.

However, as evidenced by this case scenario, the teacher parent relationship can be a complicated one. Teachers may have certain expectations for individual students, and parents may have another. The teacher felt that the child, Tom, "demonstrated competency at the appropriate level" while the parent believed that Tom was not progressing and required more challenging work. The parent also stated that he didn't think the teacher was doing his/her job. It made me wonder whether this was the first time the teacher and parent had ever discussed Tom and his education.

Effective communication between teacher and parent is all about establishing a good relationship. Parents need information about what and how their child is learning, and the teacher needs important feedback from the parent about the child's academic and social development. It is important to remember that the focus of this relationship lies in the uniqueness of the individual student. Both teacher and parent have knowledge and experiences that – when brought together – can greatly benefit the child. Not surprisingly, research shows that the more parents and teachers share relevant information with each other about a student, the better equipped both will be to help that student reach his/her potential.

Personal contact between teacher and parent is essential in building an effective relationship. Today, teachers can be in touch with parents through a variety of different means including: parent conferences, phone calls, email, school website, parent-teacher organizations or school/parent councils, and weekly or monthly folders of student work sent home for parent review and comment, to name a few. Communicating with parents should be viewed not as a one-time event, but rather as an ongoing component in relationship-building. It should also be noted that sharing positive news of the child's accomplishments is just as important as discussing the challenges and obstacles.

There are three important elements in the situation that, I believe, provide valuable lessons to educators. The teacher needs to receive necessary support and guidance from the principal. The teacher also needs to engage in self-evaluation to ensure s/he is meeting the needs of all the students' needs. Lastly, the teacher needs to plans to work with the parent in a more strategic and effective manner.

CONNECTING TO PROFESSIONAL PRACTICE

The commentary writers highlight to the importance of establishing appropriate, regular and informative communication with parents regarding program expectations and achievement. They question the professional judgment and actions of both the teacher and the principal in this case. The importance of including the student in the resolution of issues is recommended by the commentary writers. Discuss how you might support a colleague or a principal in a similar situation.

CASE NINETEEN: PARENT FAITH IN SCHOOLS

I held the letter from the school in my hand and stared in disbelief. I was shocked at what I was reading.

Dear Mr. and Mrs. Kramer,

In consultation with the principal, Mr. Brook, it has been decided that if there are any questions as to the activities Kate is doing throughout the day or any other communication that you may want to have with Kate's teachers, resource teacher or teaching assistants that it would best occur during a pre-scheduled face-to-face meeting. The teaching assistant assigned to Kate will no longer be expected to send notes home on a daily basis.

It is not general practice in high school to write to a parent on a period or daily basis. If you have any concerns in the immediate future, we would encourage you to attend the Riverview's regular parent/teacher meetings scheduled for next week.

Sincerely
Mr. F. Lacey
Resource Teacher
Riverview Secondary School.

Kate is my daughter. She is a nonverbal and severely challenged child. Kate is now in high school. All through her elementary school years Kate had always had a daily log to let me know how her day went and what activities she took part in during her time at school. The daily log that we began her first year of school allowed me to be part of her school day. The log tells me if she has suddenly become sleepy, if her classmates have included her in math activities, identifies her successes and achievements for the day and outlines any challenges that I needed to be aware of as a parent. The log includes me in my non-verbal daughter's school and life. The log in many ways becomes a voice for Kate. The log shares with me all the details that my two other children are able to tell me as they bound through the door at the end of a busy school day and I ask them, "How was your day at school?"

But at high school, it seems that they do not want me to know what is going on with Kate. Could the answer be that no meaningful programming is going on and that Kate is not progressing? Could it be that Kate is being so difficult that the teachers are trying to avoid dealing with Kate and her family? Could it be that the teachers in high school don't understand how important daily written communication is for her family? Are we perceived to be meddling parents out to cause trouble at the school? All these questions and more run through my mind.

Her father and I have put so much faith in the teachers and principals that were part of Kate's life in elementary school. Several months before Kate left her middle school we had a meeting regarding Kate's transition to high school that included Mr. Lacey, the high school resource teacher. We reviewed her current individualized education plan and went over her programs that were in place and currently working in the middle school. We discussed what high school life would be like for Kate.

Mr. Lacey said that gym, music and art classes would be available. We all felt that she would be able to take part in these activities. He indicated that Kate's general physical needs would be addressed. We felt that Mr. Lacey did not provide many details about individualized programming but that the meeting seemed friendly and positive.

Although going to high school for any teen is a big step, I felt that as parents and educators we all should put an extra emphasis on preparing Kate for this important and significant transition. Likewise, the high school should also prepare and plan for our Kate.

Dan, Kate's dad, and I discussed this transition nightly. We would ask ourselves, "Have we forgotten anything?" We combed over the medical reports, past practices and successful strategies.

We even reread Kate's log, trying to ensure the move would be as successful as possible. I remember saying to Dan, "There will be a few bumps along the way, but I'm prepared to step up to the plate and help in order to make it easier for all concerned." He smiled, knowing that there would always be bumps - but that we would always do whatever we could to support Kate and the school. This had proven to a successful approach during Kate's elementary years. The teachers knew that they could always count on us for anything.

I recalled when Kate first went to kindergarten. "Dan, do you remember how hard it was to trust someone with our special child?" He nodded and we shared a smile. "Yes", he added, "we were green behind ears. We had no idea what to expect from the school system - or what the system expected from us. It was difficult at first but we adapted. The school and teachers adapted as well."

My thoughts returned to our daughter and Kate's transition from her first school to her new middle school. "Dan, do you recall that we were so concerned that we choose to hold her back an extra year. In the end, middle school was the best three years Kate had in school." We exchanged a smile. These were positive memories.

Kate's high school is located just a block away from Kate's middle school. There is a school population of about 1300 students. Riverview is the same school that I had once attended and had graduated from more than 20 years earlier. In some ways it was comforting to me to know the layout of the school, the location of the library and the slope of the entrance where Kate would push her wheelchair.

It was stressful meeting all Kate's new teachers, entering unfamiliar surroundings, planning for different routines and anticipating the resource teacher's expectations. Always ready to help out and work in Kate's best interests, I went with Kate on her first day to high school. I thought that it would be helpful if I offered to assist the teacher assistant or the teachers in addressing any of Kate's basic needs. I could also reassure any of the school staff members who had concerns about accepting Kate into their classrooms.

What an eye opener that first day was for me. I had forgotten what high school life was like. I suddenly felt old and out of touch as the students brushed by me. Some openly stared at me, making me feel even more out of place. A few of them even snickered as I passed by.

I walked into Kate's morning classroom. "Hello, I'm Mrs. Kramer, Kate's mother." I told the teachers and two teaching assistants a bit about Kate and said that, "Since it was almost lunchtime, I could stay for awhile and help Kate to eat." I wanted to support the staff - but in a way that did not interfere with their work. I believed that an extra helping hand was always useful.

At Kate's middle school, the teaching assistant and teachers greeted me warmly and I really did feel as if I was part of the team. I could sense already that the situation was different at Riverview. I could feel a tension in the room as soon as I had walked in. The teacher and teacher assistants were polite but did not talk to me while I was with Kate. They even seemed to be avoiding making any eye contact with me during the hour that I spent in the room.

The following week, I had thought that routines might have been established. I made the trip back to Riverview. This time I thought that I could help in setting up some of Kate's program work.

I knew there was a lot of material in her file explaining about Kate's specialized program. I also knew it explained about her vision and why things were done the way they were. I felt that reading this information and applying it were quite different. I knew this from personal experience. I did not claim to be an expert in these fields. I thought that, with my help, at least the school could get started on Kate's individualized educational plan.

It would be several weeks before the resource staff with expertise in Kate's area could get into the high school. Kate would become bored waiting. I wanted to help the staff make the transition for Kate. At the same time, I tried hard not to alienate the teachers. I wanted to work in the best way possible to support Kate in this new school and with her new teachers. I wanted to be part of the team.

The resource teacher, Mr. Lacey, was responsible for many individualized educational programs and students. He did not seem to have the time or the knowledge to get Kate's specialized programs up and running. I spent several hours with the teaching assistants, talking about the resources that Kate had used in the past and the how's and why's of the different programs. I felt, as did the teaching assistants, that the basic work could get started and Kate's day could become much busier. I also reminded them that a brief note describing Kate's day and any questions that they had would really be welcomed. I would do my best to help.

I felt as if things were shaping up. Kate was settling into her new surroundings and the assistants and teachers were becoming familiar with Kate. It was hard to know for sure though because I was not receiving any information on how Kate's day-to-day experiences and accomplishments were going. There were very few questions being asked. I assumed that all was going great.

It was about the third week of school and I decided that I would drop in to the school and offer further assistance. I could also see how Kate was doing in her new setting. The lack of information coming home was beginning to make me nervous. I wondered, how much in-class time was Kate experiencing? Were any of former classmates from her middle school in her new classes? Were the teachers and teaching assistants having any problems?

When I arrived at school it was nutrition break and I found Kate in the resource room having her snack. She was with a large group of students with special needs. I asked the teaching assistant. "How much time does Kate spend here in the resource room?" She responded, "About 90%." My facial expression must have showed my horror. I thought that she was taking part in gym, music and art classes. I also thought that she was attending homeroom and being included in other classes. I thought she was working on her individualized learning program on a daily basis.

Later that day, I called Mr. Lacey and asked, "When can we have a meeting? We need to be on the same page here." I spoke calmly and tried to convey my concern without sounding angry or hysterical. I just wanted to help fix any mis-understandings there were about Kate's program. Kate's father and I wanted high school life to be rewarding for her. We wanted her to be part of school life and to be accepted by the students and teachers at Riverview. It was not about us. It was not about blaming anyone. We were just advocating for our daughter, Kate.

A week later, my husband and I were sitting with Kate's teachers and resource team once again discussing Kate's individualized program. We talked about the appropriate classes she could attend. We talked about program work that the pro-vincial education authority had set up. We talked about Kate socializing with her peers and reconnecting with former friends from her days at middle school. We talked about appropriate resources. We talked about communication between the school and home and why, because Kate is non-verbal, that is was so important that I know what was happening at school. I also offered the school any help that I could provide. All they had to do was ask.

By mid November, I was beginning to think that high school was a mistake. Perhaps Kate should have stayed in middle school. At the middle school Kate had friends, went to classes, attended assemblies, and even sock hops. She was a social butterfly. All of the students and teachers knew her.

I asked Dan, "How can we fix this problem?" We still believed that things could be worked out. We waited a bit longer. The next three or four weeks seemed to improve somewhat. There was some communication back and forth. Questions were being asked about Kate's individualized program. The names of her peers were being mentioned. We relaxed a little.

After Christmas break, I decided to check on Kate's progress for myself. Commu-nication with us seemed to have stopped. Perhaps there was a problem. I knew that Kate could not tell me herself about any problems. I went to the school and spoke to one of the teaching assistants. Kate again was spending most of her day in the resource room. She rarely attended gym or art classes. She did not go to her home-room class. It was located on the second floor and there was no elevator to transport her chair. Kate's school world had shrunk to the four walls of the resource room. My husband and I were shocked and disappointed.

We scheduled another meeting. The school indicated that the meeting would need to take place at the end of January. Teachers were busy preparing for exams.

We waited. Should we have kept Kate at her middle school? Could she return after attending Riverview for nearly five months? These questions and many more ran through our minds.

The meeting finally took place. We told the group that we needed to know what was happening with Kate at school. "How hard was it to take Kate to her classes and let her participate in any way she could? What about socialization with her peers? What about being included in high school life? What about Kate and her needs?"

I wanted to scream in frustration. Why didn't these people do anything for Kate? How could they not understand Kate's needs? I dreaded sitting at this round table with twelve individuals: teachers, administrators, and caseworkers. It felt like it was twelve against two. They shuffled papers, quoted reports, looked at the clock, whispered quietly to one another and never really tried to provide answers to our questions or address our concerns. We felt like we were being bullied. We felt like these educators believed that we were wrong. We felt unheard.

I knew that we needed help. We called the provincial Association for Community Living and told them our story, our concerns and what we felt we wanted. They told us we were not being unreasonable as we were asking only for Kate's rights to be respected and that she was entitled to an inclusive education.

We met with the school again. All those in attendance at the meeting agreed Kate would attend classes. She would participate and her program would be followed. Perhaps this time it would really happen.

In April, doubt, once again, set in. Very little communication was coming home. Were more exclusion and lack of class activity Kate's reality? I was confident if I broke down Kate's day into class periods and asked what she did in these time slots that it would give us a better idea of what Kate was accomplishing at school. I phoned the school and asked for this information and offered to provide a copy of a class period chart that the teachers could use.

My response was the letter from Mr. Lacey.

PROFESSIONAL INQUIRY

Commitment to Inclusion

– Discuss the commitment of the parents towards inclusive education.
– Explore the extent to which the school was committed to inclusion.
– Consider Kate's perspective regarding inclusion and her possible responses to the programming that the school was providing.
– Generate recommendations for making the Individual Education Plan a living and meaningful document for all involved.

Parent Involvement

– Critique the school's actions related to parent involvement in this case.
– Discuss the communication methods employed by the school.
– Analyze the meetings that took place between the parents and the school.
– Reflect on this case from the perspective of an advocate for Kate and her parents.

Challenges and Barriers to Inclusion

- Identify the challenges and barriers to inclusion that exist within this case.
- Explore the purpose and implications of Mr. Lacey's letter to the parents.

CASE COMMENTARY REFLECTIONS

After reading the commentaries reflect on the following:

New Insights
Identify new insights gained from reading the commentaries.

Understandings
Discuss the impact of the commentaries on your understandings of inclusive education.

Questions
Identify questions that emerge for you from reading the commentaries.

CASE COMMENTARY 1

Diana Carr

Effective school and home communication can be the cornerstone of a strong and enduring relationship. After receiving such a letter why should the parents have faith in their daughter's school? The parents have done their part and the school has not, they have "dropped the ball" on the obligation to provide Kate with an education.

A number of key issues emerge, such as the lack of inclusion in an inclusive school setting, members not working as a team, poor implementation of the Individual Education Plan and ineffective communication. In my experience, if communication is established effectively it becomes a valuable tool that will support all the other areas of need in Kate's school life.

Establishing a form of communication right from the first meeting does elevate many issues and challenges. All involved need to agree on the format, how to use it and to have it indicated in the Individual Education Plan. A communication book becomes a voice for the student, parents and school. Kate's right to communicate has been ignored. Doesn't the family have the right to information regarding Kate's daily progress? This communication becomes a record to support the Individual Education Plan, show what the school is doing and by involving the student it can become a learning tool, as there are many interactive models available. A communication book keeps parents part of the team while allowing them to know of Kate's daily interactions and activities. Exchange of information from home, such a change of routine, a new skill acquired or a favourite event, can affect behaviour at school. Once consistent, a communication tool can save time, since when all parties are "on board", there is less time required for phone calls, notes and face-to-face meetings.

Through home and school communication, all members of the team can participate and be accountable for the successful inclusion of the student and implementation of the Individual Education Plan. When a school team commits time and effort to plan an Individual Education Plan it is a waste not to use it. If the plan is not effective then team needs to collectively re-examine the process. Parents are part of the process, inclusion means to include all. Adults' sitting around a table does not constitute a team. Working together makes a team and it takes a team to support a child with special needs. The school has a team in place that could be used more effectively without adding a burden of time. Kate faces daily challenges and needs an advocate. She should be able to count on her parents as well as the school for this.

CASE COMMENTARY 2

Inés Elvira B. de Escallon

The meetings for the transition are fundamental in the series of events that follow in the school year. Kate's parents wanted to be give the information regarding their child. Mr. Lacey failed to explain thoroughly how the school planned to work with Kate. As a result, school started with every one having a different idea of what to expect.

Communication between parents and the school personal (principal, teachers, teaching assistants) is a process that takes time and requires trust. Well intentioned, knowledgeable parents might challenge some teachers in relation to their practices, skills and knowledge.

Parents' participation in secondary schools is very different from the way it is done in primary/middle schools. Parents of adolescents are less aware and know little of what is going on at the school. The system then has been built from many assumptions of communication between teachers, students and parents at this level.

A student with significant educational needs requires educators who are know-ledgeable, skilled, flexible and collaborative. Everyone involved has to be committed to working together. To listen, respect and include one another.

As all partners work together they will be able to design the right balance of information sharing to respond to the needs of parents in knowing what is happening in the school, ways they can support their son or daughter and the teachers when needed. Parents have to balance giving time and space for teachers to understand their child's needs and at the same time be vigilant of their child's schooling. Only through building communication channels will the school and parents be able to work effectively together. Parents will be able to trust the school when their voices, vision and expertise are genuinely included and heard. Quality inclusive education that has high expectations for every student is achievable when collaboration, communication and exemplary programming is in place.

CASE COMMENTARY 3

Miguel A. Verdugo

When attitudes of teachers and other school staff towards special needs students are negative, nothing works well. The first point in school, and social inclusion, is to change the model of thinking; that is, the way people think about students and persons with disabilities. Continuous education for all involved is a commitment that schools need to embrace. Inclusion will not occur unless collaboration, communication, effective planning, individualized programming and enabling practices are consistently employed by all involved.

The rights of students with disabilities need to be understood, recognized and honored in every school. Mothers and fathers who are working towards the acknowledgement and respect for the rights of their child to an inclusive education must be respected and invited to be full participants in the educative process. Their voice must be heard regarding access issues, policies, protocols, programming and resource support.

CASE COMMENTARY 4

Sarah Elizabeth Barrett

This is a case in which the goals of the parents for their child and the goals of the institution seem to be at cross purposes. Kate's education goals are purely social. The high school's education goals for students are essentially academic with, arguably, social concerns addressed only when they get in the way of the academic.

As a teacher, there were many times when the Individual Education Plan seemed to demand more time and expertise than I felt I could spare in light of the needs of my other students. I also recall the ways in which we teachers often viewed and labeled parents: the Meddler and the Absentee, for example. A partnership between parent(s), teachers and the school is essential for a student with special needs to be successfully integrated into a regular classroom. In Kate's case, no real partnership seems to exist. Kate's mother has been labeled a Meddler and is now being managed. How did it come to this?

In the high school in which I taught, there were two classes of students who were developmentally delayed. We were proud of the fact that they ate in the cafeteria with the rest of the student body and had student mentors visit their classrooms. Many had friends outside of the class. I suspect, however, that the author of this case would not consider this to be a satisfactory level of inclusivity. Our perspectives regarding inclusion are not the same.

Kate's situation requires more honesty on the part of the school in their dealings with Kate's parents and more understanding on the part of Kate's parents on differences in priorities between elementary and secondary schools. Kate's parents are the experts on Kate and the school staff and administrators are the experts on the school's resources and routines. Neither can help Kate to realize her social goals without the other.

The central question is who decides what accommodations are reasonable? Also, how can the parents' expertise be integrated into the school system in a way that feels comfortable for all involved?

Once characterized as a Meddler, a parent faces an uphill battle when dealing with school staff. In order to improve the situation, Kate's mother needs to understand how Kate's case looks from the school's perspective. Also, the school staff and administration need to shift away from managing Kate's parents to working with them in making the system and its limited resources work for Kate and her social goals.

CONNECTING TO PROFESSIONAL PRACTICE

Communication and collaboration with parents are the main issues raised by the commentary writers in this case. The commentary writers also have differing views of inclusion. Analyze and critique the different perspectives of the commentary writers regarding inclusion.

Reflect on this case from the perspectives of the following individuals: *the school -principal, teaching assistant(s), classroom teachers, director of education and members of the public.* Generate recommendations for professional practice that reflect the ethical and professional responsibilities of educators and that honor the rights, dignity and goals of both the learner and the parents.

CASE TWENTY: IT WAS A MEMORABLE DAY IN OUR FAMILY

After years of struggle, negotiations, and support, Julián was finishing his elementary school at the Gimnasio Campestre in Bogotá. It was a good school. We had managed to make many difficult things happen.

In the 12 years since he was born, we had achieved the unthinkable. A private school accepted the challenge and worked with us and other professionals to provide an inclusive education for Julián. We had managed to support him, his peers and his teachers on the journey. We worked through good and not so good times. Graduation from the school was certainly something to celebrate.

When Julián was born, expectations for him were low. Gloomy attitudes could be felt from everyone around us and we knew that opportunities for Julián were few and not always the best. However through hard work and by working as a family, we had managed to create a dream and vision for Julián - a dream full of hope and expectations.

As I reflect back on my memories of that last day of elementary school for Julián, I think of the school ceremony we went to take part in. My husband, my daughter and my sister joined me at Julián's school to share this milestone with him. We were anticipating it as a day to remember.

After a brief general assembly for all the children in the school, the families were asked to go to the classrooms where the students would get their final reports for the year. So we joined other families as we strolled through the hallways to Julián's classroom. We mingled with his classmates and their parents and sat down for what was going to be one of the great moments in our lives – for Julián and his family. We were all anticipating this occasion.

We had made it to this moment and it seemed many times that we had to travel a long and rocky road to get here. Our hard work led us to the firm conviction that Julián's place was here with his classmates. The classmates and teachers he had spent 7 years with.

We knew that our next challenge would be secondary school. However, we had a sense of confidence that we were going to succeed. We were going to continue to use an inclusive approach in the high school just like in this school - educating all kids together. We could think back on efforts thus far and see them as investments that paid off by bringing us to this moment. There had been struggles, happy times, challenging times and not so happy moments, but my overall feeling was of a tough job well done – with good results.

Little did we know that our sense of accomplishment was not there to stay. We sat in the classroom and heard the teacher call the names of each of the students in the class. We watched as each student received their report card. Warm and distinct compliments were expressed for each student by the teacher. Soon it was winding down and we realized that Julián was not going to be called.

I was confused. I didn't understand what was happening. My heart broke for him and – to be honest - for myself. What was going on? How did they forget Julian? How was he feeling? How should I react?

All these things went through my mind in seconds, but, as always in good or bad times, my initial concern was for Julián and his feelings. I knew I did not want him to be emotionally hurt. So immediately, I went over to his side and assured him that there was some mistake. I told him I would find out what happened.

He trusted me so much that he waited on his chair for things to happen and I needed them to happen right for him. I went to the teacher and asked her what happened? She very matter-of-factly explained that Julián was going to receive his report card from the elementary school director in her office; they thought doing it that way would be "special" for him and that we – his parents – and Julián would like it better that way.

When I heard this I found it hard to believe she could think such a thing. I must confess I was outraged. I remember bursting out in tears from frustration and hurt. It was almost the same as the crying I did that first day when we were given the news that Julian had Down's syndrome.

How could the school think that this was the best way to recognize Julián's success at school? Were they serious in considering this to be educational "best practice"?

I thought it was amazing that after 7 years of working with my son, they still did not get it. They did not understand the simple things we want for Julián. Never mind the philosophy of what inclusion is about and what it should look like in a school in terms of instruction and learning and more. We wanted and want our son to be treated like other students and to do things with them. It's as simple as that.

The teacher and some of the other parents were clearly wondering why I was so annoyed. The teacher spoke to the elementary school director and she too was surprised that I was so upset. Why did it matter so much where Julián received his report card – and besides the director was of a higher rank than the teacher!

Despite my frustration and anger I managed to tell them why it was upsetting. I explained what their actions meant for Julián and for us as a family.

We explained that we wanted Julián to be part of the community. We wanted him to feel like just like his classmates and his friends. We explained that it was being part of the ordinary things in school and at home that made our son belong. I had thought the teachers and the school understood this and that they shared our common sense approach to inclusion. "Inclusion" means everyone doing things together – doesn't it?

That day I had to start explaining again to all of them what inclusion is and what it should look like. What a set back! I felt so frustrated and wondered if we would ever see change.

As I talked on about how I felt, the teacher and the other school staff seemed to come to understood why I was so upset. I think they even accepted that I was right to be upset and disappointed. They quickly scurried around and brought some of Julián's friends and their parents into the room so he could receive his report card with them present.

I should say that for Julián it was a very happy moment in his life, which he will always remember as a great day. As for me, I have to say that it made me realize that inclusion was not fully in place; that much work still needed to be done. I knew then that I had to persevere and keep up the struggle.

As it turns out, inclusion for Julián was, is and will be - a struggle for many years to come, until *EVERYONE GETS IT.*

Today Julián is older. Our struggles are different but they continue. They seem to be unending some days. We are now at the stage where we are looking for job opportunities for him. He is a young adult and we think he has proven that he is very able. But he seems to have to continuously prove it to others – again and again. We have to work hard to see that opportunities become available to him.

We won't give up. And the main reason is that Julián has never given up. As his family, we all have a responsibility to make sure he has the opportunities to participate in his own unique way. That's what inclusion is all about.

PROFESSIONAL INQUIRY

Inclusion

- Discuss the different understandings of inclusion held by the parent(s) and the school.
- Critique the planning process used by the school for the graduation ceremony and identify the implications of this process for inclusion.
- Identify and discuss the implications of the different assumptions held by the school staff, the parents and Julian for the graduation.

Communication

- Discuss the importance of ongoing and specific communication with parents in supporting effective inclusion.
- Identify strategies that could be employed to prevent the situation that occurred in this case.

Advocacy

- Discuss the advocacy role of the parent(s) in this case.
- Identify important dimensions associated with effective advocacy.
- Explore the challenges associated with parent advocacy.

CASE COMMENTARY REFLECTIONS

After reading the commentaries reflect on the following:

New Insights
Identify new insights gained from reading the commentaries.

Understandings
Discuss the impact of the commentaries on your understandings of inclusive education.

Questions
Identify questions that emerge for you from reading the commentaries.

CASE COMMENTARY 1

Dr. Jude MacArthur

This case provides a graphic example of the way in which inclusion can mean different things to different people in different contexts. It also illustrates how, in working towards inclusion, schools need to consult with students, parents and their community, be reflexive, and continuously question the values and structures that exclude some people.

Julian's family had 'created a dream and vision' for him as a fully participating and valued member of his school and community. Consistent with this dream, Julian's school had worked with his parents and other professionals to provide him with an inclusive education, and while there had been both high and low moments, Julian's parents had reached his graduation with a strong sense that his place was 'here with his classmates'. But they were badly let down when Julian was excluded from this significant cultural event.

For Julian's parents, the teacher's actions were evidence that despite 7 years of hard work and much progress, the school still 'did not get it' when it came to the 'simple things' they valued, such as all children being and doing things *together*. Julian's wish to be treated like other children and to do things with them' is very consistent with the preferences of children and young people with disabilities who have participated in our own ethnographic research. Students emphasized that they wanted to be part of the group of all children and young people at school. They disliked being separated out into 'special' groups, and being treated differently because they had a disability. These actions made them feel 'different' in negative ways, and they asked to be included and valued in all classes and in all activities alongside their peers. While Julian's teachers were well meaning in devising a 'special' arrangement for him to receive his graduation certificate, their actions might also reflect their own underlying construction of Julian as 'separate and different' from his classmates.

The tragedy for Julian and his parents is that, despite a long relationship, the school did not fully understand the family's 'common sense' approach to inclusion, and their appreciation of the 'ordinary things' that would support Julian's sense of belonging. The story illustrates the importance of schools developing inclusive values with their school community such as equity, participation, respect for diversity and having ongoing opportunities to talk with parents and students about how these values can be translated into school practices that promote belonging and partici-pation for all children and young people.

CASE COMMENTARY 2

Diane Richler

This case shows how successful parents can be in promoting the inclusion of their children in regular classes, but it also demonstrates the challenges and limitations of such an approach.

When one child is included in a school, and especially if that child is the first to be included, that child's parents assume total responsibility for addressing any school practices that may inhibit inclusion, as well as for ensuring that their own child has a successful educational experience. This means that the parents must deal with both the school administration, and the teacher – on their own. Usually in such situations, if the teacher is positive, most issues can be resolved at the classroom level. However, this also means that if there are challenges, the teacher has few resources to draw on, except for guidance from the school administration, which is usually limited if the administration has not experienced inclusion before.

Every step is new for each teacher in the school that has the student in the classroom. In the case of most elementary schools, the parents must go thought the process of developing a working relationship with a new teacher each year. In schools that do not have a systemic commitment to inclusion, it is unlikely that many resources are devoted to full inclusion. These include in-service education, problem solving teams and systematic reviews of school practices.

The "surprise" faced by Julian and his family on graduation day might have been avoided if there had been more frequent and open communication between the parents and the school. The school should have been aware that if they were preparing to treat Julian differently from the other students, that his parents needed to be consulted in advance, and a mutually agreed upon decision made.

This story reinforces the knowledge and experiences that many parents share about the continuous struggle for inclusion. Parents want to celebrate in the accomplishments of their sons and daughters, but each new stage of life brings new challenges, and all too often, inclusion does not happen without a lot of work and commitment.

CASE COMMENTARY 3

Alicia de la Peña Rode

Inclusive schools must engage in a process of mutual sharing of the dreams related to each child. This communication is essential to enable parents, students and teachers to work together towards the same goals with similar understandings. All of these partners must be actively involved in the planning and organization of the educational program. It is also important to focus on the participation of classmates as they are necessary in promoting a caring and inclusive environment. The involvement of students, teachers and families together can help support the joys and successes found within an inclusive school community.

Unfortunately, the story of Julian is an all too familiar narrative that occurs in schools across the world. Inclusion is a learning process for all involved. It requires a belief in equity, justice and community. It also requires a deep commitment to actions that honor and respect the dignity and contribution of all members of society. Families trying to promote inclusion need to be optimistic and realistic at the same time. A mistake doesn't mean that the school is not adequate, and should not affect the total process.

Parents need to contemplate the experiences of their child with both patience and perseverance. They have a right to ongoing involvement, communication and being included in the decision making processes related to their child.

This case helps to remind school personnel of the importance of engaging in a process of continuous planning with parents. Communication is the key to building an inclusive system that has the potential to transform social consciousness related to learning.

CASE COMMENTARY 4

Bernhard Schmid

The story of my own seventeen year old son Alexander with Down-Syndrome is also not a continuous success story of inclusion. It is rather a ongoing story of raising of awareness, creative interventions, patience and negotiations. There have been a few outstanding teachers and caretakers that helped to create an environment of inclusion in both the school and the community.

Due to limited communication skills it is very hard for Alex to make and keep friends. This is very difficult for him. His feelings and desires are the same as all others of his age. For many years, the children of our friends were his active friends. However, with increasing age and different interests these friends are no longer part of his social network.

In school, there are also no real friends for him, as there is no time scheduled for common activities within the school community where he could develop social bonds. The main "social life" takes place within the family. We are always searching for new friends for Alex. We look for young adults with similar needs within our networks or in organizations for common sports or cultural activities (horse-riding, swimming, dancing).

Julian's family also seems to be a very caring, loving and supportive family. In addition, they are very ambitious to teach the community to take over its responsibility for Julian: to pay attention to him, to interact with him, to appreciate his personality with all his gifts and challenges.

Parents like them are crucial for promoting a commitment to inclusion. Unfortunately, not all parents have the skills and the endurance to always struggle and be active advocates for inclusion. Families want their children and siblings to be accepted in open environments that enable full participation and inclusion. For families that do not want or cannot take on the very difficult role of being advocates for inclusion, I would suggest that they try and educate one person at a time. Do not aim at changing the system! System change is often very slow.

Aim at changing the mind of just one person that is currently in touch with you and your son or daughter! Finding a compromise is sometimes better than to endlessly chase a high-level-target in vain! Be satisfied with small steps of success, but keep the big "vision" of an inclusive society always in mind!

CASE COMMENTARY 5

Maribel Alves Fierro Sevilla

This case reminds us of how challenging is to build an inclusive school community. Communities are diverse and promoting inclusion implies recognizing that we are all different in one way or another, at a specific period of time or under certain circumstances.

Julián's case exemplifies this issue by telling us about the steady work of understanding inclusion and special needs at the school. It shows us the barriers that can exist in schools. It reinforces the concepts of community that parents and children desire. In this case, the graduation ceremony reported to us represented all that was accomplished in the long journey that Julian and his family had gone through to promote inclusion in his school community: a truly steady work of patience and determination.

They overcame the barriers for learning and built a sense of belonging. Unfortunately, all seemed to be ruined when segregation was still a choice for the school administrators during the graduation ceremony. The school administrators did not understand that Julián's success could be addressed in the same manner as the success of the other students. This case illustrates why inclusive schools are so important. It is in school where we learn to understand differences and to be able to deal with it comfortably, without prejudice. Inclusion has to take place in an authentic way at school, because inclusion is about all of us. Inclusion is about living together in a just, equitable and accessible world. Schools can help us to respect and embrace difference without prejudice.

We might be searching for the consolidation of a common value and a collective identity that recognizes and integrates several demands and needs of the population. Only by building them up, will we be able to move toward more peaceful and happier lives with the predominance of democratic interests over segregation. Inclusion educates citizens to live together understanding differences in individual needs and to promote harmonic confidence instead of fear.

CONNECTING TO PROFESSIONAL PRACTICE

The commentary writers seem to deeply understand and relate to the issues and experiences depicted in this case. Consider the statements in the commentaries that refer to building inclusive school communities based on principles of democracy, equity, diversity and justice. Discuss how the case commentaries can inform your own understandings of inclusion related to these principles. Identify the insights you gained from the case and the commentaries. Explore the implications of these insights for your own professional practice and beliefs.

CASE TWENTY ONE: EDUCATING EMILY

Sending my daughter to school at the age of three seemed like a good idea when she was one and two. When she turned three and the reality of school loomed nearer, the idea lost some of its appeal.

By the time Emily was one year old, I was already talking to the principal, telling him that Emily would be coming to the school, and discussing our options. I offered to talk to the staff about Emily and her learning needs as we understood them. I thought it would be good to talk to all of the staff because, in a small school every teacher would be in contact with Emily in one way or another, even if it was only during recess supervision. This school, with two hundred students from kindergarten to grade twelve, seemed ideal for Emily. The principal's response to my offer was "Oh no, that won't be necessary. We have dealt with lots of students with special needs so we know what we are doing."

Early entrance into school or day care became viable options as Emily has Down syndrome. Our town has no day care facilities so we could have had Emily taxied to the next town to attend day care. However, we decided to send her to school. Here, we rationalized she could learn the routine of the school in addition to modeling the behaviour and speech of the older children. Besides, having her three older sisters at the same school offered us some consolation in the fact that they could be looking out for her small blond ponytail throughout the day.

Emily's birthday is in January so she began school after the winter break in February. At her first of three kindergarten graduations, Emily sat in the back corner, tumbling out of her red chair more often than she was sitting upright. The teacher did not correct her or ensure that she was participating. Every child in the class had an opportunity to demonstrate a skill they had learned over the year – some kids wrote the numbers one to ten on an easel, others recited short poems. Emily did not participate. She was always last to receive her diploma and graduation T-shirt. Even though Emily's last name is near the end of the alphabet, the rest of the children received their items in a random order. Somehow, Emily always held the last position.

After a sleepless night, I went to talk to the teacher. When I asked why Emily did not get to demonstrate a skill like the other children, her reply was "I forgot." She had forgotten to include Emily in kindergarten graduation. Her teacher was not only the kindergarten teacher but also the resource teacher in our school.

The next year was not much better. As the children were preparing for graduation again, Emily was not forgotten. However, when I suggested that it might be advantageous for Emily to practice their performance songs in a small group at a slower pace, her teacher obviously did not agree. She told me that if it was her child that was asked to participate in the small group, she "wouldn't want him to be held back academically to help some other child". I replied to the teacher's response by explaining that when peers help a classmate with or without a disability, they learn compassion when they get the opportunity to help a friend.

Each year in Emily's school life has brought a new teacher, a new attitude, and a new understanding of the meaning of inclusive education. Classroom teachers need to take responsibility for all the children in their classroom. In grade three, the educational assistant had to explain to one of Emily's teachers how to plan ahead and adapt a lesson plan to include Emily in classroom activities. In grade one, two and three, Emily sat most often in the back of the classroom with her assistant right beside her. In grade four, Emily was moved to the front of the row because we obtained a note from her optometrist requesting this. Emily's teachers seemed reluctant to use peers as a teaching resource. No child wants to listen to adults constantly telling her what she can do, and, more often, can't do.

Emily's behaviour, depending on who interprets it, has gotten her in trouble over the years. In grade one, Emily chose swearing as her way of receiving attention. This was an especially unfortunate choice as her teacher happened to be a nun! The note that I received from school insisted that she could not continue swearing at school. The school suggested putting numbing cream on Emily's tongue (like parents use for teething babies) every time she swore. I talked to a psychologist. Phone consultations between ourselves and the school, as well as a educative session for the school staff, remedied the problem. I paid the entire $3,000 bill.

Emily's behaviour is seen as defiant when she gets angry or throws pencils when she is taken out of the classroom to go to a resource room sessions. Emily's attitude is never viewed as what it truly is – a reaction to being taken out of the classroom and away from her peers. Emily notices when she is being treated different. Her classmates notice, too.

In grade four, the classroom teacher was unsure of his role with Emily and with the educational assistant. At the onset of the year, the comment to the educational assistant was: "Since you've been hired to work full-time with Emily, I'll let you take care of it." "It" was her entire grade four education. This became most evident when she did not participate in the first novel study her classmates were required to read. Emily did not even get a copy of the book. I was not informed that the class was reading the novel. She also did not get a grade four math textbook. It was after Christmas before Emily got the book and only because I became aware of the situation and had to ask for the textbook several times.

We were able to access speech therapy through the school, but the focus was on articulation rather than building the language aspect of Emily's program. The 45 schools in our school district were served by one occupational therapist. Emily was ten before she had an initial consultation. To compensate for the inadequacies of the school district, we have been using and purchasing services outside of our province for many years. In addition to speech therapy, reading, and occupational therapy consultations, we connected with outreach services. Whenever we used these services, my husband and I felt supported as members of Emily's learning team because we were totally included in these processes.

As we approach the end of grade four, one of Emily's teachers for next year has already contacted me and asked questions regarding inclusive education. This is encouraging, but now I feel pressured to come up with ways to prevent failure. Because there isn't a good model of inclusive education to follow at our school, I feel like the teacher is relying on me instead of all members of Emily's learning team for strategies for adapting lessons and including Emily in the classroom. I want to be part of the team, but I don't have all the answers.

Our family has struggled throughout Emily's seven years in school. I spend a lot of time researching, learning and understanding Emily so that I can give her the best chance for independence and fulfillment in the future. We have three other children, but I am not able to devote as much time to them as I would like. We have invested thousands of dollars in Emily's education. We travelled to access services. We attended as many conferences and workshops as we could to stay up to date with information. Helping our child has been a priority in our lives.

I have always felt that our school district places too much emphasis on the process (*i.e.*, paperwork) rather than on the implementation of services at the grass-roots level. Classroom teachers don't receive the skills or support to deal with the diversity in their classrooms. School administrators tell us that they believe in inclusive education, but I don't believe they understand what that entails.

It is frustrating to battle year after year. My biggest fear is that Emily will follow the same path as the older children in our school with special needs – swimming every Wednesday afternoon, sorting the recycling, getting the mail, handing out milk for the milk program, and washing dishes in the staff room. Our expectations and goals for Emily go beyond these kinds of tasks.

To parents that have children with special needs entering the school system, my advice would be to stay involved at every stage of your child's school career. Learn the process and take nothing for granted. If one year is good, there are no guarantees that the following year will be successful.

Do your own research. Ask questions. Know your rights as parents.

And most important, never give up on what you believe your child can be and accomplish. We're not sure where Emily's journey will end, but we will persevere!

PROFESSIONAL INQUIRY

Values and Assumptions

- Identify what this case reveals about how schools and society value students with diverse needs.
- Analyze the values and assumptions held by the educators in this case.

Inclusive Education

- Describe what it means to you to be an inclusive educator.
- Discuss what this case reveals about the status of students with diverse needs.
- Explore and discuss the superficiality of inclusive education policy and practice that exists in many schools.
- Describe what inclusive pedagogy might have looked like in this case.
- Discuss the possible impact a principal committed to and knowledgeable about inclusive education might have upon Emily's education.

Parental Involvement

- Identify lessons that can be learned from the way Emily's mother approaches preparing the school and classroom teachers for Emily's education.
- Explore how parents might use their knowledge and passion to move inclusion beyond paperwork to educational work.

Teacher Education

- Explore the purpose of teacher education from the perspective of inclusive education.
- Describe what an inclusive teacher education might look like.
- Discuss how teacher education can build upon the skills, knowledge, understandings and dispositions required of teachers to educate all children.
- Identify professional learning experiences that may have supported the educators in this case towards acquiring a deeper understanding of the development of the necessary skills for creating inclusive educational environments.

CASE COMMENTARY REFLECTIONS

After reading the commentaries reflect on the following:

New Insights
Identify new insights gained from reading the commentaries.

Understandings
Discuss the impact of the commentaries on your understandings of inclusive education.

Questions
Identify questions that emerge for you from reading the commentaries.

CASE COMMENTARY 1

Roger Slee

Emily's story reminds me of the vulnerability of people with Down Syndrome in a world determined to consign them to history. Shielded by the clinical distance of scientific medical screening, we fail to recognize the resurgence of old fashioned eugenics. The reference to Emily by her teacher as "IT", demonstrates the way in which people with disabilities are shunned and depersonalized. This depersonalization goes unnoticed even though such expressions are felt like a plunging dagger in the heart of loved ones. Emily's mother's reflection on her daughter's journey through schooling is a story of pain and triumph in a world that cannot live up to the values it espouses. Once again, we are reminded that inclusion is reserved for some not all; that democracy means the participation of some not all.

We can draw useful lessons from this case study. Emily reminds us of the ground we need to cover before we can claim that our schools are staffed with inclusive educators. This vignette shows us that ordinary teachers in ordinary schools have not been prepared to teach all students. I hasten to suggest here that this <u>does not mean that teacher education needs to have all teachers prepared in special education</u>. Special education will reinforce teachers' beliefs that children with disabilities are defective and require an education characterized by separation and lowered expectations. An inclusive teacher education program must commence from a re-examination of our values and an education in the ubiquity, naturalness and importance of difference.

Teacher educators have much to learn from the knowledge, skills and commitment of the many parents like Emily's mother. This story underlines the importance of building strong networks and communities to lead a new education of teachers and teacher educators. Building these new learning networks will advance inclusion beyond the capabilities of our existing educational institutions and policy frameworks. Inclusive education is community work, it is people work and not, as Emily and her mother remind us, paperwork.

CASE COMMENTARY 2

Robin Crain

The dissatisfaction shared by this parent is not uncommon when children with special needs begin school. As a parent, I have experienced the fears and frustration associated with a child who does not immediately fit within traditional classrooms. As an educator, I still found it difficult to work with his teachers to explore the maze of educational programming for my child. As this parent states, s/he does not know all the answers. Nobody does. Each child is an individual.

There are few educators who would say they do not believe in inclusion. The difference lies in whether they say "I believe in inclusion but….." or "I believe in inclusion and……"

This difference speaks to the complete belief that all children belong with their peers in their neighborhood school. The most important question is how do we problem solve to support that child to grow into the person they can be. This is the crux of this case. We see a lack of people coming together to problem solve an educational program for this child.

Policies, resources and training are necessary components for a system to be successful. Without a process to engage in collaborative problem solving, however, little will be done.

Using effective practices as a base, we then need to gather with expertise and with personal knowledge of the student together to look at what is working and what is not. Parents are essential partners. How does this child learn? Instead of band-aids, like teaching assistants to contain inappropriate behaviours, we need to ask, "How do we teach what the child needs to learn?" It takes creativity, a willingness to look at things differently and the understanding that everyone has a vested interest in helping the child. The use of formal problem solving leads to a culture of informal ways of looking at challenges.

CASE COMMENTARY 3

Alan McWhorter

Two questions emerge for me from reading this case. The first one is, *Why have a few teachers over several years been permitted to demonstrate lack of concern, poor performance, and apparent contempt for inclusion?* The second question is, *Why have these behaviours not been effectively addressed by educators in positions of responsibility?* The key issues in this case are:
– Parent understanding and commitment to inclusion.
– Lack of effective leadership in the school.
– Role of resource teacher and educational assistant
– There is a misuse of resources, especially the educational assistant.
   I would believe the following actions need to be taken in this case:
– Supervisory officer should discuss this issue with the principal.
– Provide a high quality professional development for the teaching staff.
– Define the role of educational assistant in terms of assisting the classroom teacher to include the child with special needs, ensuring that the child is not made to seem more different by the activities of the staff. The educational assistant should provide general assistance in the classroom and enable inclusion in part by freeing up some of the teacher's time.
   A child of a personal friend in grade 7 was recently "assessed" as having Attention Deficit Hyperactive Disorder (ADHD). I have known this boy since his birth, and I know him to be friendly, socially skilled for his age, and athletic. He did well in school until the last two years when he has had to endure less than stellar teaching. Acting out in class appears to be a coping strategy that he has developed. This is an incident of blaming the child for ineffective teaching. This is similar to Emily's swearing. Like Emily's parents, my friends have engaged outside professionals at their own expense. Their problem is still not remedied, but hopefully it will be soon.

CASE COMMENTARY 4

Zuhy Sayeed

Emily's family deserves great praise for 'sticking with' the issues they have faced and the learning they have had to do for their child. It's unfair and unnecessary that the challenges we families go through just to ensure; almost minute to minute; the success of our children in school and classrooms all over Canada and indeed, all over the globe.
   The issue that seems to be the largest is inculcating a school culture where inclusion is understood and respected for all children. Emily's peers will grow up learning that 'some' of their classmates do not play a role in the class and that their

learning is different, separate and that they themselves don't have a 'citizenship' role that they must play.

The costs and work that Emily's parents have borne are not right; the School District should be responsible for all of that. We, as parents of a young man with different abilities (as he calls it) faced the same issues at one time. His elementary school years were filled with some of the same experiences and bullying became a huge issue for our son. Teachers attributed our son's lack of success to his 'behaviour' and 'attitude' and we were questioned as to what we did to create his negative attitude towards school!!

We went over the heads of the teachers and resource teacher who had, without our knowledge, done certain 'assessments' on our son to validate their findings; and took him to a child psychologist who performed the appropriate assessments which we paid for.

It was only when our son was diagnosed with clinical depression and withdrawal, that we realized that his developmental disabilities were being compounded by the way he was being treated in school... and that it was time to call in the District Staff and get loud, verbal and downright angry.

The District paid for the assessments, worked through meetings and discussions with us... and we never had a meeting or a case conference without the senior District staff being present ever again.

In fact, no school personnel ever turned our requests down for a meeting at any time! And... this was our second child with developmental disabilities that we put through these same schools, worked with the same teachers and successfully removed barriers one at a time. We had two very different experiences with the same schools.

It also strikes me that Emily's mother did not mention the involvement of a Resource Coordinator or Resource Teacher at all. Albeit a small school, the District must have access to a resource person who would coordinate, plan and supervise the implementation of Emily's Individual program Plan. Schools in most provinces in Canada do have access to this level of support.

Emily's mother and other parents should ask for access to a Resource Coordinator. Access to a Coordinator or Case Manager is vital for teachers like we have just read about. It is the work of this Coordinator to do just what that title suggests- plus- keep abreast of all the experiences, research and professional development in inclusive education that is now available in plenty to us all.

This research is also available to us as parents; we must avail ourselves of the thirty plus years of knowledge and expertise that has been developed in inclusive education and community living.

This case study makes me wonder where the Local Association for Community Living is; what role the provincial Association for Community Living plays in small communities all across our provinces and territories. It points to the desperate need for the Canadian Association for Community Living to expand its human and knowledge based resources to every corner of this country and partner with both local parent groups, schools and associations to provide information to every teacher and parent in Emily's mum's position.

After all- it is really about families helping families and teachers helping teachers that will create a welcoming, diverse and inclusive environment for all our children.

CONNECTING TO PROFESSIONAL PRACTICE

The commentaries raise issues related to teacher education, values, professional responsibilities, professional learning, parent advocacy and school policies. Explore how these concepts have influenced your own practices and beliefs related to inclusive education.

CASE TWENTY TWO: OF CHESS AND LIFE

Tentatively, my son places his pawn–the simplest piece of his life he will ever acquire–upon a square. This game board is completely unfamiliar to him and he fumbles with the figure, trying to get it to stand on its own. He could pause here with his hand upon the piece, taking time to consider this choice and make sure it is the right move. But he is unfamiliar with the rules and game etiquette. He is unaware of the other pieces around him and how they should help shape his move and future play. This skill and knowledge will not come as naturally to him in his life as it does to others. There will be a lot more practice, learning, trial and error for him as a player and for us, his parents, as we act as his coaches.

Bruce was born with DiGeorge and Asperger's syndromes. He began his preparation for this game by having to prove his tenacity at a very early age. He endured and persevered through corrective heart surgery at 14 days old, then cleft palate reconstruction at a year, and beyond that has endured many illnesses, tests and hospital stays throughout his preschool years. He managed to get most of his necessary pieces to the game board save a few: fine motor, gross motor and social skills. Some of the others–memorization, letter and shape recognition and reading–he acquired very early on and if the game were solely based on the facts of the solar system, he would have had it mastered by three. But the game, as we know, is much more complex than that.

We are currently learning to play this game with our education system. Bruce is nearly six now and about to enter the first grade. Our opponent is not out for checkmate, or to bully us into resignation. Like Bruce's grandfather who patiently sat with Bruce on either side of a chess board, the school is helping Bruce along, teaching and challenging him to become a better player. Like Bruce's grandfather, the school moves with the hand of experience, but has never taught anyone quite like *this* grandson.

To help Bruce get all his pieces of the game in their proper places, we decided to enroll him in an early entrance program with the school at the age of three. Our reasoning was that he could begin familiarizing himself with the school, its building and grounds, the students and scheduling. We were unsure how long it might take him to feel comfortable enough or how long it would take him to learn how to stand in a line or raise his hand. He also needed to develop his social skills and this was the best environment to facilitate that. We spent many hours in preparation for this first introduction to school. We met with the staff and those who worked with him directly in an attempt to paint a vivid picture of our son. We needed to express our hopes and concerns for his future at this school. What we learned was that Bruce needed a full time coach, guiding him throughout the day. He is a quiet player with a mind filled with thought. He does not demand attention nor communicate freely that he needs assistance or clarification. He is a perfect candidate for slipping through the proverbial crack. After one year of half-days every other day, he surprised us all in most areas of his readiness and thus began full days of the kindergarten game at the age of four.

The beginning of the year was spent on skills and strategy he was already familiar with, how each of his pieces was supposed to move around the board. Certain pieces can only move certain ways. He had responsibilities and expectations. He learned how to sit in a desk properly, how to stand in a line and speak only when called upon.

And, finally, Bruce was ready and the real school game began…

The school moved first. They initiated a personal program plan. We informed them that Bruce's best learning environment is one that is predictable or at least a bit familiar. Keeping to schedules when possible and preparing him verbally for what is about to come all help keep the walls down around his ability to learn. Bruce responded to the move by proving this was no challenge. He achieved the objectives and goals set for him within a few months. The school made a few seemingly inconsequential moves as the schedule became routine. Bruce's comfort level grew, so the teaching assistant time decreased. The school's perception was that all was well. Our perception as parents was that it was a loss of potential, a loss of precious, early intervention time to coach and give direction to this up-and-coming player. Soon Bruce became almost purely a defensive player, making only moves that he had to or when he was asked to. Rarely did he raise an issue or challenge the school to change.

During a math exercise, the school made a very bold move without realizing it. They asked him to partake in an activity that was not acceptable to Bruce, but they persisted in trying to get him to comply. To taste the flavoured candy canes and chart the results of who likes what flavour best on the graph seemed a non-threatening demand. The school was overly confident in this move but was in unfamiliar territory. They believed they recognized his behaviour as defiance, as non-compliance to a school assignment. What they didn't understand was that there was a possibility that this child could have a strong aversion to candy, a severe dislike, a fear. They pushed for him to do as the others do. Backed into corner with few available moves, Bruce was in check, and so the walls began to rise up around his learning ability.

Bruce's next move was panic-stricken. He failed to finish the exercise and shut down. The experience went down in his mind for an undeterminable amount of time. The school perhaps didn't even notice the impact of their move, but the experience followed him home and the anxiety over candy, and trying new things, was perpetual.

As coaches, we had to step in. Shortly thereafter, with some parental consultation, the school reconsidered their move and tried to teach the skill from a different angle. Bruce's teaching assistant tasted the candy and he charted what she liked best. The skill of graphing was accomplished, but perhaps at a serious cost.

The game continued…

To ignite more initiative and incentive in Bruce, the school moved next. They introduced a reward system into his day. He received a simple check mark based on appropriate behaviour or completed tasks. We will never fully understand the results of this move until Bruce can articulate them in his own words. Whether it was the fact he liked the immediate acknowledgement or simply that he thrived on being systematic, we may never know. What we did know was that it worked remarkably well.

The school seemed to change their perspective of the game. A mutual under-standing between players was developing. The teaching assistant and Bruce were enjoying a great relationship. Gains in development and participation were evident and the events of the day were recorded in a book for us–his coaches–to read at the end of each day. We learned that Bruce made a voluntary compliment about the teaching assistant's shirt and we all smiled. This was a milestone and Bruce was becoming aware of the pieces around him. Perhaps we could raise our level of expectations. Some of Bruce's success at school was based on his supports at home. It was much easier to support him if the school relayed to us the happenings of the day, something which Bruce couldn't quite do on his own.

But then the game took a turn. The school's next move was made by the teacher. She felt that she needed more control over the teaching of Bruce, so she withdrew the teaching assistant's responsibility to fill in the communication book and took it on herself, a task that she did not have ample time to do. Therefore, the communication line from school to home was dropped.

From here, we were unaware of what was really happening in the game. In fact, it changed from a game of strategy, planning and consequence to a game of Go Fish! We didn't know about the gains or the setbacks. We did not know how well Bruce was learning or not learning. He was making moves unassisted and unbeknownst to us. He received an assessment in occupational therapy and we didn't know it until we received the written report. While he managed, he was functioning just under the radar. He was doing well enough to keep his pieces in motion on the board but not well enough to learn and improve. This was another loss of potential. We knew this time could have been much more productive.

It was here that we stepped forward again. We were beginning to more clearly understand our role as parent in this school game. We took control of the direction of the game. We had lost some of our confidence in the system and we wanted to recover it. Maybe we just needed to paint a more detailed picture and be clearer about our goals and expectations. Maybe we needed to remind the school what we thought the purpose of the game was. While the task seemed overwhelming and a bit daunting, from this point on we knew that we had to be evermore present in the beginning stages of our son's education.

We became more than observers, more than coaches. We became players with Bruce. Our next move was to be a fly on the wall. I observed in the classroom, giving the school a few moments notice of my arrival. I needed to gain insight and develop a reference and a comparison point. There was going to be a change of teachers in the near future and I wanted to be able to provide a full description of what was working and what wasn't. I was surprised at what I observed. The teaching assistant time had diminished to only a few hours a day. The statement in his program plan about preventing dependence on a teaching assistant was being taken very literally by the school and, in our opinion, a bit too aggressively. We were still under the impression that he was being provided the support of a full-time teaching assistant. Perhaps the lost communication book could have made us more aware of his circumstances earlier. I knew that there was nothing I could change about the past; I could only create a better future. I made an oath to myself that I would observe more frequently until I was confident I was getting the full picture of how the game was being played out.

The school made an incredible move; it was just a recommendation in their eyes, I believe, but the impact was significant. Bruce could participate in games, a track and field day for children with special needs. Based on this recommendation, the relationship and trust with the school began to heal. We saw the school foster Bruce's strengths and encourage his classmates to support and cheer him on. The school may never fully understand the impact this event had on Bruce and our lives. The word 'no' never crossed Bruce's lips that day, a phenomenon I will never forget. It was a day of great accomplishment and personal satisfaction. He might not be able to say it in so many words, but it was written all over his face. "I am playing well!" As parents, we now see ourselves volunteering for this event on an annual basis. If it can make such a difference in Bruce, it can do the same for another child.

As summer approaches and the game winds down for the year, I see that all players have learned so much. The school will now know that Bruce's parents will not give up or go away; we are players, too. We have learned how to be tenacious from our son and for our son. We have to be crystal clear in our goals for Bruce in this game–the education system–and persistent as to their delivery.

Bruce's sixth birthday approaches as the game goes on…

We want Bruce to lead the way and conduct the kind of game that works best for him. We want him to make his own moves and someday, just maybe, he'll be able to create his own strategies in the larger game called Life. That's what school is all about, a preparation for the bigger board. When that happens, we can be assured we've averted a stalemate and can celebrate a victory; we can step down as coaches and simply watch him play.

PROFESSIONAL INQUIRY

Inclusive Education

– Discuss what can be learned about inclusive education from this case.
– Explore the vision of inclusion held by the staff at this school and the parents.

Collaboration

– Critique the level of collaboration that was apparent in this case.
– Comment on the importance of trust within this case and the significance of trust for families and schools working together towards a shared vision of inclusion.

Teacher Education

– List recommendations for the initial and ongoing education of teachers in this case.
– Discuss the knowledge, understanding and skills teachers require to work effectively with teaching assistants within the context of inclusive education.
– Identify the professional and ethical responsibilities programs of professional teacher education, the school system, the school, and individual educators have

to ensure teachers have the necessary professional knowledge, skill and dispositions to effectively support learners with diverse needs.

Learning from Parents

- Discuss the professional insights regarding inclusive education that you gained form reading this case written by a parent.
- Identify the knowledge and skill that the parent in the case possessed about her child that could benefit educators and school personnel.

Teaching Assistants

- Explore the benefits and issues associated with utilizing teaching assistants in schools and classrooms.
- Describe your vision for the role of teaching assistants in schools and classrooms.
- Critique the use of teaching assistants in this case.
- Discuss the perspectives of the parent regarding the role and benefits of having a teaching assistant(s) involved in the education of her child.
- Identify actions and decisions that a school principal might employ when trying to foster a community of inclusion in this school regarding the role of teaching assistants.

CASE COMMENTARY REFLECTIONS

After reading the commentaries reflect on the following:

New Insights
Identify new insights gained from reading the commentaries.

Understandings
Discuss the impact of the commentaries on your understandings of inclusive education.

Questions
Identify questions that emerge for you from reading the commentaries.

CASE COMMENTARY 1

Bruce Rivers

Today's education system is being tested in many ways. Students with special education needs are a diverse group. In the past, many students like Bruce would have been sent to segregated classes and schools; including them in regular classes is just one of the many challenges currently being faced. Teachers are held to high professional standards to ensure that every student in their class is learning and progressing to the best of their ability. "Of Chess and Life" raises issues of responsibility, trust and conflict. How these issues are resolved early in the school year are critical.

One questions how prepared the teacher was to receive a student with the unique learning needs of Bruce. Was the teacher offered the opportunity to participate in additional courses? Did the school identify that the teacher would need additional information, resources and supports beyond that of a fulltime educational assistant? Was there a clear expectation that case conferences and brainstorming sessions would involve the family?

Bruce's learning challenges present themselves early and yet initially they are not recognized as such but instead interpreted as defiant behaviour, something that must be corrected, not accommodated. This is the first indication that we get that the teaching staff and parents are not meeting on a regular, consultative basis to ensure that the education plan the school has put in place meets his needs in all areas. Potentially, this could be a source of conflict that will impact on his learning for an unknown amount of time.

The parents have difficulty understanding the teacher's sense of responsibility for the learning of all students. Yet we must remember that the teacher will be held responsible by the school and the board should students not demonstrate success within that learning environment.

CASE COMMENTARY 2

Inés Elvira B. de Escallon

Children with high needs challenge the people around them. This includes parents, family members, doctors, teachers... requiring them to be knowledgeable and aware of the child's strengths and weaknesses.

The only way teachers can learn to support students is when they have them in their classrooms as participating members. Only then will they have a learning curve that will benefit the child with high needs, his fellow students and later other students that have educational needs as well.

Parents have to have the courage to take risks when they want an inclusive approach in the education of their children. They also have to be aware that things will not always work out or even look like what they wanted.

This doesn't mean they should not always challenge the system, the school and the teachers. Having high expectations for their children is the best recipe for success but also they should remember that they also have learned over the years and allowed new teachers, new principles that come into contact with their son/daughter to experience and learn from sharing on a day to day base with him/her. Time and patience is needed and parents' should provide both in order to build a team that trust each other and that as a group will provide the best support for the student on the long school journey.

We all have to remember that no single person can make inclusive education work. Inclusive education takes hard work and it has to be a team effort. Building teams is part of an inclusive education success story.

CASE COMMENTARY 3

Julie A. Stone

This case clearly illustrates the breakdown in communication between the school and the home. The parents have very high expectations for their son and for the education system. The parents are very involved in Bruce's education, to the point of showing up in the classroom with very little notice. This could be very intimidating for a teacher and demonstrates a complete lack of trust in the teacher and the system. It also indicates a complete lack of respect. I was wondering if the teacher felt intimidated in writing in the journal on a daily basis. Not everyone has the same writing talent. Or, the teacher didn't feel there was anything to report on some days or simply didn't have the time.

The metaphor of the chess game was very powerful. Parents need to be reflective and strategic in their interactions with the school. Often schools do not want to be placed in a position of check or checkmate and the response to being under this pressure from a family may cause the school to act in ways that can be interpreted as defensive. Students and families also do not want to be placed in similar confining places. Unfortunately, the rules of the game often need to be uncovered by families because the game of chess used in schools sometimes uses different rules and strategies that are known to only the school insiders.

Strategies that may be employed by the parents to support a more inclusive approach and to enable them to gain insider knowledge of the school game could include:

- Make an appointment with Bruce's new teacher before school begins in the fall.
- Set up a schedule for calls, classroom visits and journal days. If a visit becomes necessary for peace of mind, call ahead and let the classroom teacher know.
- Plan for program planning and follow-up times, so you and the teachers will know when to have files and paperwork ready.
- Decide on a case manager for Bruce's school program. A case manager would see that all school personnel, outside specialists and the family were involved in Case Conferences and the like.
- Continue to hold high expectations for Bruce's involvement and progress and for the school's diligence. Be prepared for the unexpected at times, for that is the way school is for everyone.
- Work with the teacher to find ways to make Bruce as independent as possible. Many students with a social and/or learning needs become very adult dependent and find it difficult to face the challenges that get more complex with time.

CASE COMMENTARY 4

Dr. Jude MacArthur

To support children well, teachers may need to learn about a student's disability and its effect on their learning and social experiences. Bruce's parents used their knowledge to carefully ease the way for their son and his teachers. They knew that he needed adult support to prevent him from falling between the cracks, and they were keenly aware of situations that he found difficult. The candy cane incident demonstrates a gap between parental and teacher understandings, and the devastating consequences for Bruce when he 'shut down' at school then took his grief home. Learning is sustained through trusting and caring relationships between teachers and their students. What is the impact of this event on Bruce's developing relationship with his teacher and the teaching assistant? How can he trust them?

Frustratingly, this case turns out to be a roller-coaster ride for everyone, with relationships damaged and healed. Teachers developed an effective reward system. A home-school notebook was completed daily by the teaching assistant, facilitating the flow of valuable information. The raising of expectations in relation to Bruce's learning was a profoundly important outcome of these two school initiatives. But the teacher took over the home-school notebook, resulting in the notebook and its vital communications being dropped. Teaching assistant support was cut back and Bruce's progress fell 'under the radar'. Relationships soured and Bruce's parents moved into observation and surveillance mode. School triumphed with its positive decision to enter Bruce in the 'I CAN' games, and relationships improved again. All of this occurred in the space of one year.

There is a cost to parents who feel pressured to maintain a critical position with their school. Bruce's parents are active players, ensuring their goals for him are met through quality education, and this case illustrates the importance of parents and teachers working together from the outset to share their knowledge, goals and expectations. Secondly, these parents had prepared well for Bruce's transition to school. Assessments, observations and teacher knowledge from his early entrance program should have accompanied Bruce into his first year of school, providing his teachers with a valuable data source for planning and teaching. Perhaps mistakes at school could have been avoided.

In our own research we have been impressed by the active approach taken by students with disabilities themselves to change things at school for the better, and to improve their own situation. Bruce is also an active player, and he will already be doing what his parents hope for – 'making his own moves… and creating his own strategies…' Effective teachers will recognize Bruce's attempts to shape his own social and academic experiences, and they will encourage and support his moves.

CONNECTING TO PROFESSIONAL PRACTICE

The importance of professional knowledge, skills and dispositions towards caring and inclusion are identified in the commentaries. A school's ability to access and include the unique knowledge of parents was also recognized as essential by the case commentary writers. Reflect on the ways in which you and your colleagues have honored, respected and actively accessed the knowledge and guidance of parents in the education of their child. Identify the professional knowledge and insight you gained from this process.

CASE TWENTY THREE: ROSA'S WORLD

Welcome to Rosa's world. Our daughter Rosa was born in May 1995 at 26 weeks gestation; her doctors called her "extremely premature." With a birth weight of one pound, 11 ounces, they gave her a two percent chance of surviving the first 48 hours of her life. After that, no one really knew what would happen.

When you have a critically ill premature baby in the Neonatal Intensive Care Unit, you learn fast how fragile life really is. I can still remember the big city obstetrician on call who performed my C-section. He asked me if I was sure I wanted them to do all they could to help my preemie baby live (i.e., full resuscitation). Of course I wanted them to do everything they could. How could I not? In hindsight, I suppose they felt they knew something I didn't. That 'something' was the increased odds of a preemie like Rosa going on to develop significant developmental problems, namely cerebral palsy. I suppose in the science and practicality of their hearts, they wanted to spare us the hardships of dealing with a child with a disability. I certainly didn't see it that way.

Thirteen years later, my husband and I are the very proud parents of a busy pre-teen who is doing well in a mainstream classroom at her school. She is our miracle. And yes, she does have cerebral palsy (CP). Her CP is what we call mild spastic diplegia[1]. That means she can walk, just not really well. It means she also has a wheelchair that she needs only sometimes. It means she's smart as a whip, and academically learns just as capably as a typical child without CP. It also means that she can "pass" for a typical child depending on the situation, of course. So, we walk the fence of ability/disability, never really sure where she fits. In the final analysis, she has a bit of both. She is what I call "bi-able." Sort of like being bilingual, but instead of language we use physical ability as the definer. Oh, I should add that Rosa is an only child. We never did have any more. Sometimes fate works that way.

Our school experiences to date have been multi-experiential; a mixture of really good, good, bad, and very bad. But, luckily for us, the majority of our experiences with the education system have been good. Let's start with the very bad and get that one out of the way first. To do so, I have to tell you about our experiences with kindergarten. We live in a small city with about 12 different elementary schools to choose from. So, like any good investigative parent with a child with atypical needs, we did our homework. My husband and I selected one particular elementary school based upon its reputation in the community and the fact the building was only 10 years old and all one level. The demographics of the student population seemed to indicate that the kids were coming from average middle class homes, perhaps even some affluent ones.

We'll call this first school that our daughter attended King Richard (KR) School. We started off pretty good with KR. We had a school team meeting prior to the first day of school (at my insistence). We involved the principal in this meeting, and the kindergarten teacher, all of whom were strangers to us at this point. We even brought in our physiotherapist and occupational therapist to attend this first team meeting, just to ensure that we were all on the same page. The meeting went well! I was so optimistic that we had picked the right school.

215

By Christmas that feeling of optimism changed. It was our opinion that the school didn't know how to best meet our daughter's needs and even though they were well intentioned, they were struggling. They weren't the experts I thought they were. They weren't the experts they thought they were.

For example, our kindergarten teacher (Miss Bee) had experience as a resource teacher in her previous job. Great, I thought! Who better to have as your kindergarten teacher than a resource teacher? Someone who would really understand a child's disability and the supports needed. I was wrong.

What I failed to realize was that all resource teachers are not the same. They are people first, with opinions, attitudes, and lives outside their work. And all these things affect their abilities to do their jobs well. It became somewhat obvious that Miss Bee had the attitude that insisted, "I know all about kids with special needs because I've worked with them more than anyone else; therefore, I'm the expert." She seemed to assume that Rosa was less than academically typical because she wore the CP label. In my opinion, Miss Bee assumed all kids with CP are not academically typical. And that's wrong.

Then there was the Christmas concert at King Richard School. Rosa was wearing AFO's (leg braces) at the time to help her with her balance and gait. To make things safe for Rosa, I asked Miss Bee to make sure Rosa stayed off the risers the night of the concert. I requested that Rosa stand on the level ground of the gym floor. I assumed that meant that Miss Bee would ensure that the first row of kindergarten children would stand in a row on the floor level with Rosa and then the other rows would go up on the risers behind them. What we found when we got to Rosa's first ever school Christmas concert was that she was the only one standing on the floor and all the other typical kids were behind her up on the risers. She looked scared. She had to sing her two little Christmas songs segregated from the rest of her peers. And yes, she stood out. Someone whispered behind us, "Why is that little girl just standing there by herself?"

My husband and I were devastated. We felt so bad for Rosa. She was clearly uncomfortable. And then so were we. Still, I took a picture of this less than warm and fuzzy scene. I called the principal the next day, filled with frustration, hurt, and anger – not just with the Christmas concert, but also with other things that had been going on in the kindergarten room. The concert was the last straw, and I started to lose it. At that time, I worked in another city. I commuted to work every day about 75 km each way. That meant I wasn't in the same town as Rosa during school hours Monday to Friday. It also meant I had to do all my communicating with the school over the phone, long distance. Principal Ron of KR School and I had a good relationship. But that phone call after the concert was heated–on my end. And I know it was all Principal Ron could do just to calm me down. He did volunteer to speak with Miss Bee about our concerns with the concert and said he'd get back to me. He wanted to talk to Miss Bee before I did! So I let him talk to her first. Principal Ron got back to me the very same day with what had happened.

A week went by and I cooled down. I went to see Miss Bee. We talked about the concert. I showed Miss Bee my snapshot picture of the concert. The picture that showed Rosa looking scared, alone, unsure, standing all by herself in her pretty little red velvet Christmas dress that she was so proud of, with her pretty white leotards showing off her leg braces. Braces designed to help keep her safe, not make her stand out. And yet there she was, standing out. She was standing all alone with her little hands clasped together looking at the music teacher. She was likely just looking for a friendly smiling face she knew. She needed someone to reassure her that it was okay for her to stand out like this. And all she saw was the face of the music teacher who could only focus on the performance–not the performers–and least of all Rosa. How do you explain this to a five-year-old?

I left Miss Bee with that picture. After a few more days went by, I met with Miss Bee again, this time about something entirely different. She confessed to me that after she saw the picture of Rosa at the concert, she understood our concerns. She confessed that until she saw the picture she didn't see what all the fuss was about. And she admitted to me that she wasn't assertive enough with Miss Royal. She should have insisted that Miss Royal change the configuration for the kindergarten children on the floor and the risers. And Miss Bee felt bad. Well now, that made all of us.

I wish I could say that was the only bad experience at King Richard School. But there were others. There were some good experiences, too. But it seems the bad outweighed the good. I'll never forget the problems we had with retaining a teaching assistant for Rosa's Kindergarten year. And to this day, I don't know why that was. We started off with one teaching assistant (Miss Smith) and then she quit right before Christmas. Then she was replaced with Miss Rock. Then Miss Rock quit after a few months, and then we had an assortment of substitute a teaching assistant thereafter. When I asked Miss Bee about why all these changes, she would always say that they just decided to move on to different things. After about the fourth change, I talked to Principal Ron about it. He admitted that he didn't really know why this was happening either. It was very disrupting and hard on Rosa to keep working with a different aide every three months (if they lasted that long). Principal Ron always assured me that it wasn't he who was doing all the teaching assistant changes. I got the impression that this situation was being caused by the "higher ups" in the School Division administration. To this day, I'm not sure.

And so if the multitude of teaching assistant changes wasn't bad enough, we never met with King Richard's resource teacher once. Not once in two years. We had no written personal program plan from the resource teacher (Mrs. Silverwood). We had nothing. And we didn't know any better. My husband and I didn't know we were supposed to have a personal program plan in writing. No one told us that. We found all this out later towards the end of our time with King Richard School. I remember asking Principal Ron about why the resource teacher at KR school was never involved in our case? He admitted that she was having personal life problems and that her work hours had been reduced. He didn't seem to think that was right, however, he explained that he didn't have any control over the resource teacher at King Richard School. Again, the message we were getting was it was the "higher ups."

Then, the icing on the cake came when we were having our year-end meeting with Miss Bee and Principal Ron (at my suggestion). It was the end of Rosa's Kindergarten year. I didn't feel Rosa was mature enough to progress to Grade 1. I wanted to hold her back and do Kindergarten again. Miss Bee disagreed. At that year end meeting, I explained to Miss Bee and Principal Ron why I wanted Rosa to repeat Kindergarten. Mrs. Bee turned to Principal Ron and said, "But we usually don't hold back those types of students," and then quickly looked at me and smiled. "Those types of students" is a phrase I'll never forget.

Miss Bee totally devalued Rosa as a person when she said that. It was all I could do but not verbally lambaste Miss Bee at that very moment. But I took a deep breath and kept my comments to myself. Instead, I persisted with my request to have Rosa repeat Kindergarten and that was all there was to it. It took me many days to cool down from taking offence to that discriminatory remark. In the end, I forgave her ignorance with the comfort of my favourite Biblical expression: "They know not what they do." I had to forgive Miss Bee and move on, as hard as that was. We had a repeat year of Kindergarten to go through with her.

But Principal Ron and Miss Bee couldn't leave well enough alone. They were adamant that we supplement Rosa's Kindergarten year (the repeat) with half a day of Grade 1 also. Apparently, this had been done with other students before and had yielded excellent results. We agreed to try it even though I had my reservations. This meant the morning session was Kindergarten for Rosa, and the afternoons were Grade 1.

Year 2 in Kindergarten at King Richard School was somewhat better. We retained the same teaching assistant all year long. Mrs. Duncan, the new teaching assistant, was excellent. She was experienced. She was our bright light at King Richard School. But the way this school division changed teaching assistant s, I knew I couldn't be fooled into staying at King Richard School simply because Mrs. Duncan was the best part.

By spring of that repeat Kindergarten year, my motherly instincts were telling me to switch schools; it was a gut feeling. While Rosa was having a bit better Kindergarten year, her half days in Grade 1 were less than desirable. The Grade 1 teacher had no idea what she was supposed to do with Rosa academically. She had no guidance from the resource teacher, Mrs. Silverwood, and no guidance from anyone else for that matter. This was all confessed to us in the spring report card meeting that we had with Miss Chelsey, the Grade 1 teacher. Rosa's Grade 1 report card was dismal. She was failing nearly every subject. Miss Chelsey said she didn't know what else to do. She didn't know how she was supposed to grade Rosa.

As Rosa was only in Grade 1 in the afternoons, she missed all the morning Grade 1 learning experiences which, Miss Chelsey told me, was where she taught the Grade 1's the harder subjects because they were more awake and less fatigued. This wasn't the way things were supposed to be for Rosa. In what we thought would be a better year at school. Even though Mrs. Duncan, the teaching assistant, was doing her best to help Rosa, she wasn't a teacher and she had no authority to help improve things. As painful as leaving Mrs. Duncan was, we decided to leave King Richard School. It just wasn't worth the gamble to keep Rosa there. We had given KR school two full years of Rosa's life. And it was a struggle that just never ended. It was my opinion that King Richard School was designed and staffed for typical kids, normal kids. That's how I saw it. They lacked real experience with accommodating special needs. Even though they thought they knew what they were doing, they didn't. So, sometimes you have to disengage yourself from a school that just isn't getting it. And I know we are blessed to be living in a city where we can leave one school for another. We had a choice.

So, we left KR school. We gave them a three-month notice. Principal Ron was very interested to hear why we were leaving so I went over a few things with him. But I was still pretty emotional, hurt really, about a lot of our bad experiences. So I didn't want to get into all of it with him. Besides, I wasn't sure how much was "real" versus how much was our perception. Once burned, twice shy, as they say. All I knew within my heart of hearts was that I needed to get Rosa out of that school. We "grinned and bared it" it until the end of Rosa's Kindergarten/Grade 1 year at KR school. By then I had arranged for transfer for Rosa to a different school in the fall and it was chosen with a slightly different lens.

I was no longer as concerned with school population demographics. I chose a school in a different school division. I still chose a school without stairs, all one level. But this time, I chose a school where they had demonstrated evidence of experience with special needs kids. I knew better now the questions that needed to be asked.

This new school, St. Raphael, was a breath of fresh air for us. We decided after those two tumultuous years at King Richard School, we would put Rosa into full time Grade 1 at St. Raph's. The Grade 1 teacher at St. Raph's was nervous about teaching a student like Rosa. But, at least she was honest with us about it. She was never a resource teacher before–and we thanked God for that! Mrs. Honey was only two years away from retirement, but she was still willing to learn with us. She was awesome. She had a no-nonsense attitude, with a straight-up and in your face kind of personality. And, it worked for us. She loved Rosa. And it showed. She advocated for Rosa. She stood up for Rosa. She believed in Rosa. She didn't see the label of CP; she saw Rosa first. She "got it" and that was the most inspiring thing I had seen in two long years with the education system.

Thank goodness for Mrs. Honey. She restored my belief in teachers and in the education system. And we had a wonderful Grade 1 year. There were small problems here and there, but by then I had learned how to communicate better. I took the effort to get to know Mrs. Honey. Not just Mrs. Honey the teacher, but Mrs. Honey the person. And I showed her who I was too. Not just Mrs. Monterey the parent of Rosa. Plus, by then I had switched jobs. We realized that working out of town wasn't enabling me to keep linked with the school like I needed and wanted to. I had to drive Rosa to school each day and pick her up afterwards because St. Raph's wasn't in our neighbourhood. That enabled me to be in school every day, twice a day. This allowed me to have daily chats with Mrs. Honey and/or the teaching assistant assigned to Rosa. We did not talk about Rosa all the time. We just talked: about the mall, about our community and about our shared love for travel. We had lots of laughs. Mrs. Honey, teaching assistant and I had developed a special relationship. That's where I learned that this whole school experience doesn't have to be so serious. I could lighten up a bit.

Then, after our utopian Grade 1 year at St. Raphael, we had to move to a different city due to my husband's job. In the new city I chose another school using the same lens as with St. Raphael. We choose St. Martin School, and we had a wonderful Grade 2 there. Good like St. Raph's, but a different good. And I learned that people are people no matter where you go. There is good in everyone. Good in every teacher. As a parent, you just have to know how to find it. You have to want to find it. And if you do, it will be there.

At St. Martin, I kept working on my new and improved parental communication style. And it continued to serve me well. I chose not to work outside the home in our new city. I wanted to take some time off and focus on Rosa and her school needs. Rosa had elective orthopedic surgery in our new city the summer before Grade 2. I was not working so it was great to have the time to focus on her post-surgery rehab. That also allowed me to drive Rosa to school each day and to be physically present in the school twice a day. I got to know the Grade 2 teacher, just like I got to know Mrs. Honey. Mrs. Woods wasn't Mrs. Honey and I didn't expect her to be. But Mrs. Woods was just as good a teacher. And we had a wonderful rapport.

Before we could get too attached to St. Martin's school, we moved back to our same small city. And, by choice, back to St. Raphael school. There Rosa started Grade 3. This time we had two teachers to get to know. Mrs. Kay and Mrs. Collins job shared grade 3. I had trouble at first trying to figure out how this was going to work.

I'd only ever had to worry about one teacher before. But, with their help we made it work. And we had a really good grade 3. We all wanted to have a good year. And we all worked hard at it.

However, the bad part of this school experience at that time was that the school playground was not "Rosa friendly." It wasn't accessible for anyone with a physical disability like her. It wasn't safe. It was meant for normal kids, I guess. Kids without spastic diplegia, I guess. At this time also, we were going through a new principal every year. I don't know why that was, it just was. So, I tried talking to the principal (of the day) about making improvements to the playground. Each of them said that they tried to get our School Board Office to make some improvements to the playground equipment/set-up. But nothing ever happened. And I waited and waited, patiently.

Finally, we were told that if we wanted to improve the playground, we had to raise the money ourselves through the school council. So, I jointed the PTA. But there, I found only a few allies. Everyone with the school council was intent on raising the money for new playground equipment – but for the typical kids. The "extra" stuff needed for kids like Rosa was going to cost a lot more money and so "we'd have to look at that later on." At some undefined time in the future.

But, if the playground was the only bad experience with this school, I was willing to put up with it because there were so many other good things about St. Raph's. And people kept telling me "there was no such thing as a perfect school." Yes, I settled. I settled for "good enough." I didn't fight for what was better. For what was right. And yes, I blame myself for that. We went through Grade 3, 4, and 5 waiting for some magic solution to make the playground more accessible for Rosa. But that day never did come. So, the question is, "What does a physically disabled kid like Rosa do at recess"? Good question. I don't know. Her teachers just assumed she'd figure out how to play with the other kids, I guess.

Rosa is lucky enough to have one little friend at school that plays with her at recess willingly, even though Rosa can't physically play like the other kids. At least she has one friend who over looks her disabilities and still likes her. But what does Rosa do when that little friend misses a day at school? Quite frankly, I don't know. I guess Rosa just walks around the playground by herself. The thing about Rosa is that she is very shy and very passive. In this regard, she is not outgoing enough to go join a group of her peers and play with them unless invited first. They play physically when they're this age. And Rosa knows she can't do those things they do. So, how does that make her feel? Left out and standing out. It was just like being alone at the front of the Christmas concert. What does that do to her self-esteem? How does that build her social skills?

Now, Rosa is getting ready to go into Grade 7. It is now too late for her to enjoy an accessible playground. She's grown out of that stage. But the good news is that there are other physically challenged kids at St. Raph's now and I'm a part of a new and improved parent advisory council determined to change the playground. We want to make it accessible. We want to do the right thing. We trust we will and soon.

We only have two years left at St. Raphael before high school. We're lucky that our city has four high schools to choose from. All of them have their strengths and weaknesses. There is no perfect one. This I know. I've already pre-selected the one of choice. It is accessible. It is in a decent area of town. St. Vladimir's High School has a good reputation in the community and it's a smaller high school than the rest. It's in the same school division as St. Raph's and so, we can have continuity of our Christian faith permeating the curriculum. And to us, that's important.

I have no doubt we'll have issues with the odd thing here and there in this next phase. For one thing, we'll have many teachers to deal with. More than one teacher equals more than one challenge. We will have teachers who will have preconceived notions about students with cerebral palsy. And we will prove them wrong. We will have teachers who "get it" right off the hop, and we will embrace them with gratitude! We will run into parents who stereotype kids like Rosa, and if we can't reach out to teach them a better way to think, then we will ignore them. And as for Rosa's friends when she hits high school, who knows what that will look like?

I can only hope that everything we taught her about saying no to drugs, alcohol, and other bad things will stay with her. I do know that Rosa will meet her academic goals. And yes, it will take much effort sometimes. But I know that we will continue to do everything we can to help her with what she needs. And I know that she will graduate with her Grade 12 diploma – with a little help from everyone.

Rosa's education journey won't end with completion of Grade 12 either. Ever since she was knee high to a grasshopper, she has told me she wants to be an artist when she grows up. Okay, we can handle that. She knows that if she wants to be an artist she has to complete her four-year undergrad degree in Fine Arts at university. We started saving the money for her university education when Rosa was one year old. The financial resources should be there for her. If university doesn't pan out, then she will pursue other post-secondary programs that will enable her to realize her dream of being an artist. And she will do this because she's who she is.

PROFESSIONAL INQUIRY

Inclusive Philosophy

- Explore the different understandings of inclusion held by Miss Bee, Principal Ron and Rosa's mother.
- Explore how the educational philosophy held by Mrs. Henry enabled Rosa to be more included in the school.

School Level Planning

- Discuss the issues related to Miss Chelsey's professional knowledge in the area of assessment and evaluation that became apparent through Rosa's report card.
- Critique the ability of King Richard's school to effectively plan and program for Rosa's education.

Access

- Discuss the different perspectives held by Rosa's parents and the various schools regarding an education that was accessible to all students?
- Identify the visible and invisible barriers that prevented Rosa from having full access to the educational opportunities available to other children.
- Discuss the impact and implications upon students and families when access to learning opportunities and experiences are denied.

CASE COMMENTARY REFLECTIONS

After reading the commentaries reflect on the following:

New Insights
Identify new insights gained from reading the commentaries.

Understandings
Discuss the impact of the commentaries on your understandings of inclusive education.

Questions
Identify questions that emerge from reading the commentaries.

CASE COMMENTARY 1

Bendina Miller

At this time in education, we ought to expect that all school divisions/districts have a clear understanding of and commitment to equal access to appropriate education for all students — that means leading edge inclusive education. My personal and professional expectation regarding inclusion means that all teachers have the professional skills and understanding to meet the broad/diverse learning needs of students. While this may seem idealistic, I believe that as long as we rely on specialty staff to address the inclusive education needs of students we will never have true inclusion. All staff must have the knowledge and capacity to include students in their class instruction.

'Understanding by Design' is one professional strategy which truly engages the teacher in such inclusive practice. At the same time, the provision of extraordinary support staff within the classroom may be necessary to support successful inclusion of students, however, the more we can rely on normal/generic support the more authentic inclusion will be.

For instance, the support of a peer buddy gives a student far greater opportunity for inclusion both in learning and in the social dynamic of the class and school than does the provision of a special education assistant. Most often I have seen the assignment of a special education assistant as a practice that excludes students and separates them from their peers. I recognize that there will be times when an adult specialist will be required to support the unique student needs in order to ensure success, however, I urge schools to explore generic/peer support prior to making a 'staffing' determination.

Rosa and her family are a clear example of a family that would benefit from the application of a broad vision of support. With each move, with each staff change Rosa and her family were expected to make adjustments and learn about the new organizational dynamic. Parents must be passionate advocates for their children – and – school systems must be thoughtful, professional learning leaders.

Together the passionate advocates and learning leaders will be successful in building capacity among the staff and, most importantly, in ensuring successful learning and inclusion for all students. It's about parents as advocates, it's about parents as partners in learning, it's about school divisions/districts providing learning leadership, it's about success for all students!

CASE COMMENTARY 2

Dr. Lauren Hoffman

Rosa seems to have been defined throughout her education by her label of cerebral palsy. The label has led to deficit thinking whereby expectations are lowered and her needs are seen as pathological. Although the parents have been satisfied with several of the instructional assistants throughout her education, it appears that Rosa's education was mainly the responsible of assistants, not the teacher. This Rosa's education was mainly the responsibility of teaching assistants, not the teacher. This raises the question of whose responsibility it is to ensure that Rosa's experience is challenging, empowering, and authentic. Although Rosa was in the general education classroom, her differences and needs seemed to set her apart from her peers. She was not really included as a full member of this classroom.

The relationship between the teachers, principals, and parents seems open at times, but strained when difficult and critical issues arise. Although there was communication, it is unclear if a culture of authentic dialogue was ever established in order to openly deal with Rosa's educational issues and needs. Dialogue requires more than talk, and requires a commitment to confronting difficult issues and being open to new perspectives and understandings. Leaders need to model and engage teachers and parents in this type of dialogic culture.

It is questionable how much systemic support was provided for Rosa and her family. It appeared as if each situation required new thinking and problem solving, which can be productive at times, yet cumbersome as well. It is critical that school leaders build their knowledge and understanding of cerebral palsy and provide support for teachers in order to enact an equitable and socially just education. Leaders should be responsible for ensuring pathologizing and marginalizing practices are not practiced in their school.

It is also critical to engage the perspective and voice of students. Rosa's voice should have been heard in terms of how she sees herself, her education, her questions, her desires, and her future. It is unclear how much voice Rosa had throughout all of her educational changes and challenges.

CASE COMMENTARY 3

Dr. Scott A. Thompson

Parental/Guardian Advocacy
The first thing that jumps out for me in this case study is the need for parental support simply in the areas of negotiating the systems so prevalent in the various helping professions. Teaching parents to advocate for what they can reasonably expect, indeed what is often required by law, from educational institutions is a good learning lesson for potential teachers. I also think about the many powerful parent groups that I have witnessed over the years, in which parents/guardians really are learning from each other—not only about advocacy, but about many other things: such as, best educational practices, counselling support, perspective giving, etc.

Self-Advocacy
Despite this case study being all about Rosa, there is very little of her voice in the story. She is described as passive in the case study, and that got me thinking that issues around self advocacy could be explored. I have some conceptual difficulties with self-advocacy. I struggle with the concept of giving often the most vulnerable person in an education institution the sole responsibility to self-advocate or teaching self-advocacy in a way that is not empowering. I am thinking here of something like a discrete step-wise implementation of self-advocacy in planned, overly scripted, IEP meetings. Nevertheless, I think that some interesting conversations could flow from this case study—if self-advocacy were framed within the disability rights movement within schools.

Transition Planning
Transition planning and long-term planning can be a cumbersome job, but I think that this case study demonstrates what can happen when things are not in place. There are different ways to facilitate transitions for students with disabilities and their (future) placements. I have facilitated some MAPS sessions in my time (McGill Action Planning System), and these processes can be overwhelming for parents, but opening up these conversations for student teachers is a good strategy to get them thinking about the implications of life-long learning for students with disabilities.

CASE COMMENTARY 4

Melanie Panitch

The story of the Christmas Concert hit a nerve with me. For my commentary I'd like to respond by telling another story, with a different outcome. At its 2003 convocation, Ryerson University graduated its first class of disability studies students and marked the historic occasion by bestowing an honorary doctorate on the internationally recognized, disabled film-maker, Bonnie Klein. Bonnie Klein arrived from British Columbia a day before the ceremony to meet with the convocation organizers for a rehearsal in the Theatre. She drove her scooter down the processional route in the Ryerson Theatre which the dignitaries follow to get on to the stage. She anticipated the bagpipes and music; the presidential party, the Chancellor, vice- presidents and deans; the embellished caps and gowns, including her own, specially designated for the occasion. This was the procession which she was invited to join as the honorary guest. However, at the rehearsal, she encountered a set of stairs rising from the theater floor to the stage.

She was faced with a dilemma. On the one hand, she could park her scooter and with assistance walk slowly up the stairs holding onto the banister and the arm of a companion and then make it to her seat on the stage. On the other hand, as a disability activist she recognized the significance of being recognized, presented with her degree and 'hood', and delivering her convocation address to the graduates as a disabled woman, seated in her scooter. But then how could she be part of the processional party?

The answer was quickly offered by one of the assistants whose job it was to make sure everything went smoothly at convocation. "Let's bring the entire procession in from back stage," the assistant proposed. That way Bonnie could be part of the procession of dignitaries and the issue of the stairs would disappear. So instead of Bonnie having to adjust to an inaccessible environment, the environment shifted to ensure she was central in this momentous day. But beyond this particular example, the story illuminates an approach and set of practices that with creativity and generosity of spirit has a resonance for children with disabilities in educational environments everywhere.

CONNECTING TO PROFESSIONAL PRACTICE

The significance of developing and sustaining a school vision committed to an inclusive educational philosophy is highlighted by the commentary writers. They also stress the importance of authentic dialogue, advocacy and a generosity of spirit as essential dimensions that support inclusion and access. Discuss how the concepts of authentic dialogue, advocacy and a generosity of spirit are reflected in your own professional practice.

NOTES

[1] In *spastic diplegia* cerebral palsy all four limbs are affected; both legs, as well as *mild* affects in the arms are present.

CASE TWENTY FOUR: THE PERSONAL PROGRAM PLAN

I am standing in the shower, letting the warm water and my own thoughts flow. I wonder what the day will hold. Today is Mandy's Personal Program Plan (PPP) meeting at school. Within a split second, many different emotions shoot through me: defensiveness, anger, sadness, wistfulness, uncertainty about her future and above all, a "mama bear" protectiveness to make sure my daughter receives all the supports she needs. Words from a good friend come to mind; she's been traveling the same road, only a few years longer. I think about her advice and decide that I can and will advocate for my daughter and her rights. I remind myself to do it in a firm, friendly manner that fosters cooperation with the school and a willingness to work together, rather than a bullish, in-your-face manner that puts everyone on the defense. I step out of the shower; ready to be the person my daughter needs me to be.

The Personal Program Plan (PPP); sounds good doesn't it? A programming plan tailored to the individual student, designed with that student's best interests in mind. When Mandy first started school and we heard about the PPP, we thought "Great, a plan for Mandy to help her in school and to see that she gets the support that she needs in order to function her best in her classes." What nobody tells you though is that PPP's are hard work. There are many different players at the table, hammering out thoughts and ideas, with parents striving for the best for their child, and the school trying to accommodate that while keeping to their agenda. Now, in the last couple of years throw in tight budgets, and more needs being identified in the schools, and you find that the resources are getting spread pretty thin. Parents fear their children are paying the price.

My thoughts drift to my daughter. How do you describe a child like Mandy? That is a good question. People are drawn to her. When they meet her for the first time, they say she is beautiful with her long, naturally curly, strawberry blonde hair, her big blue eyes, smooth skin and freckles. Once they get to know her, they say she shines from within. They feel her peace, her joy, her compassion. They say "she's smart, she's so grown up, she's such a hard worker, she sings like an angel." And they're right; that's Mandy. She's all of these things and more.

Mandy is our daughter, our firstborn. She is a granddaughter. She is a neat big sister who loves to play–and to fight –with her younger brother. She's a good friend, popular, well liked. She's a typical pre-teen into clothes, fashion and music. She is stubborn, determined, and at times a little hard to handle. Mandy is sometimes moody. She can also be very thoughtful. She is also a reader and a dreamer. A young girl who wishes she was different.

Mandy has Cerebral Palsy. She walks with a walker or for long distances, uses a wheelchair. She has trouble with trunk control and balance. Buttons, shoe laces, picking up small items, brushing her hair and a myriad of other things we take for granted, all give her trouble. She gets frustrated with her disability. She gets angry. She has gone all over North America for surgery and therapy.

She is stuck in the middle. We know it and she knows it. If her disability affected her a little more, then she would permanently use a wheelchair and there wouldn't be so many issues to deal with. If her disability affected her a little less, then she would be independently mobile, and there wouldn't be so many issues to deal with. The school finally realized that fact this year. They now see that Mandy is indeed stuck in the middle and presents a different spectrum of challenges to solve.

I think back to the first few years of Mandy's school life. They seemed to go well or maybe we were just naïve and thought so. We met with the resource teacher, teachers, teaching assistant and principal annually and talked about what we would like to see for Mandy during her school year. They all outlined the plans and programs they were going to have in place and it sounded OK to us. There, PPP done. Sign on the dotted line. It looks good on paper. But then again everything looks good on paper.

We were welcomed into the school in those early years. We walked Mandy to her classroom and we sat in on many of her classes and observed. We spoke daily with the teaching assistant to let her know how Mandy's night went, or to show her how we would like her to work with some of Mandy's physical needs, proper walking, proper body position and such. We addressed any concerns that she had about Mandy and answered all her questions about her abilities and how to help her be independent within the school setting. It was a good relationship; respectful with open communication and a common goal of helping Mandy do her best both physically and academically in school.

I struggle to pull my robe off the hook and remember the struggles with the school that we had in subsequent years. In her grade two year, staffing changed and we had a new principal come to our school. Fortunately, Mandy had the same teaching assistant and with whom we had developed such a close relationship. However, the new principal had some sort of personal issue with the teaching assistant and that translated into trouble for us. Suddenly, we no longer felt welcome in the school. We were no longer allowed to walk Mandy to her classroom, to talk with the teaching assistant or to suggest different ways of working with Mandy that we had found to be successful at home. We were entirely shut out of her school day. How could this rejection be a sanctioned part of the PPP? We didn't sign on for that.

During those two years with that particular principal, we tried every route we could think of to re-establish the same relationship with the school that we had all enjoyed in previous years. We met with the teacher who directed us to the resource teacher who directed us to the principal (the principal we were having problems with). We met with him several times to no avail. We went higher, talking with the Regional Supervisor of Student Services at the provincial government level. We found some guidance and support there, but were told we had to follow the proper chain of command and thus were directed to the Supervisor of Student Services for our school district. We met with her and although we had found her to be supportive and helpful in the past, for our concerns with this principal, she was very cool, businesslike and unwilling to help at all. We discovered later, through the grapevine, that she and this principal were very good friends.

Our final step before taking our concerns to the District School Board was to meet with the Director of Education for our school district. There, finally, we felt like we were being heard and we were given affirmation that we had legitimate concerns. We were informed that unfortunately, he could not do a lot about it unless the issue became big enough to take to the school board. However, he doubted that they would do anything either. We asked why and–off the record–he told us basically that this particular principal had been in the district for a very long time, and was a friend of most of the Board members. He had a big ego and spent most of his time on a power trip. The Director also told us–off the record again–that this principal had a health condition and at the end of the year would be given a medical leave of absence until his retirement.

To this day, I still question why we had to be dragged through the mill and why we had to bang on so many different doors before someone would finally just be truthful with us. Why didn't the teacher or resource teacher level with us? They were gagged by the Supervisor of Student Services, of course. Why didn't we get help at the government level? We hadn't gone through the proper chain of command and besides, they can only act in an "advisory capacity." A final decision rests with the School Board. Why was the Director of Education so open and honest with us? I don't know; maybe it was because he is the parent of a child with special needs and as such could relate or maybe, he is just a nice guy. Whatever it was, his honesty allowed us to ride out the rest of the year, stealthily talking to Mandy's teaching assistant in the school when we could and making sure the PPP was followed as best we could.

But this was a challenging time for all of us. We didn't have the daily talks with the teaching assistant to find out how the school day was running, or what was working for Mandy and what wasn't. That made it almost impossible to track whether her PPP was being followed and that lack of communication made it difficult to support Mandy properly at home, too. Thankfully, we had that close relationship with the teaching assistant. She would often phone in the evenings just to "chat as friends do" and the conversation would inevitably turn to Mandy and her day in school. So we did have some communication during this whole period, even though it wasn't school sanctioned and we trusted the teaching assistant implicitly to do what was needed and what was best for Mandy.

I get dressed, hang my towel and go to wake Mandy up. I laugh at her sleepy eyes and tousled hair. Yep, she is going to be your typical teenage girl; I can see it now, sleeping till noon and still resisting the wake-up call! As I help her to the bathroom and start getting her dressed for school, I am again thankful that we made it through those couple of years and the year after with yet another new principal. At least the new one was friendly and open, willing to listen and to help (he finally got the main bathroom made accessible!). More importantly, he was happy to let us, as parents who know our child best, talk to the teaching assistant as much as we felt necessary. That year, we again felt like we were welcome in the school and the whole school atmosphere was back to normal.

I finish dressing Mandy and doing her hair before helping her to the table for breakfast. I set her waffle in front of her and sigh as Mandy's difficulty with fine motor skills lands a sticky piece of waffle in her lap. I clean that up and let her finish while I gather up backpacks and homework. My eye falls to the math assignment we spent hours on last night. Another sigh. It is such hard work for her. Children with cerebral palsy tend to have a lot of difficulty with math, with abstract concepts and with science. Mandy has a hard time with the maps in social studies, too. I grab the lunches and Mandy's shoes and orthotics.

As I help Mandy with her shoes and splints, my mind jumps to the upcoming PPP this morning that my husband, Mark and I will attend as Mandy goes off to her class. How is it going to go? How will Mark react? Will he be relaxed and open or tense and ready to do battle? I've made my notes and my list of topics that we need to review but they are different from Mark's agenda. We have both been focused on her physical needs for so many years so that is where Mark's focus is still.

Mandy has incredible potential to become independently mobile. We have worked with her physically since birth and have seen the gains she has made. Her therapists have said there is no reason why she won't be able to move independently. She has all the strength needed and her balance is coming. All that is standing in her way is her multifaceted fear – fear of failing (falling), fear of succeeding or maybe fear of becoming independent?

As we drive to school, I think we've been lucky so far to be able to focus so much on her physical needs both at home and in the school. Mandy is smart and most academic work has come easily for her to this point. She has been able to keep up so we had the time to focus on her physical needs and the school has been very accommodating for the most part. Mandy has always been at the top of her regular education class without any modifications other than for gym and Grade 5 this year was still very manageable. However, I can see that from this point on, things will start to get more challenging for her. The math concepts are going to increase in difficulty. Science and social studies will creep up there as well. She is going to need more time to have the concepts explained in detail to her so she can understand them. There is going to be a lot more written work and note taking and while she has kept up so far in the written department, she won't be able to from here on out as these later grades start preparing her for high school.

We enter the meeting room and greet the resource teacher, the Grade 5 teacher and Mandy's teaching assistant. The principal isn't able to attend but I feel that is okay. This is really only a year-end review to talk about what has worked this year and what needs to be in place for the beginning of school in the fall. The teaching assistant gives us an overview of what she feels Mandy has accomplished physically and socially this year and the areas where she has seen improvement. She was a brand new teaching assistant this year and we weren't able to guide her and teach her the ways of working with Mandy physically like we did the past teaching assistant. So while we both appreciate the areas where she feels Mandy has improved physically, both Mark and I know it wasn't that dramatic. If anything, we feel Mandy has lost a lot of ground physically this year due in equal parts to her blossoming resistance to physical therapy and the lack of the teaching assistant being in the classroom constantly to make sure that Mandy is sitting properly, keeping her wrist flat while writing, not arching backwards when speaking, and assisting with fine motors activities.

The teaching assistant's report seems to please the resource teacher as she busily jots down all the examples of improvement. Mark notes this, as do I, and he abilities and he asks how will Grade 6 be different? Will the teaching assistant be in the classroom more often to monitor Mandy's positioning? Will Mandy be able to do exercises specific to her during gym time rather than "participating" in basketball or volleyball? What is the school's stand on her continuing her physical gains? I agree with Mark that if Mandy is allowed to have bad posture and hand position then she is going to lose the skills she has now. She needs to keep those physical skill levels, not only because she has the potential to be independently mobile but so that the academic skills are easier to do as well.

The resource teacher tries to change the topic to academics while bypassing the physical concerns we have. The Grade 5 teacher states that it sounds like we want the best of everything for Mandy: physical, academic and social. Mark counters with, "Isn't that what any parent wants?" He tries to steer the conversation back to the physical concerns and the resource teacher again tries to brush them off. Mark stops her and asks, "Aren't Mandy's physical needs now and haven't they always been a part of her PPP?" His questions are thwarted yet again. The discussion is going nowhere and the resource teacher mentions that we have to wrap this meeting up as the next parents will be there in 10 minutes. I ask who the teaching assistant will be for the fall, and whether we know whose classroom she will be in. We are told it will likely be the same teaching assistant but the classroom is not decided yet. We all agree to leave things as they are for the start of the new school year and will make changes as needed at the September PPP meeting.

Mark leaves the meeting feeling very frustrated. He says he felt rushed through the meeting and feels they were sweeping his concerns under the rug. I agree with him but I can also see the school's point of view. They are concerned with her academics and social development and preparing her to be independent in those areas as she nears high school. As a result, they are pulling back the support of the teaching assistant. I understand that, but they don't get the fact that without the physical ability to do her academics, Mandy will never be independent in academics. Without the physical abilities and dexterity necessary to open her pencil case, sharpen her pencil, and open her textbook to the correct page, Mandy will never be truly independent. And as for social development, she is young yet. I have seen her work ethic at home. She will grow in maturity over the next few years and begin to look after her own needs and concerns.

As we drive home and I listen to my husband vent his frustrations, I sigh again, for the hundredth time today it seems. What will the PPP in the fall bring? Will they be willing to take our concerns seriously, or will we be rushed through that meeting, too? Will Mandy get all that she needs? How often will the teaching assistant be in the classroom? Just for transfers and washroom needs or for more constant monitoring of her physical positioning? Does it ever end, this fighting the system for what is best for your child? Where does Mandy fit in all of this? Come fall do we get her to sit in on the PPP and begin to voice her thoughts and concerns, if any? She is definitely getting to be old enough to have a say about how she wants her days to operate.

I am beat and the day has hardly even begun. I want to crawl back into the shower and let the water run. Being a parent is tough; being a parent of a child with special needs goes beyond tough. Being the child with the special needs goes way beyond that.

I know in my heart that it will all work out in the end and that Mandy will be just fine despite what her PPP says, what it does or what it doesn't do. She will grow and mature and find her own place in the world.

I sigh again and for the hundredth, millionth, billionth time since she was born, I give thanks for who she is and who she is one day going to become, PPP or no PPP.

PROFESSIONAL INQUIRY

Individual Education Plan/Personal Program Plan

- Analyze the extent to which the Personal Program Plan or Individual Education Plan is responding to Mandy's needs.
- Critique the school's approach and response to the parents at the program planning meeting for Mandy.
- Identify the implications associated with inviting Mandy to the program planning meeting.
- Generate recommendations for enhancing the Personal Program Plan development and implementation process.

Principal Leadership

- Discuss how the philosophy and actions of a school principal can impact upon a culture of inclusion within a school community?
- Explore the possible ethical issues associated with the relationships between the school principal and the supervisor of student services.
- Discuss how this case can be used to advance inclusive education with a school or school system.

Parental Knowledge

- Identify the knowledge that the parents possessed regarding Mandy that may have contributed to the enhancement of the Personal Program Plan.

CASE COMMENTARY REFLECTIONS

After reading the commentaries reflect on the following:

New Insights
Identify new insights gained from reading the commentaries.

Understandings
Discuss the impact of the commentaries on your understandings of inclusive education.

Questions
Identify questions that emerge from reading the commentaries.

CASE COMMENTARY 1

Agnes Gajuwski and Anne Jordan

The main challenges currently facing the parents are to make their views heard by the staff at the school, and to be able to advocate successfully on Mandy's behalf. The Personal Program Plan (PPP) review meeting did not go well. Communication, or lack of it, was a key issue. After the meeting, we still do not know what resources are currently available to Mandy. If resources are in place, the parents are unaware of them, suggesting that communication between home and school is still lacking.

From the perspective of parents, we know very little about Mandy's communicational, academic and physical needs in the classroom. Her social needs are not considered at all. She has achieved well to date, but her parents' concerns about her future are justified. There does not seem to have been any discussion or plan to assist Mandy in the transition between grades, or to prepare her for secondary school. We are not told of Mandy's levels of readiness for assuming a greater degree of self-sufficiency in Grade 5. We do not know if there are technological resources available to her, nor what steps if any have been taken to prepare Mandy to use them. Other resources, such as the availability of the resource teacher, teaching assistant, peer supports, outside agencies need to be made clear for all involved if full inclusion is to be achieved.

Everyone seems to subscribe to greater independence for Mandy. However the participants have differing views about what form this will take. Her father sees the teaching assistant as important to monitor Mandy's seating and posture. The school seems to understand independence as phasing out dependence on the teaching assistant. However, neither position will be successful unless Mandy herself learns to self-monitor her seating and posture, and this may require an instructional intervention by all parties to move her toward this goal, and further, to help her learn to advocate for her own needs. The next meeting should not address whether Mandy needs to assume more responsibility for her learning needs, but how to get her there.

The September meeting should also be used to address Mandy's academic needs. It should devote some time, preferably without time constraints, to initial plans for short-term and long-term transitions to subsequent grades and to secondary school. It should also consider details of the accommodations that will maintain Mandy's excellent academic record, including a plan to evaluate the success of those accommodations. If Mandy's physical skills are likely to impede her progress, technological resources should be considered, such as voice-activated word processing. Her potential difficulties in mathematics and science could also be addressed, while her strengths in other areas could be highlighted. For example, is Mandy developing skills in languages, the arts and literature, and if not, what is needed to make sure these are not neglected?

The parents' expertise about Mandy's physical needs should be represented in further plans. The members of the PPP meeting should also be clear that parents are full participants in the planning and transition process. As participants they should be able to keep track of Mandy's progress in much greater detail than at present. The classroom teacher and resource teacher should be the primary contact people in this partnership; the teaching assistant should not carry this responsibility.

CASE COMMENTARY 2

JoAnne Putnam

This case illustrated the challenges that parents can face in advocating for their child's education. While parents vary in their knowledge and expertise concerning disabilities and education, Mandy's parents are well informed and highly committed to their daughter's success at school. They are actively involved with PPP planning and have persevered through trying times. As "senior partners" in the planning process, their perspectives should be honored through a process that maintains open lines of communication, promotes consensus building, clarifies roles, and has clear procedures for resolving disagreements.

Effective collaboration requires that planning team members reach consensus regarding expectations for the student as well as expectations for school supports and services. We know that high expectations for students with special needs improve outcomes. Mandy's parents would like to see more focus on physical outcomes, as Mandy is at the top of her class academically. The resource teacher is more concerned with academics and social functioning. A consultant may recommend greater use of instructional technology to enhance Mandy's fine motor skills and written expression.

Differing expectations are understandable and to be expected. Unfortunately, in Mandy's case it appears that time constraints in the planning process cut off important discussions prematurely. The parent's questions about plans and support personnel for the next year received vague responses in the rush to end the meeting. More time is needed for thoughtful planning.

It appears that the general educators need to be more involved in the PPP discussions, as they are responsible for Mandy's curriculum and instruction. Have co-teaching models for the resource teacher and general educator been explored? And what are the roles of the general educator and the teaching assistant? The lines of responsibility do not seem clear. Finally, how and to what extent was Mandy involved in the PPP planning?

Transitions require more advanced planning if next year's teachers are to pick up where last year's team left off. Delays in start-up time at the beginning of each school year translate into lost opportunities for learning. Parents also need to know that the school is following through with the Personal Program Plan. If the plan is simply on paper without an effective process for reporting on progress toward stated goals, it may fail due to lack of feedback and evaluation. Formal strategies such as narrative reports during the grading period and informal communication through communication books, phone calls, or electronic communication through e-mails or websites are examples of techniques.

Mandy's parents needed a mechanism for addressing and resolving their concerns. Some schools have student support teams that meet regularly to consider parent and teacher concerns, for example. Formal mediation procedures should be available in school districts. With improvements in PPP planning processes and procedures for addressing concerns, many of the difficulties Mandy's parents encountered can be prevented or resolved.

CASE COMMENTARY 3

Marie Schoeman

The case study explores the trajectory of the parents' experience of inclusion of their daughter, Mandy, who has cerebral palsy, over a number of years at a particular school. As is often the case, there are good times and there are bad times, supportive individuals and obstructionists. And throughout, parents usually see themselves as the staunch and fierce protectors of their child's best interests. A successful inclusive system and school is one that establishes structures, cultures, policies and practices which are strong enough to withstand the influence of individuals with negative attitudes. It is of course problematical if the school principal, who should be providing visionary leadership, is the one who is causing the problems. Unwillingness to be flexible and accommodating in applying the rules of the school and to allow natural partnerships and communication with the parents to be harnessed in the best interests of a child can become a serious stumbling block.

Parents, who feel strongly about their child's rights to attend mainstream school, are often confronted with power plays on the part of principals at the school and district levels. Education departments should recognize this as a potential area of difficulty and set in place measures to prevent principals from intimidating parents. From my own experience, a school-based support team which consists of a number of teachers who are advocates for inclusion can often be the catalyst between the school and the parents. It is very important to solve problems in context and as they arise so as to prevent a situation where the parents have to call upon the next level of authority. This is often very difficult for parents, especially if they are not as empowered as Mandy's parents.

Where it can be considered natural that parents would want to be involved in the education of their child in the early years, they need to start withdrawing and trust the school to support the child in the most appropriate way as the child becomes older. Parents should not be encouraged to interfere in the classroom which is the domain of the teacher. The teaching assistant of the child should also not take over the responsibility of the teacher. Provided sound communication systems have been established, the parents should step back. In many under resourced systems such as the one in which I work, a teaching assistant for each child would in any case be out of the question.

Personal program planning is increasingly recognizing the right of the child to have a voice in the process. Although the commitment of the parents to ensure the optimal physical development of their children, must be admired, they also have to realize that they cannot control all processes related to their child's development and need to allow her to indicate how she wants to gain her growing academic and social independence.

Even a child with a severe disability, remains a child first and has a right to a life of her own which is not controlled by caregivers and professionals. Striking a balance and applying common sense are keys to successful inclusion.

CASE COMMENTARY 4

Anne Kresta

The key point in this case is the need for true collaboration in the Personal Program Plan(PPP) process so that the educational outcomes are prioritized in an appropriate manner and all team members feel validated. Too often personality issues and agendas take over (in the case of the second principal, for example) and voices are not heard or appreciated. Sometimes parents are left out of the *real* discussion because they are viewed as wanting too much for their child at the exclusion of all other children or staff at the school. It is difficult, from the case study, to know what each party's interests are when it comes to Mandy's education and knowing this could help the team work more collaboratively together. For example, if educational assistant time is an issue, or understanding of the consequences of not maintaining correct posture is not present, then these should be on the table and open for discussion.

Actions that may be taken to alleviate this situation include having Mandy as an active team member and enlisting the services of an advocate who can help to keep the conversation on a professional level and help to delve into what exactly the issues and interests are for each of the planning team members. It may also be useful to have someone knowledgeable come to do a presentation to the group that would elaborate upon the needs for continued physical intervention so that Mandy can continue to develop independent movement skills. This may be a physiotherapist or an advocate from the Cerebral Palsy Association. This person could also elaborate upon the learning challenges that Mandy faces and the need for reduced work load and adapted curricular outcomes in certain areas of her education. This technique has been quite helpful in my experience with two sons who have both Asperger Syndrome and Tourette Syndrome. By in-servicing the teachers and the resource staff, we were better able to work together towards what we all viewed as relevant goals.

Another avenue to explore would be to have a longer range plan facilitated by an outside agency or person with all the stakeholders around the table. This plan, along the lines of a PATH (Planning Alternative Tomorrows with Hope) would enable all participants to dream along with Mandy of what her future will hold and then to work together to choose relevant, positive and possible goals to be set in the PPP. Every time the PPP is revisited it can be measured in terms of how well it is preparing Mandy for her future. This would take the onus off of any one individual member of the team and make it truly collaborative.

In any case, it is important for the parents to document the results of conversations and meetings with various school system staff and to reiterate these meeting "minutes" in the form of letters or memos to the staff in question. These letters should be strictly professional, restating the facts and concerns that were raised by the various parties. If there are possible solutions to some of the problems that are reasonable and achievable, they also may be part of the letter. Having this kind of paper trail enables the parents to document the meetings, their outcomes and helps them to more effectively travel the chain of command when they need to. I have found the use of the paper trail very effective when advocating for increased supports or a change in approach when it comes to how educational programming is set up for my sons.

- Some questions to raise with regards to this case are whether the PPP updates could be done more frequently (at every reporting period for academic marks) and whether the planning team could be expanded to include the clinicians that are working with Mandy outside of the school system to help her gain independent mobility.
- I also question the professionalism of the school board and the superintendents when they are reluctant to address valid complaints regarding the actions of a school principal.
- On a day to day level, I wonder if a communication book could be implemented to help the parents to understand how Mandy's school day is progressing so they do not feel obligated to be present at the school and in the classroom so often.
- There may also be a role for each of the classroom teachers to play in ensuring that more correct posture is used and curriculum is adapted to better respond to Mandy's needs.

CASE COMMENTARY 5

Isabel Killoran

This case study provides insight into the experiences of parents in the Personal Program Plan(PPP or also known as an Individual Education Plan) process and the frustration and anxiety they can feel in preparing for and participating in meetings related to developing and/or reviewing objectives. People often forget that parents' objectives involve an understanding of their child that school staff just cannot have in the few hours a day that they are with the student. Sometimes the objectives of the school and parents do not match. Finding a way to make sure that all the voices are heard and understood is very important. There are effective ways of collaborating with parents (such as MAPS – Making Action Plans/McGill Action Planning System) so that everyone is an equal and active participant (including the child).

The description of Mandy at the beginning of the case is a perfect illustration of what would be included in the MAPS process. Mandy's mother sets the stage for wanting to really get to know who Mandy is. This is a very different approach from how most meetings begin. In practice, meetings are rushed and parents are often bombarded with all the things their child is not or cannot do. Rarely have I witnessed a truly holistic image of a child being presented at a non-MAPS meeting (i.e. IPRC or IEP review). What have your experiences been? Imagine if those meetings had been structured like MAPS where you had the opportunity to listen to positive descriptions from Mandy and all of the important people in her life. Would the tone have been different? Would the outcome have been different?

This case also presents the parents' perception of having to do battle with the school. This is not an uncommon experience. If parents feel this way then meetings are less likely to be productive. What can schools do to create welcoming and colla- borative environments? As demonstrated in this case, the principal is key to setting the tone and the overall culture of the school. Mandy's parents have had principals who have been welcoming and another that had a closed door policy. Imagine how it must feel to a parent to know they are not welcome in their own child's school. If they aren't welcome how could they possibly trust that the school is capable of educating their child? This approach creates an atmosphere of distrust. During a child's time in a school there are often several people who serve as principal. Each time, parents can feel like they are starting over. The transition between administra- tion and the impact that has on students' PPP's and parents' experiences cannot be overlooked.

To compensate for the lack of communication with a "team" parents may come to depend on educational assistants (EA) to fill them in on what is happening with their child. Research has shown that EAs are often used ineffectively; they frequently take on the role of "teacher" as many classroom teachers abdicate their responsibility for the planning and including of children who work with EAs. Generally, an EA's preparation does not include how to modify or accommodate yet they, the people with the least training in this area, are being left to do just that for the students with the highest needs. Research has also shown that EAs can interfere with the social interaction of the child if the EA is not aware of strategies to avoid this. Finding creative ways to use personnel support, such as EAs, so that a child works toward independence can be challenging but it is ultimately beneficial to the child. The key is collaboration.

CASE COMMENTARY 6

Dr. Kathryn Noel

Because most parents engage daily with their children in settings outside of school, they may have important information to share with school personnel about the child's struggles and progress in relation to the Personal Program Plan(PPP). Moreover, parents need to feel that their input is valued and respected, for the child ultimately belongs to them and not to the school.

It is in the best interests of the child, the parents, and the school personnel to include in suggestions for activities to be done at home in the PPP. The child then benefits from the consistent reinforcement of skills, behaviours, and concepts both at home and at school.

Specific categories for observations as they relate to the PPP might be suggested to all those who participate in the meetings. In that way, particular topics can be the focus of the discussion, and all relevant information and concerns can be shared within the time scheduled for the meeting.

CONNECTING TO PROFESSIONAL PRACTICE

The commentary writers discuss a number of issues that emerge in this case. The need to clearly define and monitor the role of educational assistants was identified as very important in promoting and sustaining inclusive learning environments. The influence and impact of the school principal upon the inclusive culture of the school and ensuring effective transition planning processes were in place were highlighted by the writers. The significance of including the voices and perspectives of the student within individual education plans or personal program plans was also stressed.

Select one of the issues identified by the commentary writers and discuss how your experiences relate to this issue.

CASE TWENTY FIVE: SCATTERED NOTES FROM A SCATTERED MOM

Daniel's educational career when he started at the age of four with early entrance all the way through to his high school graduation has been a road of frustration, exhaustion, and a few sunny patches now and then when we thought the clouds might be letting in a few positive rays. Writing something about it–something I thought would be a bit of a catharsis–turned into a form of water torture. I'd sit down ready to write with the summer horizon before me and I would begin to remember the many painful school experiences. My mind would start to sift through all those times when people just didn't understand Daniel or when they invented creative ways for supporting him. I remembered the people who wished all the best for Daniel, my boy with autism. However, they would also indicate that it would be great if he could get the support somewhere as far away from them and their school as possible.

Daniel is 18 now. We're in a new phase of life, our family of six. We've sold the farm. Dan is taking a shot at living in the city with his brother in an apartment. After weeks of thinking about what Daniel's school years were like, I felt almost paralyzed to write anything beyond some scattered recollections. So pardon my lack of cohesive storyline as I share some memories of my son's time in school. I guess the brain has ways to protect our hearts from too much pain, so it seems there are fuzzy memories and some that have disappeared altogether.

At four, Daniel went off to school in our small rural community, riding the bus with his siblings. The school hired an educational assistant. Ironically, Dan was the first person with a disability since his Uncle Francis, my husband's younger brother.

For Dan, kindergarten and grade one was a fairly good experience. They tried to make inclusion work, however, you could see the frayed edges showing. The communication book that traveled to and from school was good, but the content needed to be more useful. I didn't really need to read how frustrated the educational assistant was, nor did she need to "tattle" on everything Dan might have done during the day. Anyone supervised that closely is going to make a mistake. When other students might daydream or look out the window, it's not a huge concern. But when Daniel did it, he was labeled "unfocused."

As he moved on to grade three and up, things deteriorated. The number of times Dan was pulled out of the classroom increased and teachers and staff found more differences, more reason to isolate him. In a flash of real ingenuity, they created a Time Out room in a storage closet and he probably spent more time in it than the mops and brooms ever did. Dan's classmates told me it frightened them when he was put in there.

When Daniel's breakdown happened, it was both physical and mental. He was aggressive and unhappy. After many doctor visits, he was suspended from school for four months and the principal was pushing us hard to send Dan to a special school. We went to meeting after meeting, trying to convince them there had to be an alternative. It wasn't until we met the Special Education Coordinator that we felt for the first time that these meetings were about education and she insisted Dan get back into school. It would happen even if it meant hiring all new staff.

It's here that I go into my freefall of notes as I think about what followed for awhile. As I look back, some of it doesn't even make any sense to me:

The teaching assistant travels on the bus with Daniel to our farm daily. Daniel saw a behavioural consultant and is prescribed medication.

Many struggles and both my husband's and my job was impacted greatly. We'd get calls at work to pick Dan up from school. There would be a half hour drive to work, only to have to turn around and drive back to get him.

I often wonder what it would feel like to have an immediate opportunity for a break. Parents do the job of raising their child 24–7. Throughout the struggles, it was not the professionals that provided support to us but other parents. We burned up the phone lines as we received ideas and techniques to try, ears that listened and shoulders felt comfortable and safe to cry on.

We could see plainly that the more Dan was included with his age peers, the more he learned. Pullouts and isolation can never prepare our children for the future.

Dan's siblings played a huge role; my other sons and daughters and their friends included Dan. They would stand up for him at school.

When Dan entered high school, inclusion became even more difficult.

It was at this time I was offered a job as a teaching assistant in Dan's school. I saw it as an opportunity to bring the philosophy of inclusion into the school. This wasn't easy. While the students were accepting and willing to help and support peers with a disability, every class had a different mood depending on the teacher. What inclusion is not? Please remember there is nothing inclusive or "special" about having the desk for 'that' student in the back corner of the classroom. It is even less special so to be educated separately from your peers and that only serves to widen the gap and makes differences more evident. I recognize that some students needed fewer distractions to complete their work, but this must be monitored carefully. Maybe a goal for the classroom is to adapt to noise, adapt the presence of someone who acts a bit differently. Teaching assistants should not be educating a student with a disability on their own away from the classroom.

We started attending the meetings about Dan's transition after high school. I realized quite soon and with some horror that the "options" for Dan's future centred on which group homes and sheltered workshops might be most suitable, including a huge workshop in Saskatoon with over 350 people in it. My arguments included concepts like Daniel owning his own home, further education, creating a meaningful job he enjoys doing. The talk for Daniel started to focus on the dreaded "life skills approach." The suggestions were pretty wimpy. He could have a paper route. Maybe deliver milk. Please, let's be creative. They started to insist Dan have two teaching assistants with him "in case something happens." In truth, Dan's 14-year-old sister can provide the support he needs, yet the school was all wrapped up in some sort of protection model.

As the end of grade 12 draws closer, we get called to a meeting. The big question: "Who will be responsible for Dan on graduation day?" After all this time, this is the concern for our son on the day he moves from school into his adulthood. I think it needs to be said that after much planning and negotiating, Daniel graduated and was a star that evening. All the staff commented on how well it all went and we were very proud. As I look back now, it really didn't matter about all of our planning the staff and I did. Daniel chose it to be a great time.

Daniel always loved English. He doesn't write but he loves the spoken word. For some reason, he has a great appreciation for Shakespeare. One smart teaching assistant adapted his assignments so there would be oral readings and she used other students to read to Dan. Last summer, he bolted from his mentor on the University campus. Where was he found? On stage with the actors in a Shakespearean play. He cannot tell us about his interests and passions, but he can certainly show us.

So now, we lurch along into Dan's future, trying a few things out, trying not to worry, trying to relax. He's living in an apartment with his brother and we're providing some supports. We are a family who knows who Dan is. Adam lives with him and supports him because they are brothers. Adam believes in Dan and I've no doubt the reverse is true.

Is Dan prepared for his life? Are we? I am not sure but we'll take that road together and Dan will do his best to let us know how we're doing.

PROFESSIONAL INQUIRY

Inclusive Education

– Critiques the educational programs provided to Daniel and identify the processes that were not consistent with inclusive education philosophy.
– Identify proactive responses to systemic barriers to inclusion that exist in schools.
– Generate strategies for helping to change the way teachers and other professionals think about their work, their roles and their practices in relation to inclusive education.
– Identify approaches for reviewing inclusionary practices in schools.

Social Justice

– Explore counter narratives that can be introduced to disrupt the model of disability that positions students labeled "disabled" on the margins.
– Explore how students can be given a voice in the construction of their own identities.
– Discuss how inclusive education is concerned with how we understand and engage with difference in valued and respectful ways.
– Explore methods to assist teachers and other professionals to re-construct their beliefs and values related to student's right to education and the vision of inclusive education.
– Respond to the following statement, "A belief in the right to choice and freedom and in the agency of students labelled "disabled" and their parents is critical to the achievement of the goal of inclusive schooling".

School Culture

- Discuss how inclusion needs to be linked to fundamental changes in the culture of schools, communities and societies
- Respond to the perspective that inclusion is about asking important questions about the way in which the school as an organization is structured and how the organization can be transformed to ensure the inclusion of all students.

CASE COMMENTARY REFLECTIONS

After reading the commentaries reflect on the following:

New Insights
Identify new insights gained from reading the commentaries.

Understandings
Discuss the impact of the commentaries on your understandings of inclusive education.

Questions
Identify questions that emerge from reading the commentaries.

CASE COMMENTARY 1

Carla Digiogio

This is a heart-wrenching account of what it is like to be a parent of a child with learning and social challenges in school. I felt for the parent as she told of the stress of working while trying to provide support to her child. The need to leave work to pick up her child when he had difficulty is very common and must have a devastating effect on parents' work and home lives, not to mention their marriages.

The support that the student's siblings gave him and continue to give him is inspiring. I feel that siblings and friends should have their own support systems to discuss and plan for the success of a their sibling or friend. They should educate educators on how to better support students with challenges in the school. The support network for the parents is also very necessary as this mother attests. It is sad though, that the school was not as supportive as it could have been.

A big issue for me is the separation that took place in the child's life at school. The physical and academic separation probably had long lasting effects on his learning and his self-esteem. The lack of problem solving skills or willingness to try, is no excuse for isolating children from their peers, neglecting their learning, or forcing them to spend unreasonable amounts of time with an educational assistant outside of the classroom. This is unacceptable.

I have seen many cases where parents became employed by the school to be able to have a say or impact in some way the teaching of students with learning challenges. It is good to see them in this setting and able to give their view of what should be. Their experience is immeasurable. However, sometimes they are seen as biased and unprofessional when they get involved in other children's cases and advocate for parents in a way that is seen as threatening to other staff in the building and system.

There is a lack of respect in many cases for parents and educational assistants due to their perceived lack of education or power in the school system. Yet, they have more first-hand knowledge of students with challenges as they spend the most time with them. These key participants need to be invited and heard at the table when planning and ongoing reporting of progress is being discussed. They need to be respected for their ideas and listened to.

Finally, I applaud all students like this one who have the inner fortitude to continue in the face of all of this adversity. I also applaud their siblings and friends for supporting them and feel we need to see these peers as the key to individuals' health and wellbeing in and outside of schools and include them in our planning.

CASE COMMENTARY 2

Marilyn Dolmage

Of course, we are left to wonder how Dan's school staff would have described his education. This story is recounted by his mother, but this is a parent who has also worked in a school. There is a need for real teamwork – where members understand and respect each other's perspectives while keeping the focus on serving the student.

Despite what we often hear from school systems and teacher federations, it does NOT seem to me that Dan's problems arose because of a lack of resources. The school system was willing to pay to maintain and expand segregated programs or to plug in additional support staff. They were not willing to change – at least for Dan.

While much is discouraging about Dan's elementary and secondary school education – and all those important years could have been used so much better – it is great to know that his life has improved so much now. Someone whose future was seen as very limited now lives in a home of his choice and is furthering his education. Where there is a will, there can be a way!

Also encouraging here is the fact that young people can make a difference. Dan's brothers and sisters remain so much a part of his life – and they have become even more resourceful as adults. His mother has worked in the school system and knows that other students can learn well together, in spite of (or perhaps because of) their differences. My experience tells me that those other children who saw Dan treated badly by educators as a child might have the social justice perspective needed to create real change.

It's really all about listening to students like Dan. And if they do not communicate with words, we must learn to hear with more than our ears! There are challenges, but accommodations can be found. Let's remind ourselves of all of Dan's strengths and how he is motivated by what interests him: he loves English, has a passion for Shakespeare! That's what is exciting about education; everyone can learn and change: students and school systems alike.

No progress can be made to improve education when the focus involves removing students from schools and classrooms. It is difficult for parents to trust the system, when their first contact may be with an administrator who proposes that their child leave, go somewhere else, to a segregated program away from his or her own community. Teachers isolated Dan – whether by punishing him in a closet or by forcing one- or even two-to-one educational assistant support without seeming to clarify educational roles. His school's inability to resolve issues meant that Dan was denied education altogether, suspended and sent home.

What is striking is the lack of real solutions on the part of Dan's school staff. They didn't seem to adapt their approach to accommodate and respect Dan. They appeared to create was an archaic and probably abusive "time out" room: and their planning involved suggesting segregated adult programs and a paper route. By contrast, Dan's family was creative, changing their lives and taking risks to find a better life for him – selling their farm, helping Dan and his brother to share an apartment, now involving him in university. It's no wonder that Dan's mother said their best help came from other parents, not professionals. One special education consultant finally made a difference by putting the focus on Dan, willing even to risk hiring all new staff.

Collaboration will not improve unless responsibilities are agreed upon and roles are clarified. In this story, it seems that the school's goal was control, while his family wanted Dan's world to expand. The family wanted inclusion, but says the school too often isolated him. When he was removed from school, staff had less work while his family had more. Although additional staff were always available – one or two educational assistants – there seems not to have been agreement about their roles. The communication book should not just report on problems perceived as the fault of the student, but can be used to improve collaboration and change school team behaviour.

CASE COMMENTARY 3

Nithi Muthukrishna

This case study makes one more aware that prejudice, exclusion and discrimination which largely emanate from a medical and deficit view of disability are still major issues confronting children labelled 'disabled' or 'special' in school settings. The hegemonic psycho-medical model positions students labelled with disabilities as the 'other', marginal, with deficits and deficiencies, and in need of *expert* intervention. This social "mothering" results in teacher and professional mindsets and educational practices that are exclusionary and in opposition to the philosophy of inclusive education. For example, conceptualizing the educational needs of students labelled 'disabled' as located outside the general curriculum, positions these students as the other and as marginal. The case study foregrounds the power of the traditional form of special education and educational psychology and the capacity of these sectors to retain control over inclusive education settings in pervasive ways. The case study draws attention to the fact that the voice of the professional expert continues to be privileged in schools that have included students labelled 'disabled'. This without doubt impacts the nature and forms of inclusion and exclusion.

In South Africa, debates have focused on the issue of what discourses are embedded in professional training and development programs. Such debates have highlighted the need for professional development programs that provide counter narratives to disrupt the psycho-medical model. Such perspectives should reflect a social rights model and a view of inclusive education as a moral and ethical imperative. Our policies call for an engagement with inclusive education in the context of systemic discrimination and deep structural barriers to educational access. Such counter narratives should engage with the issues such as: the nature of diversity in the classroom, school and in society and how diversity can be embraced; education as a human right; the need for political critique of social values, priorities and the structures of schools; the need for continual constant critique of exclusionary school practices within so called inclusive settings; the agency of students labeled 'disabled' and their parents; the need to challenge stereotypical notions of lowered expectations and categorical, technical approaches to teaching students labeled disabled; and developing innovative, creative approaches to curriculum access for all children.

Professional development programs have to prepare teachers and support professionals to interrogate the power structures within schools that serve to reproduce injustices and oppression. This would involve examining questions such as: Who is affirmed? Who is marginalized and relegated to the status of 'other'? Who gets what? Who is given voice? Who makes decisions? Who benefits from such decisions? Who loses out from decisions made? Which students are more valued and which are not? Who is not given voice? What are the disabling and oppressive practices, beliefs, assumptions within the institution?

CASE COMMENTARY 4

Penny Milton

My Daniel is older than yours. He's a beginning teacher - a teacher who I believe will strive to understand a child like yours, one who will want to really know each child – their intentions, aspirations, interests, personalities, ways of learning and ways of relating to their worlds - because he deeply believes in the essential humanity and worth of every child. And he likely thinks that way because he of his own experiences of exclusion – different, yet in some ways the same.

As the youngest of four boys, I sometimes wondered if Daniel had a fair share of love and attention at home or at school. Handsome, bright, athletic, musically talented, you'd have thought school would be a breeze. Yet it was those adolescent years when adults – parents as well as teachers - jump to conclusions, misunderstand intentions and try to control when what the youngster needs is support. I remember the high school principal who told me he was afraid of Dan but could offer no reason for his fear. Dan left school at sixteen and eventually found his way without a graduation diploma.

Both your son and mine encountered educators who cared, who listened, understood and knew how to connect with them in ways that facilitated learning. But these essential features of diverse classrooms are not yet systemic in education systems.

There are two truths in these stories – every parent wants the best for their child; every child can learn. Inclusion must mean that each child is valued and recognized as a learner, and as a person who belongs in the community, not simply allowed in under certain circumstances. We need to recognize that all students benefit when every child participates and is an active and valued member of the school community. When we talk about children who are different, children with disabilities, or children with exceptionalities, who are we comparing them to? In the march for higher standards, are we running a real risk of standardization of the human condition and a reduced tolerance for the diversity of people, a risk of implying a greater worth of some than of others? The language is difficult. We do need to provide supports that allow all children to learn but 'accommodation' is often a weasel word. Sometimes we seem to mean "making fit" but if we are committed to inclusion it can only mean "to make room for, to hold without crowding, to allow for…"

Inclusion is fundamentally an issue of values. To bring about inclusion, these values must be translated into educational design – of facilities, of curriculum, of pedagogy, together with the foundational principles of recognition, justice, respect and community.

CASE COMMENTARY 5

Alex Dingwall

This situation reminds me of our experiences in the early days of "integration". For a vision of inclusion to take hold, it requires a change in the way that parents, educators, government agencies and communities view the approach to supporting quality education. Every individual within the education system had to be oriented and trained to serve students with disabilities and individual needs with the vision that they will be successful, contributing members of their community after graduation.

Without this common vision, supported by policy, resources and community involvement, children would be exposed to a myriad of different approaches not based on sound developmental and educational principles. While "mom was asking for support and help", she probably was dealing with a school system that was very poorly equipped or able to meet her son's needs.

We have learned that to make significant and meaningful change in the education system requires a process that takes extra-ordinary effort and time. It requires a leadership and understanding at all levels from government to the classroom.

One can only hope that Daniel's experience challenged his school and community to start to think on how they may move towards inclusion in a pro-active and positive manner.

CONNECTING TO PROFESSIONAL PRACTICE

Social justice emerges as a significant theme in the commentaries. Consider how your own values, beliefs and practices reflect and align with the social justice principles inherent within inclusive education.

SIGNIFICANCE OF LIVED EXPERIENCES FOR INCLUSIVE EDUCATION

Dr. Vianne Timmons
President and Vice Chancellor
University of Regina

This book was an innovative project, bringing together real-life experiences in inclusive education to enhance learning for students studying to be teachers and experienced teachers. It is critical that we share our stories and experiences, because through this sharing we can advance our collective knowledge about inclusive practices.

I have been promoting inclusive practices since the 1980s. At times, I rejoice at the research and changes that have taken place over the last three decades. We have very few segregated schools, in many elementary schools inclusive classes are the norm, and we have many universities and colleges in Canada providing education for young men and women with intellectual disabilities.

At other times, however, I feel great frustration at how little progress we have made. In many cases, for example, our secondary schools have not embraced inclusive education as I would have hoped. Many teacher education programs have not infused their curriculum with inclusive practices, and we have fewer and fewer researchers working in the field. Yet we know that all children can benefit from inclusive educational practices, so it is critical at this time to ensure that we recognize and communicate the importance of inclusive educational practices.

Using narratives such as those in this book brings to life the reality of teaching in a complex system. There are many issues faced in classrooms that require innovative solutions and partnerships. This book of 25 cases which illustrate that children, families, teachers and schools are interwoven and multi-dimensional.

The case commentaries provide an opportunity for the reader to hear the reflections of other educators on each case. Through the case studies and commentaries, the reader has an opportunity to experience guided reflection and participate in a discussion of the lived experience of others.

In Theme 1, *Commitment to Inclusion*, we are introduced right away to the challenges principals face in promoting inclusive practices in their schools. Leadership is a critical component in any school that wants promote inclusive practices, and principals must support innovative approaches to education for a school to adopt an inclusive philosophy. In Theme 1, we are also introduced to the challenges a school faces to be truly inclusive. It is not only about meaningfully including children with intellectual challenges, but also children of different races, religions and cultures. Some of the most challenging children to include are those with behavioural difficulties who have become disenfranchised and become school leavers. The importance of partnerships with families, other teachers and social services is also evident in this Theme. Educators need to know how to initiate and support collaborative relationships to enhance learning opportunities and to ensure consistency for children.

Theme 2, *Professional Knowledge and Practice*, challenges us to recognize that our beliefs and values influence our behaviours. To be effective educators and leaders, we need to reflect on and learn from our past decisions. Sometimes it takes colleagues to help us see the influence our assumptions can have on our teaching. Sometimes it takes courage to challenge colleagues' behaviours and assumptions. Teaching is filled with contradictions and complexities, and it is only through recognizing this that we can manoeuvre through the relationships and challenges faced every day. In Theme 2, the case on "Six Girls and a Bully" demonstrates the importance of being thorough and of ensuring that students' safety is paramount in our schools. That is a responsibility we cannot take lightly, because students cannot learn in an unsafe environment. We know this; however, it is challenging to keep our classes, halls and school spaces safe. It requires an observant eye and vigilant supervision. Inclusive education does necessarily mean that everyone is meaningfully included and can learn a given educational environment.

Theme 3 looks at *School Level Planning and Practices*. This section is critical for schools, as collaboration is a critical component of inclusive schools. School Teams are reviewed here, together with the challenges that exist in implementing them. As mentioned earlier, family involvement is also part of a collaborative approach to education, and the role of parents in planning is also explored in this section.

Challenges and Barriers to Inclusion are explored in Theme 4, a section which provides us with rich information on the multi-dimensional aspects of inclusion. This section is a great illustration of how we can learn from each other. Language and treatment of others are highlighted in this section, because ror a school to be inclusive we need to ensure that people are treated with dignity and respect. Advocacy should be embraced and supported because advocates not only provide critical information for teachers, but also challenge us to do the best we can for children.

The Voice of Parents is central to Theme 5. Teachers often overlook the rich resource they have in parents, viewing them as their agents rather than partners. This section highlights the challenges of advocating for inclusion in a system that does not always embrace parents' views and desires. For many families, advocacy has had to become a way of life. They have had to advocate throughout the school system, encountering resistance to inclusion for their child over and over again. They know that their child will live in an inclusive society and the school should be a reflection of that society. Hearing parents' voices gives teachers an opportunity to step out of the educator role and experience the frustration and challenges many parents face. For true partnerships to be formed, hearing parents' voices is crucial.

This book explores many aspects of inclusive practices, and in doing so positions relationship and respect as central to the discussions. I found myself nodding as I read through the cases and the commentaries, reflecting on many similar situations I myself have experienced as an educator and as a parent. I hope you felt the same as you read through the stories, thoughts, dreams, frustrations and reflections of principals, teachers and parents. This book captures the challenges and the benefits of inclusive practices, and in doing so shows us both how far we have come and how far we still have to go. Taking the time to read, think about and learn from others' experiences it is a privilege. Sharing the stories presented in this book within teacher education and leadership development programs will hopefully help to make inclusive education a reality for all children and families.

FINAL REFLECTIONS

Exploring Inclusive Educational Practices Through Professional Inquiry invites reflection, exploration and critique of the educational practices and processes that can impact upon a vision and lived reality of inclusive education.

The narratives captured in this text illuminate the dimensions necessary for all students to be fully included in schools. Inclusive attitudes, beliefs and commitments are an essential first step in welcoming and inviting all students and families into the school system. These dispositions must be combined with extensive professional knowledge, relevant curriculum, effective practices and enabling policies for inclusion to be supported and realized.

The voice of parents is privileged and included in this educational text. The lived experiences of parents can serve as powerful pedagogical and curriculum resources for the professional learning of educators, researchers, community personnel and policy makers. Innovation, communication and collaboration enable flexible and accessible learning environments to be adapted in response to individual student strengths, interests and needs.

It is hoped that the narratives in this text will help support inclusive education. This book can be used as a pedagogical and curriculum resource within teacher education, leadership formation programs and in professional learning sessions for educators, policy makers and school support personnel. This collection of stories, inquiry processes and commentaries are intended to help open the minds and hearts of educators and policy makers towards a vision of inclusion that embraces and honors all students.

ABOUT THE EDITORS

Gordon L. Porter, C.M., is a consultant, trainer, researcher and teacher. He was instrumental in developing an inclusive approach to education in schools in New Brunswick, Canada, recognized as an example of good practice by UNESCO and the OECD among others. He retired in 2006 as a professor of Education at the University of Maine at Presque Isle, in the USA. He has also taught at the University of Prince Edward Island, the University of Calgary, McGill University in Montreal and Ryerson University in Toronto.

Gordon Porter is Director of Inclusive Education Canada, an initiative of the Canadian Association for Community Living and is active in supporting inclusive education in Canada. He is editor of the website – www.inclusiveeducation.ca. He was a co-editor of *Changing Canadian Schools*, a book that focused on strategies and practices for building inclusive schools in Canada.

In 2007, *The Canadian Education Association* named Dr. Porter the recipient of *The Whitworth Award for Education Research*. The Award recognizes Dr. Porter's substantial contribution nationally and internationally at both a conceptual level and a practical level to building inclusive classrooms. In 2009 he was awarded a Doctor of Education Degree, Honorus, from the National Pedagogical University of Peru. He has conducted training and provided consultation on inclusive education in countries in many parts of the world, most recently in Portugal, Germany, Spain, Peru, Columbia and Ethiopia. Gordon Porter was inducted as a member of the Order of Canada in November 2010.

Déirdre Smith is the Manager of the Standards of Practice and Education division of the Ontario College of Teachers. In this capacity, Smith has led the collaborative development, with 10,000 educators and members of the public, of a set of ethical standards and standards of practice for the teaching profession that provide a collective vision of teacher professionalism in Ontario, Canada. These standards or principles of professional practice are a foundational core of teacher education programs in Ontario. Smith has also co-ordinated the policy development of over 300 Additional Qualification courses and programs for teacher and leadership education. As well, she has led the development of provincial multimedia inquiry-based resources and educational texts to support teacher education and leadership formation programs.

Smith teaches graduate courses in Educational Leadership with Niagara University and facilitates educational sessions across the Canada. She is co-editor of *Exploring Leadership and Ethical Practice through Professional Inquiry* and *Cases for Teacher Development: Preparing for the Classroom*. Smith has presented nationally and internationally on ethical standards, standards of practice and the relationship of these to teacher education and teacher professionalism. She has been published in the areas of cases, teacher education, leadership, inclusive education and ethics. She received the Principal of the Year award from the Geneva Centre for Autism for her commitment and leadership in the area of inclusive education. Her experience as a school principal, education consultant, special education administrator, teacher educator, youth counselor, classroom teacher and professional facilitator inform her work in policy development, teacher education, leadership formation and professional learning.

ABOUT THE CONTRIBUTING PARTNERS

Vianne Timmons is the President and Vice Chancellor of the University of Regina. She is a teacher and has spent the last 30 years working, researching and promoting inclusive practice. She is the mother of a young woman with Fetal Alcohol Syndrome Disorder and has experienced the challenges of advocating for an inclusive education.

She has worked nationally and internationally researching and presenting on inclusive education. She is the President elect of the International Association of the Scientific Study of Intellectual Disabilities and is the Chair of their World Congress being held in Halifax, 2012. Dr. Timmons is presently the Education Lead on a Social Science Humanities Research Council (SSHRC), Community University Research Alliance grant, looking at the relationship between policies and practices in inclusive education.

Dr. Timmons is involved in Inclusive Education Canada, a group of researchers and practitioners brought together by the Canadian Association of Community Living (CACL). She was the recipient of the CACL Inclusion Educator Award in 2010. She is an advocate of programs that provide inclusive education experiences at the post secondary levels. She is committed as a parent, teacher and administrator to support inclusive practices.

Brian Kelly is the Director of Education, Student Services, New Brunswick Department of Education. Brian Kelly's work has focussed on inclusive education for children since working on a deinstitutionalization project in Newfoundland in the 1980s. As a volunteer, he has been a board member and chairperson of his community's early intervention agency and residential living board, serving individuals with special needs. Brian is currently the chair for US/Canada Committee for the Council for Exceptional Children.

Diane Richler
Diane Richler, C.M. is Past-President of Inclusion International, a global federation of national organizations of people with intellectual disabilities and their families in over 115 countries. She was a leader of the NGO effort to have the United Nations adopt the Convention on the Rights of Persons with Disabilities. Diane was formerly Executive Vice President of the Canadian Association for Community Living. She was inducted into the Order of Canada for her work in disability rights.

ABOUT THE COMMENTATORS

Ulla Alexandersson
Ulla Alexandersson, MA, is a lecturer and director of studies at the Unit of Special Education, Department of Education, University of Gothenburg, Sweden. Ulla's research focuses upon inclusion in practice and classroom studies concerning students with intellectual disabilities. She has worked for the Swedish Government on a committee with the mission to investigate how the Swedish school system can be built to include students with intellectual disabilities.

Carson Allard
Carson Allard is a Program Officer in the Standards of Practice and Education Unit at the Ontario College of Teachers. He has studied, promoted and supported teacher inquiry over a thirty year career in teaching. His current inquiries centre on ethics in teaching practice as well as First Nations, Métis and Inuit epistemologies and curriculum.

Shelley Arsenault
Shelley is an English as an Additional Language Itinerant teacher for the Department of Education and Early Childhood Development on Prince Edward Island. The first 7 years of her career were spent in a remote Inuit village in Northern Quebec teaching ESL at the elementary level. In 1998, she returned to PEI to teach for the Western School Board. For the last 11 years Shelley has taught upper elementary, grade 1, Reading Recovery, elementary resource, and EAL. In 2008, she began a Masters of Education in Inclusion at UPEI.

Angèla AuCoin
Angèla AuCoin, PhD., began her career as a classroom teacher and later developed her passion for inclusive education when she started working with students of different cognitive and physical abilities as a resource teacher. Today Angèla AuCoin is an associate professor at l'Université de Moncton and has been teaching courses on differentiated instruction at their Faculté des sciences de l'éducation since 2003.

Sarah Elizabeth Barrett
Sarah Elizabeth Barrett, PhD., is an assistant professor at York University's Faculty of Education, where she teaches both prospective and practicing teachers. She taught high school science for 10 years. Currently, her research interests include teacher education, inclusive curriculum and teaching science for social justice.

Tracy Beck
Through social, voluntary, professional and educational experiences, Tracy Beck has spent the last twenty years in passionate support of people with disabilities. Having worked in segregated, integrated and inclusive settings, at workshops, summer camps, group homes, recreational programs, schools and an institution,

she has a wide variety of experiences that have shaped and guided her beliefs. A graduate of Ryerson University's School of Disability Studies, she currently teaches at White Oaks Secondary School in Oakville, Ontario

Alice Bender

Alice Bender is a teacher, principal and educational consultant who lives in Montreal. She worked supporting the development of inclusive education in English schools in Quebec for several years and contributed a great deal to progress in that province. Alice has taught courses on inclusion at McGill University and conducted training in many schools and districts. She is a visionary leader with a passionate belief in teachers and students and the potential for success with inclusive education.

Sheila Bennett

Sheila Bennett is a professor and former chair of the Department of Teacher Education at Brock University. Dr. Bennett has worked in the field of special education for more than 20 years and is currently involved in a number of research projects, including an international project on rights and advocacy for persons with disabilities. She served as co-chair, with the Honourable Kathleen Wynne, on the Ontario Ministry of Education's Working Table on Special Education. Her published monogram on *WHAT WORKS? Research into Practice: Including Students with Exceptionalities*- published by the Ontario Ministry of Education in January 2009 is a used in many school boards in the province.

Diana Carr

Diana Carr is an educator based in Montreal, Quebec. She has accumulated a wealth of experience working as a classroom and resource teacher, special needs consultant, and Coordinator of the Centre of Excellence for Autism Spectrum Disorders. Presently she works on a project supporting the ten English school boards in Quebec in the area of teacher professional development and delivery of services for exceptional students.

Krista Carr

Krista Carr is Executive Director of the New Brunswick Association for Community Living. Krista is responsible for the overall operation of NBACL/ANBIC but has focused on policy and practice related to inclusive education in New Brunswick. She has worked with families, schools and the Ministry of Education to move inclusion forward in her province.

Edith Clarke

Edith Clarke, M. Ed., has worked as an educator for more than 30 years to support and implement instructional support systems for educating all students within general education settings. Edith has worked as a classroom teacher, special education consultant and part time instructor in the McGill University Inclusive Education Certificate Program. She is presently Assistant Director of Student Services with the English Montreal School Board.

Robin Crain
Robin Crain has supervised the Student Services programs in School District 14 in Woodstock, N.B. She has worked as a classroom teacher, Special Education teacher, Employment Counselor, Guidance Counselor, Principal and as an adjunct professor at the University of Presque Isle. She has demonstrated a distinguished career-long commitment to social justice and inclusion.

Carla DiGiorgio
Carla DiGiorgio is an inclusion specialist in the Faculty of Education at University of Prince Edward Island. She teaches courses and supervises thesis students in the Bachelor of Education, Master of Education, and the PhD programs at UPEI, as well as teaching for University of South Australia. Carla was a teacher for 15 years before becoming a professor. Dr. DiGiorgio researches in the areas of inclusion, including learning disabilities, cultural and linguistic inclusion, and enrichment.

Alex Dingwall
Alex Dingwall is Superintendent of Schools in School District 18, Fredericton, N.B. He has been a Superintendent/Director of Education in Dalhousie and Saint John and Director Of Student Services within the Department of Education in New Brunswick. He has represented Canada on the panel of CERI, a research program of the OECD, Paris.

Marilyn Dolmage
Marilyn Dolmage is an Inclusive Education Consultant. She assists schools and families to work together to improve education. She communicates with a broad network of allies across Ontario, sharing information and inspiration about the law, research, provincial policies, effective education practices, career development and advocacy strategies. She has co-ordinated a variety of projects of The Ontario Coalition for Inclusive Education and its member associations since 1995.

Tammy Dunbar
Tammy Dunbar is the Principal of the Southern Carleton Elementary School, District 14, Woodstock, New Brunswick. She has enjoyed the roles of classroom teacher, Method and Resource teacher, District Consultant, Vice Principal and Elementary School Principal. She has supported inclusive education work in all her educational roles.

Emily Dwornikiewicz
Emily Dwornikiewicz is a Developmental Services Worker. Her experience supporting learners in a variety of educational and community programs has enabled her to address issues of advocacy in collaboration with parents, educators and community groups. As an Inclusive Facilitator, she has supported children and youth to achieve success through being authentically included within schools, recreational programs and the community.

Inés-Elvira de Escallón

Inés-Elvira de Escallón has personal experience with inclusive education through her son Julián and professionally in her work with an NGO in Bogotá, Colombia She is also a consultant with Inclusion International. Inés now lives with her fsmily in Toronto, Canada.

Jackie Fewer-Bennett

Jackie Fewer-Bennett is a Consultant for Inclusive Education at the Department of Education, Newfoundland and Labrador. She has 17 years of teaching experience at various grade levels, spending the majority of this time as a high school special education teacher. Jackie has an education degree, special education degree and a master of education degree from Memorial University.

Cindy Finn

Cindy Finn is Director of Student Services at the Lester B. Pearson School Board in Dorval, Quebec, the largest English-language School Board in Quebec. Cindy holds a Ph.D. in Educational Psychology from McGill and worked as a school psychologist prior to moving into administration. A frequent lecturer at Montreal-area universities, Dr. Finn has also published research in the area of inclusive education, particularly related to best practices for students with emotional and behavioural challenges.

Agnes Gajuwski

Agnes Gajewski is a doctoral student at OISE University of Toronto. Her research interests relate to the ethics of special education.

Tiffany Gallagher

Tiffany Gallagher is an Assistant Professor in the Faculty of Education at Brock University in St. Catharines, Ontario. She is a member in the Pre-service Department of the Faculty of Education. She teaches courses in educational psychology and assessment and evaluation. She has co-authored the texts, *Educational Psychology* (1st and 2nd Canadian Ed.) and *Classroom Assessment: Concepts and Applications* (1st Canadian Ed.). Tiffany's current research interests include literacy assessment, reading and writing strategy instruction, the role of the special education teacher, teachers with learning disabilities and post-secondary education for persons with disabilities.

Odet Moliner Garcia

Odet Moliner Garcia, PhD., is Professor of Education at the University Jaume I in Spain. Her main research interest is in the area of inclusive education. Odet is recognized as a leader in inclusive education in Spain. She is involved in studies related to cooperative learning, diversity in secondary schools and school transformation.

Dan Goodyear

Dan Goodyear has worked in the education field for over 30 years. For 12 of those years Dan worked as a regular classroom teacher, special education/resource teacher and as a district level program coordinator in the K-12 education system. From 1990–2007 Dan was a faculty member of College of the North Atlantic where he held various positions in the Student Support Services Department. Dan is currently Director of Student Support Services with the Department of Education, Government of Newfoundland.

Anke Grafe

Anke Grafe is a native of Halle/ Saale, Germany. She now lives and works in Buchholz, a city near Hamburg. She has been teaching within inclusive education settings since 2002. Anke also provides professional learning for teachers in the methods of cooperative learning and supports schools in the development of inclusive processes.

Seamus Hagerty

Professor Seamus Hagerty, PhD., is Chair of the International Association for the Evaluation of Educational Achievement (IEA). He served as Director of the National Foundation for Educational Research in England and Wales for twelve years until his retirement in 2005. He chairs the Education for All working group within the UNESCO UK National Commission. He serves on the National Council for Special Education in Ireland where he chairs the Research and Communication working group. He has advised UNESCO and other international bodies on special needs issues for over 20 years. He is founder/editor of the *European Journal of Special Needs Education*, now in its 22nd year, and edited *Educational Research* for 12 years. He has written or co-authored numerous books and papers on special education, assessment and research management.

Lauren Hoffman

Dr. Lauren P. Hoffman is Assistant Professor of Education at Lewis University. After a 27 year career as a practicing speech and language specialist, supervisor, professional development specialist, and assistant director of special education in two large suburban Chicago cooperatives, Dr. Hoffman joined the faculty at Lewis University and also serves as a Visiting Professor at Indiana University. She co-developed and co-directs the TECnet project that focuses school teams building unified systems to support all students. In addition she consults with school districts and school teams on issues related to curriculum, instruction, and assessment. She is currently helping to develop Lewis's new doctoral studies in leadership and is teaching courses on development and learning, instructional strategies, and performance-based assessment

Heather Hogan

Heather Hogan is the vice-principal of the Southern Carleton Elementary School in Woodstock, New Brunswick. Heather has been an elementary classroom teacher, a resource teacher and a district resource consultant. Her education background includes a B.A. and B.Ed. from St. Thomas University. She completed her Masters of Education at the University of New Brunswick. Heather is active in her professional association and is a director of the New Brunswick Teachers' Association.

Anne Jordan

Anne Jordan's research examines the beliefs, practices and knowledge of teachers who include students with disabilities into their regular classrooms. The result is a book, *Introduction to Inclusive Education*, published as an electronic text in 2008 by John Wiley, Canada. Anne served as a Professor of Education at the OISE, University of Toronto.

Jacqueline Karsemeyer

Jacqueline Karsemeyer is Program Officer at the Ontario College of Teachers, in the Standards of Practice and Education Department. She holds a PhD in Education, a Masters in Educational Psychology and Measurement and Special Education Specialist certification. She was executive assistant in "Equity and Women's Services" with the Elementary Teachers' Federation of Ontario. Holistic education, early years, equity and social justice are her areas of focus. Jacqueline has studied dance for over 40 years, and West African dance for the last 12 years.

Jaya Karsemeyer

Jaya Karsemeyer is a freelance artist and writer involved in international anti-racism, peace-building and education initiatives. She holds a Bachelor of Education and French qualifications and is involved in supporting learners with special needs. She has a particular interest in First Nations, racialized, LGBTQ and other groups working on human rights issues.

Lois Kember

Lois Kember is a teacher from Summerside, Prince Edward Island and mother of six. She has extensive experience with students with special needs. Her most enjoyable moments are working with children with challenges.

Shirley Kendrick

Shirley Kendrick is Assistant Superintendent of Special Education and Support Services with the Dufferin-Peel Catholic District School Board, in Ontario. With over 20 years supporting students with diverse learning needs as a teacher, resource teacher, Family of Schools contact, vice principal for Special Education and school principal.

Isabel Killoran

Isabel Killoran, PhD is an Associate Professor in the Faculty of Education and Graduate Programme Director of Critical Disability Studies at York University. Her areas of research include inclusion, teacher attitudes, equity and education. She has published in the areas of inclusive education, gender diversity and sexual orientation, teacher preparation, preschool inclusion and anti-bias curriculum. Currently, she is researching alternative dispute resolution processes related to conflicts about special education programs and supports.

Anne Kresta

Anne Kresta is a parent of three children, two of whom have Asperger Syndrome, Tourette Syndrome and Attention Deficit Disorder. Her advocacy for their appropriate education within the public school system of Manitoba has led her to become an advocate for the appropriate education of all children with special needs. She now serves Community Living Manitoba as its Inclusive Education Consultant. Anne works at many different levels within the education system to understand the driving forces behind policies and decisions. She also believes that the future of inclusive education lies, in large part, within our youth and works to increase their engagement and understanding of the struggles that people with disabilities have faced in gaining their rights and freedoms under the Canadian Charter.

Gordon Kyle
Gordon Kyle has worked for the past 30 years in organizations providing community services and advocacy support to people who have an intellectual disability. For the past 20 years he has worked for Community Living Ontario, a provincial umbrella organization for more than 115 local organizations supporting people who have an intellectual disability. At present, Gordon is the Director of Social Policy and Government Relations for Community Living Ontario and supports the Association's advocacy related efforts aimed at creating inclusive communities through improved access to inclusive education, housing, employment and other services.

Audrey Lampert
Audrey Lampert is a recently retired (2009) school administrator whose career in education spanned all levels from kindergarten to post-secondary, including working with at-risk youth in an alternate setting. She served many years as an elected school board trustee in Moncton, NB, and was appointed to the Provincial Board of Education when school boards were abolished in New Brunswick. Audrey has served as a member of the New Brunswick Human Rights Commission and the Research Ethics Board of the Horizon Health Network.

Brent Langan
Brent Langan has taught in both elementary and secondary schools with experience in the area of special education at both levels. He currently works as a System Special Education Resource Teacher for the Huron-Perth Catholic District School Board supporting school teams to implement best practice for Inclusive Education.

Darquise Leroux
Darquise Leroux is an experienced elementary and secondary school principal. She is currently principal of an elementary French Immersion school in Toronto. Her professional work experiences include roles as a school board program co-ordinator for student services, a resource teacher for special education, a supervisory officer assistant and recruitment officer and an advisor and facilitator with the Ontario Educational Leadership Centre. Her professional commitments include past membership on the Board of Governors of the Ontario Teachers' Federation and on the provincial executive of the Association des enseignantes et des enseignants

de l'Ontario. As a reflective practitioner, she has engaged in ethical decision-making research conducted by the Ontario College of Teachers, participated in several Open Space consultations relating to the development of qualification guidelines for the teaching profession and has actively supported the revision of the Ethical Standards for the Teaching profession and the Standards of Practice for the Teaching Profession in Ontario.

John Loughran

John Loughran is the Foundation Chair in Curriculum & Pedagogy in the Faculty of Education, Monash University, Victoria, Australia. John was a science teacher for ten years before moving into teacher education. His research has spanned both science education and the related fields of professional knowledge, reflective practice and teacher research. John is the co-editor of Studying Teacher Education and his most recent book is What Expert Teachers Do (Allen & Unwin/Routledge, 2010).

John Lundy

John Lundy, inaugural Director of the Laurentian University (English Language) School of Education, is a former Sudbury educator who taught in the area from 1971 to 1989. He was an Education professor at Nipissing University from 1989-2004. John was an English teacher for 17 years. He completed his doctoral degree in Education at the Ontario Institute for Studies in Education (OISE) in 1988. His teaching responsibilities at the post-secondary level have included courses in social foundations (Education and Schooling) as well as courses in Sociology and English, and Master of Education courses in Curriculum and Program Evaluation. He is actively doing research on equity of access to teacher education by Aboriginal peoples, visible minorities and people with disabilities. From 2001–2004 he was president of the Canadian Association of Foundations of Education; he is a past-president of the Association of Canadian Deans of Education.

Zana Lutfiyya

Zana Lutfiyya is Associate Dean (Research and Graduate Programs) and Professor, Faculty of Education, at the University of Manitoba. Zana completed her graduate training and post doctoral work at the Center on Human Policy, Syracuse University. She joined the University of Manitoba in 1992. Her longstanding research interest has been identifying and examining the factors that help or hinder the valued social participation of individuals with intellectual disabilities in community life. In recent years this has included facilitating the participation of individuals with intellectual disabilities in the research process, as participants and in helping determine research goals and questions. She is also a member of a newly emerging research team focusing on vulnerable people and end of life care.

Jude MacArthur

Jude MacArthur is a freelance researcher, recently retired from a position as senior researcher at the *Donald Beasley Institute* in Dunedin, New Zealand.

Her background is in primary teaching, and she has previously worked as a lecturer in Education at the University of Otago where she taught inclusive education and human development. Her recent work has looked at disabled children's school experiences as they made the transition from primary to secondary school. This study explored how factors relating to transition, culture, impairment, social relationships and school experience impact on children's identities.

Ann Marie MacDonald

Ann Marie MacDonald has taught for the past 12 years at various grade levels and in administration for 8 of those years. She teaches Grade 5 and is Vice Principal at Souris Consolidated School, in Prince Edward Island. Ann Marie is completing a Masters in Inclusive Education at the University of Prince Edward Island.

Kendra MacLaren

Kendra MacLaren resides in Summerside, Prince Edward Island where she teaches English and Alternative Education to High School Students. She is completing her Masters in Inclusive Education at the University of Prince Edward Island. Her thesis study is focused on Alternative Education and At-Risk students. She hopes to continue her work with secondary students and may one day pursue a PhD.

Joanne MacNevin

Joanne MacNevin is employed by the Prince Edward Island Department of Education as an Itinerant English Additional Language Teacher, teaching English Language Learners at the high school, junior high and elementary levels. She is completing a Masters in Education at UPEI with a focus on Inclusive Education.

Pamela C. McGugan

Pam McGugan is an Education Officer with the Leadership Development Branch, Ontario Ministry of Education. Prior to that, she was a principal with the Peel District School Board where she worked with students with special needs. Pam was instrumental in working with architects to design a school which twinned two schools under one roof in a 'school within a school concept'. This 'state of the art' school was designed to provide maximum program opportunities for students with special needs in an inclusive environment. Pam also served as chair of the Special Needs Regional Identification Placement and Review Committee (IPRC) and was writing team leader for the revision of Personal Life Management, a Peel District School Board resource guide for the School to Work /Community Transition Program, a resource document for students with developmental disabilities that reflects the most current practices and program suggestions. She has been a workshop presenter at numerous Council for Exceptional Children conferences.

Darren McKee

Darren McKee is Anishnabe, originally from Manitoba, but completed all his formal education in Saskatchewan. Darren has worked as a teacher and administrator in various First Nation communities in Saskatchewan and began working with the province of Saskatchewan in 2005. Darren held various positions including Superintendent, Director and Executive Director before becoming the Assistant Deputy Minister in 2007. Darren has presented at regional, national and international conferences specifically on educational issues relating to Indigenous education. In his current capacity Darren works closely with the Western and Northern Canadian Protocol (WNCP) and The Council of Ministers of Education Canada (CMEC) to provide support to First Nation, Métis and Inuit education. Darren has a particular interest in math and science from Indigenous perspectives and working with gifted children.

Peter McLaren
Peter McLaren is a professor in the Division of Urban Schooling, the Graduate School of Education and Information studies, University of California, Los Angeles. He is the author and editor of forty-five books and hundreds of scholarly articles and chapters, including *Life in Schools* (which was chosen as one of the 12 most significant education books in existence worldwide by an international panel of experts organized by the Moscow School of Social and Economic Sciences in 2004). Peter was the inaugural recipient of the Paulo Freire Social Justice Award presented by Chapman University, California.

Sheila McWatters
Sheila McWatters is Superintendent of Special Education and Support Services with the Dufferin-Peel Catholic District School Board. As an educator, Sheila has been a consultant, principal, Superintendent of Schools and led multiple System Portfolios. Sheila also has experience in supporting K-12 spectrum, early learning, community based collaborative and transformative practice and programs with educators and inter-ministry partners enabling success for all learners with particular focus on the needs of diverse learners.

Alan McWhorter
Alan has served as executive director for Community Living Kingston since 1987. He has been a career worker with Community Living at local, provincial, and national levels since 1969. Alan recognizes that public education is, next to the family, the most powerful means of transmitting culture across generations. He became an early advocate for children with intellectual disabilities attending neighbourhood schools with their age peers. He believes that inclusive education for students with special needs is the key to citizenship and their life-long participation in community life.

Cor Meijer
Cor J. W. Meijer is Director of the European Agency for Development in Special Needs Education. The agency is an independent and self-governing organization, established by member countries to act as their platform for collaboration in the field of special needs education. Dr. Meijer's work at the agency has involved major research projects related to inclusive education practice. He previously worked at the Institute for Educational Research, The Hague, The Netherlands.

Bendina Miller
Bendina Miller has been a classroom teacher in grades 1 to 12, a special education teacher, consultant, principal, assistant superintendent and Superintendent of Schools in British Columbia. She has been actively involved in community living for over 40 years and is President of the Canadian Association for Community Living.

Penny Milton
Penny Milton served as Chief Executive Officer of the Canadian Education Association from 1996 to 2010. She was Chair of the Toronto Board of Education, Executive Assistant for the Federation of Women Teachers' Association of Ontario, Executive Director of the Ontario Public School Board Association and served as Deputy Minister of the Ontario Premier's Council of Health, Well-being and Social Justice. Before joining CEA, Ms. Milton was Vice President, Human Resources and Corporate Affairs for ORTECH Corp. She is the author of several book chapters, numerous articles and presentations on policy issues in education. She holds a B.Sc. (Hons.) from the University of Nottingham and a M. Management from McGill University

James Moloney
James Moloney is a program officer with the Standards of Practice and Education unit at the Ontario College of Teachers and has been an elementary teacher, special education teacher, consultant, vice-principal and principal. He has experience working in the leadership development branch with the Ontario Ministry of Education. His areas of interest are leadership, ethics and teacher leadership.

Catherine Montreuil
Catherine Montreuil is a Superintendent of Education with the Bruce-Grey Catholic DSB. She has worked for 20 years in Special Education - 10 years as a Special Education administrator and 10 years as a Special Education teacher. Catherine has been recognized for her work to make schools inclusive by Community Living Ontario and the Canadian Association for Community Living.

Nithi Muthukrishna
Nithi Muthukrishna is a Professor in the School of Education and Development, University of KwaZulu-Natal, South Africa. Her research interests are in the areas of diversity in education, social justice education, childhood studies, and education quality in particular issues of rights, social justice and equity.

Kathryn Noel
Kathryn Noel teaches at The University of Western Ontario. Over the course of her career, she has been a classroom teacher, school board consultant, Ministry of Education consultant, professor, and researcher. Dr. Noel's research interests include topics related to language and learning, to teacher effectiveness, and to gifted education, and her work with teachers has taken her to a variety of educational settings including those in Sierra Leone, Mongolia, and China.

Anthony H. Normore
Anthony H. Normore is Associate Professor and Program Development Coordinator of Doctorate in Educational Leadership, Graduate Education Division, School of Education, at California State University-Dominguez Hills in greater Los Angeles. His research focuses on leadership development, preparation and socialization of urban school leaders in the context of ethics and social justice. His books include, *Leadership for social justice: Promoting equity and excellence through inquiry and reflective practice* (Information Age Publishers, 2008); *Leadership and intercultural dynamics* (Information Age Publishers, 2009, and co-authored with John Collard); and *Educational leadership preparation: Innovation and interdisciplinary approaches to the Ed.D. and graduate education* (forthcoming, Palgrave Macmillan, and co-authored with Gaetane Jean-Marie). His research publications have appeared in national and international peer-reviewed journals including *Journal of School Leadership, Journal of Educational Administration, Values and Ethics in Educational Administration, Leadership and Organizational Development Journal, The Alberta Journal of Educational Research, Canadian Journal of Education Administration and Policy, International Journal of Urban Educational Leadership, Educational Policy, International Electronic Journal for Leadership in Learning,* and *Journal of Research on Leadership Education.*

Melanie Panitch
Melanie Panitch is Director of the School of Disability Studies at Ryerson University, a position she has held since the School was founded in 1999. Drawing on her deep roots in the disability rights movement, she has recently published a history of activist mothering in the Canadian Association for Community Living titled, "Disability, Mothers and Organization: Accidental Activists."

Alicia de la Peña Rode
Alicia has advocated for inclusion for children with intellectual disabilities in regular schools all over Mexico. She has been the coordinator of an Inclusive Education Project of the Instituto Mexicano para la Excelencia Educativa A.C. Alicia was a leading participant in the international project: Working Together in the Community, sharing and learning about inclusive education with CACL (Canada) and The ARC (U.S.A.)

Darlene Perner
Darlene Perner earned her doctorate from the University of British Columbia. She is currently a Professor in the Department of Exceptionality Programs at Bloomsburg University of Pennsylvania, where she teaches courses on inclusive education, current issues in special education, assessment and moderate and severe disabilities. She has worked in public schools as a regular and special education teacher, and in provincial government as an inclusive education consultant and educational policy analyst. Her primary research areas are inclusive education, curriculum differentiation, and alternate assessments.

JoAnne Putnam
JoAnne W. Putnam is Professor at the School of Education at the University of Maine at Presque Isle. Her work focuses on inclusive education, cooperative learning, indigenous education, and diversity in education. Dr. Putnam has published several books including *Cooperative Learning and Strategies for Inclusion* and *Cooperative Learning in Diverse Classrooms.* She received her Ph.D. from the University of Minnesota and was professor at the University of Alaska Anchorage and The University of Montana.

Sharon Rich
Sharon Rich is Professor and Dean of Education at Nipissing University in North Bay, Ontario. She was previously Dean of Education at the University of New Brunswick, Fredericton and was a professor at the University of Western Ontario. She has authored several books in language and literacy education including Reading for Meaning in the Elementary School as well as many texts for classroom use. Her research is rooted in language and literacy but more recently she has turned her attention to the creation of communities in the virtual environment. Involved in education for over 30 years, Sharon has taught from Grades 1–10 in public schools.

Bruce Rivers
Bruce Rivers is the CEO of Community Living Toronto. He has previous experience in child welfare with both NGO and government. He is past-president of the Child Welfare League of Canada and International Forum for Child Welfare.

Jean J. Ryoo
Jean J. Ryoo is a doctoral student at the Graduate School of Education and Information Studies in the University of California, Los Angeles. Her research interests in the sociology of education, critical theory, and urban education towards the goal of increasing educational equity stem from her work teaching in varying contexts as an art teacher, after school program educator, English teacher for French public schools, and middle and high school Social Studies and English teacher in Hawaiian public schools.

Zuhy Sayeed
Zuhy Sayeed has lived in Canada for over 30 years, having moved from Bombay, India. She has a background in early childhood Education; taught in Bombay and managed a Nursery School in Lloydminster. She and her husband have four sons, two of who have been labelled with different abilities. Zuhy is a Past President of the Canadian Association for Community Living.

Bernhard Schmid
Bernhard Schmid is Secretary General of "Lebenshilfe Wien", an Austrian advocacy organisation and service provider for people with intellectual disabilities and their families. Bernhard is also the father of a 17-years-old young man with Down-

Syndrome. He is a keen supporter of inclusive education in his country and in Europe.

Maribel Alves-Fierro Sevilla
Maribel Alves-Fierro Sevilla is a social sector specialist working for the Ministry of Culture in Brazil. She has a PhD from Michigan State University on Education Administration and International Development. Before working in Brazil, Dr. Sevilla has collaborated with different international organizations and non-profit organizations based in USA and abroad, contributing for the development of the inclusion agenda in different social sectors: education, health and culture.

Marie Schoeman
Marie Schoeman is a Chief Education Specialist in Inclusive Education for the South African Ministry of Education. In this capacity she has been responsible for the development and implementation of national policy in the field. She has collaborated in several international research projects which investigated best practice in inclusive education. Her professional work has been enriched through her personal experience as a parent of a son with Down Syndrome and as disability rights activist.

Denise Silverstone
Denise Silverstone is Director of National Programs at the Boys and Girls Clubs of Canada (BGCC). Before joining BGCC, she worked at the Canadian Association for Community Living where she helped develop CACL's Inclusive Education Initiative. Silverstone was also a research coordinator at the Centre for the Study of Learning and Performance at Concordia University and worked for many years as an ESL teacher in Toronto, Thailand and Japan.

Roger Slee
Roger Slee is the Professor of Inclusive Education at the Department of Learning, Curriculum and Communication at the Institute of Education, University of London, UK. Before taking up this current post, Roger was the Dean of the Faculty of Education at Canada's McGill University. He has held research chairs at the University of London and the University of Western Australia. Roger was formerly the Deputy Director General of the Ministry of Education in Queensland. Roger is the author of numerous books and refereed papers on inclusive education and is the Founding Editor of the International Journal of Inclusive Education.

Jacqueline Specht
Jacqueline Specht has a Ph.D. in educational psychology. She is a tenured associate professor in Faculty of Education at the University of Western Ontario, and current director of its Centre for Inclusive Education. Dr. Specht has over 20 years of experience in the field of special education. Her current research interests encompass pedagogical issues surrounding the participation of children in the school system.

Julie A. Stone

Julie Stone has been an educator for over 40 years. She has taught at all grade levels in public education as well as at the university level. Julie has taught in the Instructor Development Program for the New Brunswick Community College system (NBCC.) Julie works for the New Brunswick Association for Community Living on a project aimed at assisting high school teachers to be better prepared to teach students with learning challenges, including those with learning and intellectual disabilities. She also works with NBCC on the Special Admissions Program which is designed to assist high school graduates who have been on Special Education Plans to be successful in a post-secondary setting. Julie is also writing and teaching on-line courses dealing with Education and Disability for the New Brunswick Department of Education. Julie is a Past President of both the National and Provincial Associations for Community Living.

Scott A. Thompson

Dr. Scott A. Thompson is Associate Professor of Inclusive Education in the Faculty of Education at the University of Regina. His research interests are inclusive education, Disability Studies in Education (DSE), the autism culture, and teacher education. Currently, he is partnering with Dr. Lynn M Aylward at Acadia University conducting a three-year investigation in teacher education and DSE, entitled *Disabling Teacher Education from the Ground Up.* His most recent article is soon to be published in the *International Journal of Inclusive Education*, entitled *Thrice disabling disability: Enabling inclusive, socially just teacher education.*

Chris Treadwell

Chris has been a principal for 25 years of schools from K-12. Presently, he is principal of Park Street Elementary School in Fredericton, New Brunswick, Canada. In 2009 Chris was recognized as one of Canada's "Outstanding Principals" by The Learning Partnership.

Miguel Ángel Verdugo

Miguel Ángel Verdugo is a professor of Psychology of Disability and Director of the Institute on Community Integration at the University of Salamanca (Spain). Miguel is also Director of the Service on Information about Disabilities (Ministry of Work and Univ. of Salamanca) and Director of the Journal on Intellectual Disabilities Siglo Cero.

Kara Walsh

Kara Walsh is a M.Ed. student at UPEI studying in the area of inclusive education. She has been working as a resource and special education teacher in eastern Prince Edward Island and enjoys the challenges each day brings. She loves living and working on PEI and couldn't imagine life without the beautiful countryside, fresh air, family and friends.

Amanda Watkins

Dr. Amanda Watkins is the Assistant Director: Project Implementation of the European Agency for Development in Special Needs Education based in Denmark. Her responsibilities include co-ordination of the Agency project implementation procedures; project Manager of a number of on-going projects including Teacher Education of Inclusion and Higher Education Accessibility Guide; responsibility for co-ordination of the Agency information dissemination procedures. Her main areas of interest are policy and legal frameworks for SNE; post compulsory provision for learners with special needs; learners with severe and profound learning disabilities. Amanda received the Myriam Van Acker inaugural award for contributions to supporting students with disability in Higher Education, July 2004.

Barbara Wenders

Barbara Wenders is a teacher from Münster, Germany. She is a teacher for children with special needs in Grundschule Berg Fidel, a German primary school in Münster. Barbara and several colleagues have been promoting inclusion and school reform in their community for several years. In 2008 she spent a month in an inclusive school in Woodstock, New Brunswick. Barbara is the co-editor of a new book on inclusive education published in November 2009 in Germany - Ungehorsam im Schuldienst: Der praktische Weg zu einer Schule für alle by Reinhard Stähling, Barbara Wenders, and Donata Wenders.

Jerry Wheeler

Jerry Wheeler is a former bilingual secondary educator and served as professional development coordinator for the integration of computers within the curriculum. He is presently a program officer at the Ontario College of Teachers conducting research, analyzing and developing policies and programs related to initial and ongoing teacher education and teaching practice. He supported the work involving the development and implementation of the College's Standards of Practice and Ethical Standards for the teaching profession. He facilitates sessions with educational leaders as well as pre-service and in-service groups at faculties and in schools concerning the integration of standards within professional practice. His work in the accreditation of teacher education programs involved reviews of faculty of education programs at Ontario universities and of Additional Qualification programs offered by faculties of education and other providers. Jerry is co-editor of the book, *Explorer les pratiques déontologiques et le leadership par le questionnement professionnel.* This book explores the leadership and ethical practices of school principals.

Margaret Kress White

Margaret Kress White is a Saskatoon educator at SIAST and the University of Saskatchewan. She has taught students in pre-service teacher education, early childhood, educational assistants, and other human service programs, in addition to early and middle-years children and high school youth with varying needs and gifts. She is an advocate for children and youth and believes all Canadian teachers can learn how Indigenous pedagogies embrace the inclusion of all persons. She is completing her PhD in Transformative Education at the University of Manitoba.

Tanya Whitney

Tanya Whitney lives in Woodman's Point, New Brunswick. She has been an educator both in the public and first nations school systems in elementary and middle schools. She is principal of Forest Hills School, a K-8 school of 750 students on Saint John's east side.

Stephanie Zucko

Stephanie Zucko is an educator who lives in Montreal, Quebec. Differentiated learning practices have permeated Stephanie's work over the years. She has designed curriculum with UNESCO partners for teachers in Mali, Africa; in the teaching of courses in the Inclusive Education program at McGill University and in workshops guiding teachers through curriculum change processes in the province of Quebec.

BIBLIOGRAPHY

Abend, A. (2001). *Planning and designing for students with disabilities.* Retrieved October 20, 2009, from National Clearinghouse for Educational Facilities Web site: http://www.edfacilities.org/pubs/disabilities.pdf

Allan, J. (2005). Inclusion as an ethical project. In S. Tremain (Ed.), *Foucault and disability* (pp. 281–297). Michigan, MA: University of Michigan Press.

Allard, C. C., Goldblatt, P. F., Kemball, J. I., Kendrick, S. A., Millen, K. J., & Smith, D. (2007). Becoming a reflective community of practice. *Reflective Practice, 3*(8), 299–314.

Bennett, S. (2009). *Including students with exceptionalities.* Retrieve October 6, 2010, from http://www.edu.gov.on.ca/eng/literacynumeracy/inspire/research/Bennett.pdf

Brendtro, L. K., Brokenleg, M., & Van Bockern, S. (2002). *Reclaiming youth at risk: Our hope for the future.* Bloomington, IN: National Educational Service.

Bogdan, R. C., & Biklen, S. K. (2007). *Qualitative research for education: An introduction to theories and methods* (5th ed.). Boston: Pearson A & B.

Bunch, G., & Valeo, A. (1998). *Inclusion: Recent research.* Toronto, ON: Inclusion Press International.

Canadian Association for Community Living. (2009). *No-excuses campaign.* Retrieved October 1, 2010, from http://www.no-excuses.ca

Carr, E. G., Ladd, M. V., & Schulte, C. F. (2008). Validation of the contextual assessment inventory for problem behavior. *Journal of Positive Behavior Interventions, 10*(2), 91–104.

Cherubini, L., Smith, D., Goldblatt, P., Engemann, J., & Kitchen, J. (2008). *Learning from experience: Supporting beginning teachers and mentors – Booklet 1: Facilitator's guide.* Toronto, ON: Ontario College of Teachers.

Commission on Emotional and Learning Disorders in Children (CELDIC). (1970). *One million children.* Toronto, ON: Crainford.

Coots, J. J. & Stout, K. (Eds.). (2007). *Critical reflections about students with special needs: Stories from the classroom.* Boston: Pearson/Allyn and Bacon.

Council for Exceptional Children. (n.d.). *Behavior disorders/emotional disturbances.* Retrieved April 19, 2010, from http://www.cec.sped.org/AM/Template.cfm?Section=Behavior_Disorders_Emotional_Disturbance

Crawford, C., & Porter, G. L. (2004). *Supporting teachers: A foundation for advancing inclusive education.* Toronto, ON: The Roeher Institute.

Darling-Hammond, L., & Hammerness, K. (2002). Toward a pedagogy of cases in teacher education. *Teaching Education, 13*(2), 125–135.

Department of Justice Canada. (1982). *Canadian charter of rights and freedoms.* Retrieved September 29, 2010, from http://laws.justice.gc.ca/en/charter/

Dufferin-Peel Catholic District School Board. (2009). *Progressive discipline response protocol.* Retrieved October 20, 2009, from http://www.dpcdsb.org/CEC/Schools/Safe+Schools/Progressive+Discipline.htm

Engemann, J., Kitchen, J., Cherubini, L., Smith, D., & Goldblatt, P. (2008). *Learning from experience: Supporting beginning teachers and mentors – Booklet 2: Using the case method in induction.* Toronto, ON: Ontario College of Teachers.

European Agency for Development in Special Needs Education. (2009). *Key principles for promoting quality in inclusive education: Recommendations for policy makers.* Retrieved October 1, 2010, from http://www.european-agency.org/publications/ereports/key-principles-for-promoting-quality-in-inclusive-education/key-principles-EN.pdf

Falvey, M. A., Forest, M., Pearpoint, J., & Rosenberg, R. L. (2000). *All my life's a circle. Using the tools: Circles, MAPS & PATHS.* Toronto, ON: Inclusion Press.

Friesen, J., Hickey, R., & Krauth, B. (2009). *Disabled peers and academic achievement.* Retrieved October 6, 2010, from http://www.sfu.ca/cerp/research/d_p_a_a.pdf

BIBLIOGRAPHY

Forest, M., & Lusthaus, E. (1989). Promoting educational equality for all students: Circles and MAPS. In S. Stainback, W. Stainback, & M. Forest (Eds.), *Educating all students in the mainstream of regular education* (pp. 43–58). Baltimore: P.H. Brookes Pub. Co.

Forest, M., & Lusthaus, E. (1990). Everyone belongs with MAPs action planning system. *Teaching Exceptional Children, 22*(2), 32–35.

Forest, M., & Pearpoint, J. (1992). MAPS: Action planning. In J. Pearpoint, M. Forest, & J. Snow (Eds.), *The inclusion papers: Strategies to make inclusion work* (pp. 52–56). Toronto, ON: Inclusion Press.

Frederickson, N., & Turner, J. (2003). Utilizing the classroom peer group to address children's social needs: An evaluation of the Circle of Friends intervention approach. *The Journal of Special Education, 36*(4), 234–245.

Giangreco, M. F., & Doyle, M. B. (Eds.), Artiles, A. (Contributor). (2007). *Quick-guides to inclusion: Ideas for educating students with disabilities* (2nd ed.). Baltimore: Paul H. Brookes Publishing Co.

Glasser, W. (1998). *Choice theory: A new psychology of personal freedom.* New York: Harper Collins Publisher.

Goldblatt, P., Engemann, J., Kitchen, J., Cherubini, L., & Smith, D. (2008). *Learning from experience: Supporting beginning teachers and mentors – Booklet 4: Implementing a new teacher induction workshop.* Toronto, ON: Ontario College of Teachers.

Goldblatt, P., & Smith, D. (Eds.). (2005). *Cases for teacher development: Preparing for the classroom.* Thousand Oaks, CA: Sage Publications.

Gonzalez, N., Moll, L., & Amanti, C. (Eds.). (2005). *Funds of knowledge: Theorizing practices in households, communities, and classrooms.* Mahwah, NJ: Lawrence Erlbaum Associates, Publishers.

Hainstock, E. G. (1997). *Teaching Montessori in the home: The school years.* New York: Plume.

Hollander, E. P. (2009). *Inclusive leadership: The essential leader-follower relationship.* New York: Talyor & Francis Group.

Hooks, B. (2000). *All about love: New vision.* New York: William Morrow.

Hooks, B. (2008). *Reel to real: Race, class and sex at the movies.* New York: Routledge.

Hooks, B. (2009). *Belonging: A culture of place.* New York: Routledge.

Inclusion classroom tips for new teachers: Teaching students with learning disabilities. (n.d). Retrieved April 19, 2010, from http://newteachersupport.suite101.com/article.cfm/inclusion_classroom_tips_for_new_teachers

Inclusion in the classroom: The teaching methods. (2006, October 4). Retrieved April 19, 2010, from http://www.associatedcontent.com/article/66531/inclusion_in_the_classroom_the_teaching.html?cat=4

Jordan, A. (2007). *Introduction to inclusive education.* Mississauga, ON: J. Wiley & Sons Canada.

Jorgensen, C. M., Schuh, M. C., & Nisbet, J. A. (2005). *The inclusion facilitator's guide.* Baltimore: Paul H. Brookes Publishing Co.

Keyes, C. R. (2000). *Parent-teacher partnerships: A theoretical approach for teachers.* Retrieved December 20, 2010, from http://ceep.crc.uiuc.edu/pubs/katzsym/keyes.pdf

Kitchen, J., Cherubini, L., Smith, D., Goldblatt, P., & Engemann, J. (2008). *Learning from experience: Supporting beginning teachers and mentors – Booklet 5: Research summary.* Toronto, ON: Ontario College of Teachers.

Kunc, N. (2000). Rediscovering the right to belong. In R. A. Villa & J. S. Thousand (Eds.), *Restructuring for caring and effective education: Piecing the puzzle together* (2nd ed., pp. 77–92). Baltimore: P.H. Brooks Pub.

Ladson-Billings, G. (Ed.). (2003). *Critical race theory perspectives on the social studies: The profession, policies and curriculum.* Greenwich, CT: Information Age Pub.

Ladson-Billings, G. (2005). *Beyond the big house: African American educators on teacher education.* New York: Teacher College Press.

Ladson-Billings, G. (2009). *The dreamkeepers: Successful teachers of African American children.* San Francisco: Jossey-Bass.

Ladson-Billings, G., & Tate, W. F. (Eds.). (2006). *Education research in the public interest: Social justice, action, and policy.* New York: Teachers College Press.

MacArthur, J., Gaffney, M., Kelly, B., & Sharp, S. (2007). Disabled children negotiating school life: Agency, difference, teaching practice and education policy. *International Journal of Children's Rights, 15*(1), 99–120.

McAtee, M., Carr, E. G., Schulte, C., & Dunlap, G. (2004). A contextual assessment inventory for problem behavior: Initial development. *Journal of Positive Behavior Interventions, 6*(3), 148–165.

McGee, J. J., & Menolascino, F. J. (1991). *Beyond gentle teaching: A nonaversive approach to helping those in need.* New York: Plenum Press.

Merseth, K. K. (2003). *Windows on teaching math: Cases of middle and secondary classrooms.* New York: Teachers College Press.

New Brunswick Human Rights Commission. (2007). *Guideline for accommodating students with a disability.* Retrieved October 1, 2010, from http://www.gnb.ca/hrc-cdp/e/g/Guideline-Accommodating-Students-Disability-New-Brunswick.pdf

Ontario College of Teachers. (2006). *Foundations of professional practice.* Toronto, ON: Author.

Ontario College of Teachers. (2009). *Living the standards* [Resource kit 2]. Toronto, ON: Author.

Ontario Human Rights Commission. (n.d.). *Accommodating students with disabilities: Principles.* Retrieved April 19, 2010, from http://www.ohrc.on.ca/en/resources/factsheets/Priciples

Ontario Ministry of Education. (2000). *Standards for school boards' special education plans.* Retrieved December 20, 2010, from http://www.edu.gov.on.ca/eng/general/elemsec/speced/iepstand/iepstand.pdf

Ontario Ministry of Education. (2005). *Education for all: The report of expert panel of literacy and numeracy instruction for students with special education needs, kindergarten to grade 6.* Retrieved January 6, 2010, from http://www.edu.gov.on.ca/eng/document/reports/speced/panel/speced.pdf

Ontario Ministry of Education. (2007). *Shared solutions: A guide to preventing and resolving conflicts regarding programs and services for students with special education needs.* Retrieved April 20, 2010, from http://www.edu.gov.on.ca/eng/general/elemsec/speced/shared.pdf

Ontario Ministry of Education. (2009a). *Learning for all K-12.* Draft retrieved January 6, 2010, from http://www.ontariodirectors.ca/L4All/L4A_en_downloads/LearningforAll%20K-12%20draft%20J.pdf

Ontario Ministry of Education. (2009b). *Realizing the promise of diversity: Ontario's equity and inclusive education strategy.* Retrieved April 19, 2010, from http://www.edu.gov.on.ca/eng/policyfunding/equity.pdf

Pearpoint, J., Forest, M., & O'Brien, J. (1996). MAPs, circles of friends, and PATH: Powerful tools to help build caring communities. In S. Stainback & W. Stainback (Eds.), *Inclusion: A guide for educators* (pp. 67–86). Baltimore: P.H. Brookes Pub. Co.

Pearpoint, J., Forest, M., & Snow, J. (1992). *The inclusion papers: Strategies to make inclusion work.* Toronto, ON: Inclusion Press.

Philpott, D. (2007). *Assessing without labels: Inclusive education in the Canadian context.* Retrieved September 28, 2010, from http://www.coespecialneeds.ca/uploads/docs/assessingwithout labelsinclusivity.pdf

Porter, G. (2008). *Making Canadian schools inclusive: A call to action.* Retrived October 25, 2010, from http://www.inclusiveeducation.ca/documents/2MakingCanadianSchoolsInclusiveGPorter.pdf

Porter, G., & Richler, D. (1991). Changing special education practice: Law, advocacy and innovation. In G. Porter & D. Richler (Eds.), *Changing Canadian schools: Perspectives of disabilities and inclusion* (pp. 9–34). Toronto, ON: The Roeher Institute.

Purpel, E. & McLaurin, M., Jr. (2004). *Reflections on the moral & spiritual crisis in education.* New York: Peter Lang.

Putnam, R. D. (2000). *Bowling alone: The collapse and revival of American community.* New York: Simon and Shuster.

Putnam, R. D., Leonardi, R., & Nanetti, R. Y. (1993). *Making democracy work: Civic traditions in modern Italy.* Princeton, NJ: Princeton University Press.

Redman, G. (2007). *A casebook for exploring diversity* (3rd ed.). Upper Saddle River, NJ: Pearson/Merrill Prentice Hall.

Rogoff, B., Turkanis, C. G., & Bartlett, L. (Eds.). (2002). *Learning together: Children and adults in a school community.* Oxford: Oxford University Press.

Rushowy, K. (2010, February 16). Special education funding falls short, Toronto board says: Costs $20 million more than province provides - report. *Toronto Star*. Retrieved October 1, 2010, from http://olympics.thestar.com/2010/article/766452

Sapon-Shevin, M., Dobbelaere, A., Corrigan, C. R., Goodman, K., & Mastin, M. (1998). Promoting inclusive behavior in inclusive classrooms: "You can't say you can't play". In L. H. Meyer, H.-S. Park, M. Grenot-Scheyer, I. S. Schwartz, & B. Harry (Eds.), *Making friends: The influences of culture on development* (pp. 105–132). Baltimore: P.H. Brookes Pub. Co.

Schon, D. (2002). From teaching rationality to reflection-in-action. In R. Harrison, F. Reeve, A. Hanson, & J. Clarke (Eds.), *Supporting life long learning: Perspectives on learning* (pp. 40–61). New York: RoutledgeFalmer.

Shapiro, J. P., & Gross, S. J. (2008). *Ethical educational leadership in turbulent times: (Re)solving moral dilemmas.* Mahwah, NJ: Lawrence Erlbaum Associates.

Shields, C. M., & Edwards, M. M. (2005). *Dialogue is not just talk: A new ground for educational leadership.* New York: P. Lang.

Shulman, J. (Ed.). (1992). *Case methods in teacher education.* New York: Teachers College Press.

Shulman, L. S. (1992). Research on teaching: A historical and personal perspective. In F. K. Oser, A. Dick, & J. Patry (Eds.), *Effective and responsible teaching: The new synthesis* (pp. 14–29). San Francisco: Jossey-Bass.

Slee, R. (2008). It's a fit-up! Inclusive education, higher education, policy and the discordant voice. In L. Barton & F. Armstrong (Eds.), *Policy, experience and change: Cross-cultural reflections on inclusive education* (pp. 177–188). New York: Springer.

Sleeter, C. E. (2005). *Un-standardizing curriculum: Multicultural teaching in standards-based classrooms.* New York: Teachers College Press.

Sleeter, C. E. (Ed.). (2007). *Facing accountability in education: Democracy and equity at risk.* New York: Teachers College Press.

Sleeter, C. E., & Grant, C. A. (2009). *Making choices for multicultural education: Five approaches to race, class and gender* (6th ed.). New York: Wiley.

Smith, D. (2010). Developing leaders using case inquiry. *Scholar-Practitioner Quarterly, 4*(2), 104–124.

Smith, D., & Goldblatt, P. (Eds.). (2007). *Casebook guide for teacher education.* Toronto, ON: Ontario College of Teachers.

Smith, D., & Goldblatt, P. (Eds.). (2009). *Exploring leadership and ethical practice through professional inquiry.* Québec, QC: Les Presses de l'Université Laval.

Smith, D., Goldblatt, P., Engemann, J., Kitchen, J., & Cherubini, L. (2008). *Learning from experience: Supporting beginning teachers and mentors – Booklet 3: Exploring professional practice with beginning and mentor teachers - Vignettes.* Toronto, ON: Ontario College of Teachers.

Stake, R. (1995). *The art of case study research.* California: Sage.

Strike, K. A. (2007). *Ethical leadership in schools: Creating community in an environment of accountability.* Thousand Oaks, CA: Corwin Press.

Strike, K. A., Haller, E. J., & Soltis, J. F. (2005). *The ethics of school administration* (3rd ed.). New York: Teachers College Press.

Supreme Court of Canada. (1997). *Brant County Board of Education v. Eaton* [1997] 1 S.C.R. 241; (1996) 31 O.R. (3d) 574 (1996) 142 D.L.R. (4th) 385.

Supreme Court of Canada. (2010). *R. v. Conway* [2010] 1 S.C.R. 765. Retrieved October 20, 2010, from http://scc.lexum.umontreal.ca/en/2010/2010scc22/2010scc22.html

Timmons, V., Breitenbach, M., & MacIsaac, M. (2006). *Educating children about autism in an inclusive classroom.* Charlottetown, PEI: University of Prince Edward Island.

Timmons, V., & Wagner, M. (2008). The connection between inclusion and health. Canadian Teachers Federation. *Professional Development Perspectives, 7*(3), 20–24.

UNESCO. (1994, June). *The Salamanca statement and framework for action on special needs education.* Retrieved September 29, 2010, from http://www.unesco.org/education/pdf/SALAMA_E.PDF

United Nations. (2006). *Convention on the rights of persons with disabilities.* Retrieved September 29, 2010, from http://www.un.org/disabilities/default.asp?id=259

Valencia, R. R. (Ed.). (1997). *The evolution of deficit thinking: Educational thought and practice.* Washington, DC: Falmer Press.

Vanier, J. (1991). *Community and growth.* Bombay: St. Paul Publications.

Vanier, J. (1998). *Becoming human.* New York: Paulist Press.

Wagner, M. (2008). *Inclusion and health: A study of the 2001 participation and activity limitation survey (PALS).* Unpublished master's thesis, University of Prince Eduard Island, Charlottetown, PE, Canada.

Wolfensberger, W. (1972). *The principle of normalization in human services.* Toronto: NIMR.

Ysseldyke, J., & Christenson, S. (2002). *Functional assessment of academic behavior: Creating successful learning environments.* Longmont, CO: Sopris West.

Printed in the United States
By Bookmasters